JUDGING DRUGS

Every day, judges determine vital questions about 'addiction', 'drugs' and the rights of those who use them. Despite the law's crucial role in handling 'drug problems', and in shaping drug practices, effects and outcomes, drug scholars have often overlooked case law. In a rapidly changing drug policy landscape, how is the law managing drug effects and harms, stigma, addiction, agency and responsibility? Why do we regulate drugs? Are drug offenders responsible for their actions? Is drug use a disability? Is drug treatment a human right? Do drugs cause harm? And might drug law itself be harmful? Authors in this volume take a variety of approaches to these questions and more. Drawing on critical theory, all consider new ways of thinking about drug problems. This vital new collection enables a deeper, critical understanding of how the law works to shape knowledge about, as well as judge, drug use and its effects.

SIMON FLACKS is Associate Professor at the School of Law, University of Sussex. He is a sociolegal scholar and criminologist with considerable expertise in researching the interface between law and critical drug studies. He has published extensively. He is the author of *Law, Drugs and the Politics of Childhood: From Protection to Punishment* (2021).

KATE SEEAR is Professor at Deakin Law School, Deakin University. She is a lawyer, sociologist and leading international expert in critical drug studies. She has published extensively on drug law and policy. Her book *Law, Drugs and the Making of Addiction: Just habits* (2020) was the winner of the UK Socio-Legal Studies Association's History and Theory book prize.

JUDGING DRUGS

Key Issues in Law and Society

Edited by
SIMON FLACKS
University of Sussex
KATE SEEAR
Deakin University

CAMBRIDGE
UNIVERSITY PRESS

CAMBRIDGE
UNIVERSITY PRESS

Shaftesbury Road, Cambridge CB2 8EA, United Kingdom

One Liberty Plaza, 20th Floor, New York, NY 10006, USA

477 Williamstown Road, Port Melbourne, VIC 3207, Australia

314–321, 3rd Floor, Plot 3, Splendor Forum, Jasola District Centre,
New Delhi – 110025, India

Cambridge University Press is part of Cambridge University Press & Assessment,
a department of the University of Cambridge.

We share the University's mission to contribute to society through the pursuit of
education, learning and research at the highest international levels of excellence.

www.cambridge.org
Information on this title: www.cambridge.org/9781009713351

DOI: 10.1017/9781009713399

When citing this work, please include a reference to the DOI 10.1017/9781009713399

First published 2026

Cover image: 'Intrigue, Want, Need' by Chazzy, hand-drawn work of pen on paper. PACE
Artist 2024.

A catalogue record for this publication is available from the British Library

Library of Congress Cataloging-in-Publication Data
Names: Flacks, Simon editor | Seear, Kate editor
Title: Judging drugs : key issues in law and society / edited by Simon Flacks,
University of Sussex; Kate Seear, Deakin University, Victoria.
Description: Cambridge, United Kingdom ; New York, NY : Cambridge University Press,
2026. | Includes bibliographical references and index.
Identifiers: LCCN 2025036378 | ISBN 9781009713351 hardback | ISBN 9781009713344
paperback | ISBN 9781009713399 ebook
Subjects: LCSH: Drugs – Law and legislation | Drug abuse – Law and legislation | Electronic
cigarettes – Law and legislation | Alcohol – Law and legislation | LCGFT: Law materials
Classification: LCC K3636 .J83 2026 | DDC 344.04/233–dc23/eng/20250807
LC record available at https://lccn.loc.gov/2025036378

ISBN 978-1-009-71335-1 Hardback

CONTENTS

FIGURES

CONTRIBUTORS

NANCY D. CAMPBELL is Professor of Science and Technology Studies at Rensselaer Polytechnic Institute, Troy, New York. She is a historian of science, technology and medicine who focuses on legal and illegal drugs, drug science, policy and treatment, harm reduction, and gender and addiction. Her most recent book is *OD: Naloxone and the politics of overdose* (MIT Press, 2020). She also studies the ethics of human subjects research, social movements and the fruitful convergence between neuroscience and addiction research. She has published two books on gender: *Gendering addiction: The politics of drug treatment in a neurochemical world* (with Elizabeth Ettorre, Palgrave, 2011) and her first book, *Using women: Gender, drug policy, and social justice* (Routledge, 2000), which was about how drug-using women figured in drug policy discourse from the 1910s to the 1990s.

ALEXANDRA DMITRIEVA is based at the School of Social and Political Science, University of Edinburgh. She received her PhD degree in sociology at St Petersburg State University in 2013. Her thesis was aimed at exploring how Giddens's theory of structuration works to explain in what forms drug use is produced and reproduced in Russia. In 2017, she co-founded the Support, Research and Development Center, a Kyiv-based non-governmental organisation aimed at conducting qualitative social research of drug use, health and medicine in the context of post-Soviet transformations in Ukraine. She has worked on numerous projects to advocate for the rights of people who use drugs in Russia and Ukraine.

MATS EKENDAHL is Professor of Social Work at Stockholm University. He was awarded his PhD qualification in 2002 on a dissertation about substance users' views on lifestyle change and compulsory treatment. Since then his research has drawn on mainly qualitative approaches to study policy and practice in the field of alcohol and other drug use. His work has covered a wide range of topics related to social work, such as motivation, mandatory treatment programmes, aftercare interventions, opioid substitution treatment, risk perceptions, service provision and user perspectives. He has also worked collaboratively with researchers in other parts of the world, including in comparative studies on the treatment of gender, alcohol consumption and violence among young people across Australia, Sweden and Canada, and in a multicentre study on the support needs of people who use cocaine and crack, conducted in eight European cities. He is an associate editor of the journal *Contemporary Drug Problems*, and a member of the international editorial board of *Drugs: Education, Prevention and Policy*.

SIMON FLACKS is an Associate Professor in criminal justice at the University of Sussex. His most recent book is *Law, drugs and the politics of childhood: From protection to punishment* (Routledge, 2021), and he is the author of more than a dozen peer-reviewed articles on aspects of drug law and policy. These have covered a range of topics, including policing, human rights, gender, addiction and family justice. He has won funding from the Socio-Legal Studies Association and is a contributor to the London Drugs Commission. He has worked with a variety of organisations, including Release, Stopwatch and the United Nations Office of the High Commissioner for Human Rights.

RENAE FOMIATTI is an Australian Research Council Discovery Early Career Researcher Award (DECRA) senior research fellow at the Australian Research Centre in Sex, Health and Society (ARCSHS), in the School of Psychology and Public Health at La Trobe University. She conducts qualitative research on the social and cultural dimensions of alcohol and other drug consumption and treatment, related phenomena such as blood-borne viruses and overdose, and contemporary experiences of health and gendered embodiment. Her research is informed by feminist theory and science and technology studies. Her research has appeared in international journals including *Social Science and Medicine*, *Sociology of Health & Illness*, *The International Journal of Drug Policy*, *Qualitative Health Research* and *Health Sociology Review*. She is an editor of the peer-reviewed journal *Drugs: Education, Prevention and Policy* and editorial board member of the journals *Health Sociology Review* and *Contemporary Drug Problems*.

HELEN KEANE is Professor of sociology at the Australian National University. Her research areas include social and cultural studies of health and medicine, sociology of addiction and drug use, embodiment, gender and feminist theory. She has published widely on discourses of addiction and drug-use practices (including smoking and vaping). She is the author of the highly influential book *What's wrong with addiction?* (Melbourne University Press, 2002), which provided the first book-length critical examination of popular and medical understandings of addiction. She is also the co-author of *Habits: Remaking addiction* (Palgrave, 2014) (with Suzanne Fraser and David Moore), which provides a new theoretical framework for understanding addiction and is a landmark text in critical drug studies. She is an associate editor of the *International Journal of Drug Policy*.

SHANA HARRIS is a cultural and medical anthropologist and associate professor in the Department of Anthropology, with a secondary joint appointment in the Department of Internal Medicine at the University of Central Florida. Her research, which has been funded by such organisations as the US National Institutes of Health and the Wenner-Gren Foundation for Anthropological Research, focuses on drug use, 'addiction', and health politics and interventions in Latin America and the United States. Her current work examines psychedelic-based drug treatment in Mexico, harm reduction responses to the co-use of opioids and stimulants in the United States, and syringe service programmes in Florida.

GEMMA NOURSE is a research associate at ARCSHS. She completed her PhD in 2022, which examined the co-constitution of performance and image-enhancing drugs (PIEDs), health and masculinity in Australia. Her PhD was supervised by Professor Suzanne Fraser and Professor David Moore and was awarded the La Trobe University's Nancy Millis Medal for outstanding postgraduate theses. Since 2022, she has published research on hepatitis C treatment and efforts to address blood-borne virus-related stigma in healthcare. She is currently working across two projects: an Australian Research Council Discovery Project exploring the relationship between trauma and alcohol and other drug-related problems, and a pilot project exploring the constitution of sexual consent in relation to alcohol and other drug consumption.

KIRAN PIENAAR is Senior Lecturer in sociology at Deakin University. She is also an adjunct senior research fellow at ARCSHS, La Trobe University, and an honorary research associate at Rhodes University. She has expertise in gender and sexuality studies, and health sociology, with a focus on LGBTQ identities and cultures; the politics of gender, sexuality and the body; narcofeminisms, drugs and the self; and the social dimensions of health. She has published on topics related to gender, drugs and 'addiction', and the biopolitics of public health and drug policy. Her research has appeared in international journals including *Sexualities*, *Social Science & Medicine*, *International Journal of Drug Policy* and *Sociological Review*. She has published a co-edited collection titled *Narcofeminisms: Revisioning drug use* (The Sociological Review, 2023) and a monograph titled *Politics in the making of HIV/AIDS in South Africa* (Palgrave, 2016).

ALLISON SCHLOSSER is a cultural and medical anthropologist with a background in public health and social work. She is Assistant Professor of anthropology at the University of Nebraska, Omaha, where she teaches medical anthropology and health humanities. Allison specialises in critical drug studies, cultural constructions of 'addiction' and related interventions in the United States. Her research draws on ethnographic and other qualitative methods to examine the moral politics of drug treatment and harm reduction; identity, subjectivity and care in relation to drug use; and socio-economic inequalities in access to services. Her current research explores lived experiences of houselessness among people who use drugs in relation to US state and regional differences in policies and practices to manage these issues, drawing on ethnography, photographic research methods and spatial mapping.

KATE SEEAR is a professor at the Deakin Law School, Deakin University. She is a trained sociologist and lawyer. She holds the prestigious Australian Research Council Future Fellowship (FT200100099) and previously held an Australian Research Council DECRA Fellowship. From 2020 to 2025, she was based at La Trobe University and undertook some of this work there as part of the Future Fellowship, with additional supports provided by the deputy vice chancellor (Research and Industry Engagement) and ARCSHS. She is the author of 5 books and more than 100 academic publications, exploring topics such as the links between alcohol, other drugs, stigma and the law; and drugs, gender, human rights and health. She convenes the Gender Law and Drugs (GLaD) programme and is the founder and convenor of the Australian Drug Lawyers' Network. Her most recent sole-authored book is *Law, drugs and the making of addiction: Just habits* (Routledge, 2020) and was the winner of the UK Socio-Legal Studies Association's History and Theory book prize.

VLADIMIR STEPANOV completed his PhD in 2024 at the Department of Sociology of Kyiv-Mohyla Academy. His thesis focused on developing an ethically sound approach to study marginalised groups, with a special emphasis on the use of photography-based methods. In 2017, he co-founded the Support, Research and Development Center, Kyiv, Ukraine. Before moving to Ukraine, he worked as a photographer and curator. His current research interests lie at the intersection of sociology of drugs, ethics of care and research, and visual methodology.

AYSEL SULTAN is a lecturer at the Science and Technology Studies (STS) Department of the Technical University of Munich, and an affiliate at the Eastern Health Clinical School, Monash University. Her interdisciplinary research lies at the intersection of sociology of health and illness, childhood and youth studies, and STS. In her postdoctoral fellowships at the universities in Frankfurt and Haifa and Monash University, she explored culturally adapted drug treatment modalities, gender-responsive drug service design and policy impact in accessing harm reduction. Her monograph – *Recovering assemblages* (Palgrave, 2022) – explores sociocultural, linguistic and policy dimensions in young people's recovery experiences. Currently, she is studying the effects of digital platforms on knowledge around health, harm and safety with a particular interest in digital harm reduction and social media drug markets. She is also the editor of the international, peer-reviewed academic journal *Drugs, Habits and Social Policy.*

ACKNOWLEDGEMENTS

This book is the product of several years of work, shaped through conversations with many people, including our friends, families and colleagues. We'd like to acknowledge all of those who provided support to us to help bring this collection to life.

First and foremost, we give thanks to all of the contributors to the collection: for their trust in us and their patience as we realised our vision for the book. Special thanks go to Dr Marie Jauffret-Roustide, who helped convene a workshop in Paris in September 2023, where early drafts of the chapters in this book were presented, and the contributors had the chance to come together and share ideas. Thanks also to Associate Professor Adrian Guta, who attended the workshop and gave helpful feedback on the draft chapters.

We are grateful to Tobias Ginsberg and the team at Cambridge University Press for their careful stewardship of the project.

Thanks also go to Dr Alejandra Zuluaga, who gave editorial assistance.

Thank you to the artist Chazzy, a Peer Arts Collective Exhibition (PACE) artist 2024, who kindly allowed us to use her artwork for the front cover, and to the team at the Australian Injecting and Illicit Drug Users League (AIVL) for their support. As AIVL tells us:

> PACE is more than a fine art showcase, it's a declaration. A moment to honour the stunning and complex creativity that exists within the community, expressed through works that speak where words fall short. Art is our language of emotion, memory, and connection. For our first edition in 2024, we released an inaugural PACE Book at the AIVL Health & Human Rights Summit in Adelaide that features 16 extraordinary artists from across Australia. With hundreds of submissions from all around the world, it's clear this is just the beginning. The dream is for PACE to grow into an international movement, one that shifts culture, opens eyes, and centres artists who use drugs at the heart of the creative conversation. Born from a community of artists who use drugs, PACE is a space to challenge stigma and celebrate the often-overlooked brilliance woven deeply into our lives. In Latin, *pace* means 'in peace', and in English, it

refers to the speed at which one or something moves. PACE embraces both meanings: an art collective that honours personal expression, peace, and creativity at whatever pace feels right.

Simon

I am grateful to attendees at the Socio-Legal Studies conference in Portsmouth, UK, in 2024, where I presented a draft of this work and benefitted from questions and feedback. I would also like to thank supportive friends and colleagues at the University of Sussex, who have helped in various ways during the genesis of this book, including Lucy Welsh, Tanya Palmer and Jess Shurson, and Professor Naomi Creutzfeldt at the University of Kent. I am indebted to wonderful colleagues at the Centre for Innovation and Research in Childhood and Youth (CIRCY), who have provided support and mentorship during my short time at Sussex. They include Liam Berriman, Perpetua Kirby, Michelle Lefevre, Lisa Holmes and Louise Gazeley. I'd like to thank Raivo, my partner, for his endless patience, love and support, and my son Joshua for providing light relief and perspective, among many other things.

Finally, I'd also like to thank and pay tribute to Dr Leah Moyle, a drugs researcher and criminologist who died from brain cancer in 2024 at the horribly young age of thirty-eight. Leah and I met a few times, hanging out at the Contemporary Drug Problems conference in Prato where I first met Kate. Her impact in the field of drug research was profound, and she left behind a body of work that, I have no doubt, will continue to inform and inspire for years to come. Her dedication to social justice was evident in all she wrote. There was more to Leah's contribution to the academic community, however. She was remarkably kind, with a natural ability to bring people together and foster a sense of belonging wherever she went. Her generosity, warmth and sharp intellect are deeply missed, but her legacy remains.

Kate

I am grateful to the Australian Research Council's Future Fellowship scheme (FT200100099), which provided the funding support to undertake this research. Huge thanks to Dr Sean Mulcahy, who worked as a research officer on my Future Fellowship and provided invaluable assistance right across the life of the project. I am also grateful to

Dr Alejandra Zuluaga, who provided research support during the project. My work also benefitted from the input of an expert advisory board, many of whom provided input on early drafts of the work I present in this book and other aspects of the project: Emerita Professor Susan Boyd, Judy Chang, Sione Crawford, Professor Patrick Emerton, Adjunct Professor Suzanne Fraser, Professor Sarah Joseph, Dr Annie Madden and Adjunct Professor Donald McPherson. Thanks also go to Adjunct Professor David Moore and Dr Steven Angelides, who provided crucial intellectual and research support in the early stages of the project's design and development, alongside advice from Suzanne Fraser. Thank you also to Sarah Schwartz and Meghan Fitzgerald for their support in gaining permission from Veronica Nelson's senior next of kin to write about the inquest into her death in the chapter I have contributed to this collection. It is both a profound sadness and a deep honour to be able to keep the conversation around her death going, in the hope for change. I am also grateful to attendees at the 'Tackling Stigma' conference, which was held at the University of New South Wales in Sydney in 2024. There I presented a draft of this work and benefitted from questions and feedback. Thanks also to La Trobe University, where I was based for the majority of the fellowship and where some of this work took place.

I am particularly indebted to the large and strong network of drug user advocates in Australia who have provided feedback and support for my work over many years. I cannot list them all here, but I want to acknowledge everyone at AIVL and AIVL's member organisations, and offer special thanks to John Gobeil, Sione Crawford, Ele Morrison, Chris Gough, Annie Madden, Charles Henderson and Nick Kent for their expertise and help over many years. And finally, to my family, especially my sister Claire Seear, my partner Stewart Dugmore and our late, beloved dog Cyril. This work would not be possible without your love and support.

Introduction

Troubling Judgments

SIMON FLACKS AND KATE SEEAR

The control of alcohol and other drugs (AOD) is an important feature of the global public policy landscape. There is widespread recognition that the 'war on drugs', rooted in international systems of drug control, has failed both on its own terms and because of the harms it has visited upon users and their communities. Although some states have moved towards liberalisation, the vast majority continue to heavily invest in punitive measures. Importantly, however, key ideas about drugs are coming under sustained pressure, and in some instances, beginning to break down, including the idea that drugs inevitably produce harms, including illness, injury and death, or that they produce other predictable, stable and consistent 'effects' (Fraser and Moore, 2011). There is evidence of this change in specific contexts including drug policy, health promotion and service provision. But what is happening in law courts? How are drugs being conceptualised in legal cases around the world? Scholars from a variety of disciplines have taken a keen interest in the 'drug problem', but there has been little scrutiny of how key cases in different jurisdictions have influenced the ways in which we understand, respond to and punish the use of various substances. The importance of such decisions extends beyond criminal matters and affects outcomes in a variety of legal spheres including immigration, welfare, family justice, education and employment law. *Judging Drugs* is the first book to chart the impact and significance of those cases in different parts of the world, and to consider how ideas about drugs are (or might be) changing across our courts. It thus comprises an important and distinctive addition to a body of scholarship that has sought to understand the ways in which drugs and 'addiction' have been subject to varying degrees of control and opprobrium. Importantly, contributors to this edited collection do not simply identify and summarise important legal cases from around the world. In this sense, the collection is not a 'textbook' of important case law. It is also not a textbook of cases with apparent precedent value. Instead, our contributors have selected cases that raised issues of interest and concern for the AOD field more broadly, including because they: raise important questions about the way we understand agency, responsibility and culpability regarding harms associated with drugs; are an entry point for exploring important intersections between drugs, race, gender and sexuality; or otherwise open up ways of conceptualising harm, safety, danger, geopolitics, biopolitics and relationality.

In each instance, our contributors read, reread, interrogate and trouble their chosen decisions in the light of theoretical and empirical advances in how we understand drug use, supply and manufacture. They also pick up emerging ideas within the case law to consider what they might tell us about the future of drugs and addiction, and how the range of 'problems' frequently associated with drugs can or might be reshaped via courts into the future. The collection highlights a range of issues of contemporary significance to global drug policy by: *identifying concepts and assumptions* about drugs and 'addiction' and their relevance to major cases, exploring the *relevance of local and global forces and factors* in shaping ideas about and approaches to AOD, considering *whether concepts and assumptions are breaking down or coming under pressure* and what this might tell us about the future of drugs, examining *whether such assumptions and concepts stand up* to theoretical and empirical scrutiny, and *exploring opportunities for disruption, resistance and reform*. This introduction draws together insights from across the case studies, including synergies and points of difference in approaches to AOD and addiction, and what it might mean for the future of drug regulation.

The ways in which laws about drugs and addiction have been interpreted by judges have profound implications, both for the individuals and families concerned and for how we understand concepts such as 'addiction' and 'drugs'. The law is, of course, only one system of knowledge by and through which truths about these concepts are stabilised, circulated and produced. Health policies, government strategies, public documents and research studies, drawing on a variety of political and epistemological perspectives, are among the many discourses to have played important roles. Yet the law – in all its forms, practices and processes – has been subject to limited critical scrutiny beyond the study of those key legislative instruments that criminalise drug use, manufacture and supply. Authors critically consider the impact and significance of a range of key court cases from a breadth of legal arenas, drawing on innovative approaches to how we think about 'drugs', 'addiction' and their purported effects. At the outset of this project, we invited our contributors to each identify an important case concerning AOD from their jurisdiction. We then invited them to undertake a critical (re)reading of each case from a particular theoretical or epistemological perspective of their choice, providing an opportunity to 're-imagine' the judgment and place it in a broader historical, sociological and cultural context. The chapters incorporate a variety of standpoints including, but not limited to, feminism (neo)liberalism, cultural studies, politics, Science and Technology Studies (STS), critical race theory, sexuality studies and sociology. In addition to providing an opportunity to reflect on the relationship between drugs, addiction and lawmaking, its interdisciplinary value lies in bringing together a spectrum of approaches in one volume.

This unique collection thus makes a number of contributions to the international literature on drug policy and law. First, in bringing together scholars from a range of jurisdictions and disciplines, and inviting them to identify cases of relevance in numerous areas of law, it serves as an important source of knowledge about international jurisprudence on AOD. Second, the collection aims to generate a better understanding of how approaches to drugs converge and diverge in different parts of the world. Authors explore the influence of locally, culturally and historically specific factors and forces in shaping ideas about and approaches to drugs and addiction. Finally, the collection considers whether these forces and factors offer any insights into the future of drug policy and law and explores whether insights from one jurisdiction offer opportunities for resistance, activism or change. We hope that this collection generates renewed interest in the study of the law among critical drug scholars. As we explain throughout this introductory chapter, there is a rich tradition of critical drug scholarship that engages with important questions about how drugs are conceptualised and practised in a range of settings, including drug policy and practice, drug education and more. Although the law plays a crucial role in shaping drug practices, effects and outcomes, there has been less sustained and comprehensive engagement with some elements of drug law, including case law, than we might expect. There are several possible explanations for this, including the disciplinary backgrounds and orientations of drug researchers, and a relative lack of legal expertise compared to other forms of expertise that tend to dominate the field (e.g., history, sociology, cultural studies). In previous work, we have both argued for the importance of studying law and legal practices in more depth (e.g., Seear, 2020; Flacks, 2021). Most contributors to this edited collection had not previously engaged with the law in this way, including through careful, detailed analyses of case law. We hope, therefore, that this collection shows others interested in AOD how this work can be done and helps to encourage more work at the intersections of AOD, law and critical theory.

Why This Book, and Why Now?

The global conversation on drug law and policy is rapidly evolving, perhaps more so than at any time since the international prohibition of certain substances in the early to mid-twentieth century. During that era, a series of United Nations conventions were enacted to prohibit or at least limit the trade in some psychoactive substances, beginning with the 1925 Geneva Opium Convention, which was a response to criticism of the opium trade, and included controls on trade but not on supply and consumption (Kendell, 2003; Bewley-Taylor et al., 2014). The 1925 Convention marked a 'turning point' (Seddon, 2020, p. 1568) and a wide range of countries implemented domestic prohibitions. The reasons for prohibiting the use of drugs in general are varied, but colonial and capitalist interests drove the speed of change in the early twentieth century (Courtwright, 2001). The Single Convention on Narcotic Drugs, adopted in 1961 and establishing the International Narcotics Control Board, has been signed by 184 of the 193 members of the United Nations – an unusually high level of support. The mood could now be changing. Decriminalisation schemes have now been explored in Colombia, the Czech Republic, France, Germany, Ghana, Israel, Malaysia, Portugal and Tunisia. A variety of reasons have been cited for relaxing controls. In Germany, lawmakers claim that the move would reduce the health harms associated with the illicit trade, particularly to young people, raise revenues and address organised crime (Oltermann, 2022). In Uruguay, the 'convergence of a specific set of problems, policy and political circumstances' (Queirolo et al., 2019, p. 1313), including concerns for public safety and security and the election of a liberal government, resulted in legalisation. Yet we must be mindful that moves towards the decriminalisation of certain substances, most notably cannabis, do not – by any stretch – resolve all of the problems associated with prohibition in different parts of the world. The disproportionate policing of racial minorities, the surveillance and incarceration of pregnant, substance-using women and gender diverse people, and the stigmatisation of illicit drug users and of those identified as 'addicted' or 'dependent' are just some of the challenges posed by drug regulation that will not simply disappear due to changes in the legal status of one substance.

Perhaps surprisingly, even though most systems of drug control are rooted in international and national legislation, there has been relatively limited critical, sociolegal research on the questions of drugs and addiction (Seear, 2020; Flacks, 2021). The relationship between drugs and crime has been the subject of a large body of criminological research (Stevens, 2011; Seddon et al., 2012; Bean, 2014), whereas sociologists, policy scholars and health scientists routinely reference the legal framework when turning their attention to the 'drug problem' more broadly. Scholarship has also explored the human rights consequences of drugs prohibition, pointing out how punitive drug polices stemming from United Nations international treaties lead to increases in imprisonment, violence against women, displacement and other human rights violations (Flacks, 2012, 2021; Bone, 2019). However, the law itself, including how drugs and addiction are constituted within cases, precedent and legal practices, has rarely been the object of study (although see Seear, 2020; Flacks, 2023), even though the meaning of AOD, including their constitution, purported effects and relationship with human behaviours, is a feature of judgments in a range of legal settings, including those beyond the criminal law (Seear & Fraser, 2014a).

Critical questions therefore remain. How does the law in different jurisdictions 'think' about addiction? How are 'drugs' conceptualised and understood by judges and legal professionals, and what are their purported effects? What does the law have to say about the reasons for drug use and the causes of addiction? Do courts frame and enact drugs and addiction in different ways across jurisdictions? How do the concepts of 'drugs' and 'addiction' interact and intersect with legal principles such as 'responsibility', 'capacity' and 'reasonableness'? Do 'addicts' have the same legal entitlements as others? How do legal decisions hinge on assessments about gender, sexuality, disability, class and other triggers for potential marginalisation? Focusing on judgments provides an opportunity to both interrogate and trouble legal approaches to drugs and addiction, while providing the basis for exploring the relationship between critical approaches to drug studies and legal discourse. The changing drug policy landscape makes it ever more important to attend to how the law understands and constitutes the relationship between AOD, addiction, agency and responsibility.

Critical Approaches to Drugs and Addiction

Authors in this volume take a variety of approaches to questions about drugs and addiction, but all are concerned with new ways of thinking about the 'drug problem' that move beyond traditional or conventional perspectives. Scholarship has long been focused on the damage caused by systems of drug control, including their legal origins, implications for human rights standards and consequences for racial, Indigenous and ethnic minorities, as well as women and children (see, for example, Becker, 1973; Musto, 1973; Berridge and Edwards, 1981; Kohn, 1992; Courtwright, 2001; Campbell & Ettorre, 2011; Stevens, 2011; Flacks, 2021). Historians have also interrogated the problematisation of drugs and addiction, and its roots in liberalism and the notion of freedom (Valverde, 1998; Reith, 2004; Room, 2006; Fraser & valentine, 2008; Seddon, 2010). Although approaches vary, most researchers agree that efforts to control the trade in licit and illicit substances has successfully contributed to the stigmatisation and dehumanisation of certain groups, particularly minorities (Weinberg, 2002; Campbell & Ettorre, 2011).

Feminist perspectives on drug law and policy have been important for drawing attention to how women's AOD use is represented as more problematic than men's. This is particularly so in the context of caregiving and reproduction where women are expected to be the incubators of the 'citizens of tomorrow'. According to Campbell and Ettorre (2011, p. 179), women's drug addiction has thus consistently been framed within the 'domain of social reproduction' in a society in which 'women are assumed to be the linchpins of social order, family life, and biosocial (and cultural) reproduction'. As a consequence, women who use drugs are represented as more risky both to themselves and others. This was seen in the 'crack scares' of the 1980s in the United States, when mothers faced criminal charges for giving birth to infants who failed drug tests – a set of practices currently undergoing a resurgence or renewal in some parts of the world, including the United States. In liberal democracies, at least, the 'good mother' is White, middle-class, moral, sober, maternal and heterosexual (Backhouse, 1999; Campbell, 2000; Boyd, 2019). Boyd notes that 'Women who fall outside of this discourse, as poor and racialized mothers do, are constructed as incapable of mothering and raising their own children.' Women may well try to conceal their AOD use from health and social services, a choice that, for Campbell and Ettorre (2011, p. 180), should be viewed as a rational response to the social stigma faced by drug-using women, and might equally be understood as a reasonable reaction to the threat of child removal (Barnard and Barlow, 2003; Kroll and Taylor, 2003). Research with service providers has found that substance use by women may be framed as 'essentially harmful' via a 'gendered responsibilisation of women as foetal incubators and primary caregivers of infants' (Benoit et al., 2014, p. 260). A recent edited collection, *Narcofeminisms: Revisioning Drug Use* (Dennis et al., 2023), changes the emphasis on AOD use as a means of controlling the conduct of women to a concern with what drugs 'do' as a feminist practice.

In respect of LGBTQ+ AOD use, important critical work has interrogated the ways in which potentially higher rates of consumption within queer communities tends to be understood as a response to marginalisation and stigma, rather than, for example, as a means of enhancing pleasure (e.g., Møller & Hakim, 2023). Pienaar and colleagues (2020) therefore examine the *productive* role of drugs in enacting queer identities, exploring how drug consumption, sex and gender shape each other across a range of settings. Kane Race's work has consistently sought to understand questions of agency in relation to drugs discourses and sexuality, drawing on cultural studies, queer theory and STS (see, for example, Race, 2017).

From a racial perspective, Koram (2019, p. 2) has identified the war on drugs as a 'contemporary arena in which difference in racialized subjectivity and experiences continue to be produced'. The suffering experienced as a result of prohibition has disproportionately affected certain groups of people, notably 'groups that were already historically oppressed through the preceding racial and colonial organization of the globe' (Koram, 2019, p. 2). It is also notable that cultural practices, such as coca-leaf chewing in the Indigenous communities of the Andes or the traditional consumption of khat by Arab and North African societies, have not always been afforded protection, such as through human rights law, from these systems of prohibition. Although there has been much discussion of the racialised consequences of the war on drugs in the United States, in which a system of mass incarceration and state violence operates (it is estimated that more than half of all federal prisoners, disproportionality Black, are imprisoned because of drug offences), Koram argues that it is important to recognise how this dynamic plays out globally. He writes that:

> The problem of race exceeds any one national narrative of racial divisions; it spans the globe encapsulating the legacies of apartheid and land appropriation in settler colonies, the hierarchy of populations produced

> through scientific racism and the notions of sub-humanity, as well as gendered ideas of stronger (masculine) and weaker (feminine) peoples, that continue to haunt the contemporary, ostensibly post-racial world.

The field of drugs studies has itself been subject to critique by, among others, Maziyar Ghiabi, who has explored the history of intoxicants from the perspective of 'decolonisation', and particularly the 'structures of knowledge' underlying the domineering relationships between the 'Global North' and 'Global South' (Ghiabi, 2019). These critiques, acknowledging and interrogating the gendered, raced, sexualised and colonial antecedents of global drug policies, have generated essential insights into the governance, production and stabilisation of AOD use and its effects, including how and why regulation sustains wider processes of marginalisation. We contend, however, that there is more scope for understanding the relationship between these processes and insights and the technical forms of practice that are central to lawmaking. This is necessary if we are to avoid treating law as a mere product of social relations, thereby valorising the 'social' at the expense of the 'legal' (Latour, 2004).

The Matter of Matter/Ontology

A particularly fertile – and arguably overarching – line of enquiry among drug researchers has involved the use of theoretical and methodological tools developed – broadly speaking – within the field of STS. The concept of 'drugs', like 'addiction', is famously slippery. Jacques Derrida long ago asserted, in *The Rhetoric of Drugs* (Derrida, 1993), that the concept of a 'drug' is 'a non-scientific concept, but is rather instituted on the basis of moral or political evaluation'. Indeed, 'medicines' may be used for recreational purposes and illicit substances might be used to improve mental and physical health. It is often said, therefore, that there is a lack of ethical or scientific consistency in the ways different substances are both described and regulated.

Historically, AOD research has been underpinned by one of two theoretical approaches: realism (or essentialism) or social constructionism. Broadly speaking, a realist approach to drugs 'assumes drugs simply to be self-evidently concrete entities possessed of intrinsic characteristics and producing predictable results' (Fraser & Moore, 2011, p. 1) in the form of various drug effects and harms. These include the purported physiological and psychological effects of drugs, such as intoxication, euphoria and paranoia, and a range of harms that can be associated with drugs, such as non-fatal and fatal overdoses, and blood-borne viruses such as hepatitis C and HIV. On the other hand, a constructionist account sees the effects and harms of drugs 'as made in discourse, practice and politics' (Fraser & Moore, 2011, p. 1). According to social constructionists, drug effects, such as intoxication, euphoria or paranoia, or harms, such as overdose or hepatitis C, are not natural or self-evident effects of substances themselves but function as an outcome of discourse, including shifting perspectives and interpretations over time and across cultures. Depending on which approach one takes, 'reality is seen as wholly (or primarily) determined by either matter (realism) or discourse (constructionism)' (Seear, 2013, p. 202). Writing about the histories of drugs, Emilie Gomart (2002, p. 95) explains why these two approaches matter, arguing that:

> The dichotomies set up by essentialists' and social constructivists' analyses rig historical descriptions of drugs. They force a choice between two kinds of explanation, which focus either on objects themselves or on human actors. Essentialists root for a substance with discoverable attributes always already there, invariable, irreversible. They shove outside their focus the impure construction of that entity, its uncertainties and contingencies. In contrast, social constructivists assume that the world of objects is fashioned by humans who project on to it representations which have no necessary correspondence with the object itself. They are blatantly silent about the question of the reality of the object and write only about human constructions.

Gomart (2002, p. 96; original emphasis) goes on to say that: 'It is not the *difference* between these approaches to drugs, but rather their *common points*, that is the crux of the problem. Both these (historians') paths suggest that the substance itself is that which by definition does not change. The substance is given and constant.' There are a number of reasons why such approaches might be problematic. For instance, Duff (2013, p. 168) argues that realist research treats causality simplistically, by claiming that it is possible to 'quantify and ascribe "causal" responsibility to individual actors, objects or factors'. Such a logic, Duff (2013, p. 168) argues, 'is premised on the assumption that individual actors, objects and/or factors may be statistically "abstracted" from their contexts in order to probabilistically determine their "contribution" to the particular state of affairs under investigation'. Such research often suffers from a central problem, however, Duff (2013: 168) goes on to say: 'Without ignoring the significance of these kinds of studies, they have not fared especially well in the treatment of counterfactuals, such as the vast majority of instances in which methamphetamine misuse does not cause psychosis, or where alcohol intoxication fails to produce violent (male) subjects.' In other words, AOD do not generate reliable, predictable or stable 'effects' and 'harms'; many people consume substances without experiencing the kinds of effects or problems often assigned to them.

Although social constructionist approaches are sometimes understood as a more sympathetic or generous account of AOD and the people who use them (Seear, 2013), they have been criticised by, among others, the Dutch philosopher Annemarie Mol (2002). One problem with social constructionist approaches in general, she argues, is the claim that objects are constructed as a once-off, never-to-be-repeated process. Based on her ethnographic studies of disease, she instead argues that objects have a 'fragile' ontology, with a complex past and a 'complex present', and that their identities 'may differ between sites' (Mol, 2002, p. 43). Mol goes on to suggest that 'maintaining the identity of objects requires a continuing effort' and notes that 'over time [those identities] may change' (Mol, 2002, p. 43). This is not simply a difference in perspective or construction, Mol argues, but is an ontological question. Suzanne Fraser and David Moore (2011, pp. 3–4) thus question where constructionism's neglect of materiality leaves us when dealing with thoroughly material problems, such as fatal drug overdose:

> Are social constructionist approaches going too far in emphasising the role of discourse in the production of reality? Do theoretically elegant ideas about reality as socially constituted fail in the face of the biological 'facts'? Who would want to dismiss, for example, a fatal heroin overdose as merely a discursive construction, as if a change in ways of talking and thinking about it would alter it or instantly prevent it from happening?

As Fraser and Moore point out, these concerns overlap with the kinds of questions being explored in other fields. Most obviously, feminists have long grappled with constructionism's neglect of materiality, fearing that the approach was too simplistic, while being simultaneously wary about matter because 'the materiality of women's bodies has been used historically to limit their opportunities' (Fraser & Moore, 2011, p. 3; see also valentine and Seear, 2020). The noted feminist theorist and quantum physicist Karen Barad posed a similar question regarding how discourse and matter are conceptualised by critical scholars, arguing that:

> Language has been granted too much power. The linguistic turn, the semiotic turn, the interpretative turn, the cultural turn: it seems that at every turn lately every 'thing' – even materiality – is turned into a matter of language or some other form of cultural representation [. . .] Language matters. Discourse matters. Culture matters. There is an important sense in which the only thing that does not seem to matter anymore is matter.
>
> (2003, p. 801)

How do we theorise and reconcile the agency of matter and discourse and their place in the production of realities, while neither ignoring nor overstating the importance of either?

Drawing on a range of insights from the field of STS, while recognising her indebtedness to feminist theorists such as Judith Butler (1990, 1993) and governmentality scholars such as Michel Foucault, Mol developed a new approach that has come to be known as 'ontological multiplicity'. Mol explored these ideas in an early piece on anaemia (Mol, 1999) in which she questioned how the term was understood, explaining that in practice, 'anaemia appears to be *performed* in several different ways' (Mol, 1999, p. 77; original emphasis), including: *in the clinic*, through observation of visible symptoms and an account from the patient; *in the laboratory*, through analyses of blood samples, haemoglobin levels and statistical levels; and through *pathophysiology*, which consists of identifying the dividing line between normal and abnormal haemoglobin levels. Although these three 'performances' of anaemia are linked together in medical textbooks, Mol also explains that, in practice, 'the three ways to diagnose "anaemia" each diagnose something different'. Her conclusions in her classic full-length book *The Body Multiple* (Mol, 2002) are: first, that realities are not singular but multiple. Second, that realities are unstable and changeable, rather than stable and fixed. Third, that realities are constituted through practices and processes of iteration and repetition (see also Butler, 1990). Fourth, we must attend to the specific practices and processes by which realities are enacted, formulated and maintained if we are to understand how realities come to be. Mol (1999, p. 86) positions her work as a form of 'ontological politics' or 'ontics'; these terms recognise the links 'between the real, the conditions of possibility we live with, and the political'.

Karen Barad's work is similarly concerned with ontologies and offers an alternative approach to the study of realities in the form of 'posthumanist performativity' (Barad, 2003). With their aforementioned starting point – that language has been granted too much power – the 'posthumanist performativity' approach sets out to revive the place of matter in scholarship, cautioning scholars not to think of it as 'merely an end product rather than an active factor in further materializations', because to do so would be 'to cheat matter out of the fullness of its capacity' (Barad, 2003, p. 810). One of Barad's most important ideas is that research intervenes in and helps to create the realities it investigates, with the research 'apparatus' playing a key role in the production of realities. For Fraser and Moore (2011, pp. 5–6), Barad's work allows us to observe that: 'Where objects do not have inherent attributes separate from the processes of observation or of intra-action with other objects, it makes no sense to see them as acting independently or consistently on other objects, or as "determining" reality in predictable ways.' So, they argue, universalising or blanket claims about the 'actions', 'properties' and 'effects' of drugs cannot be sustained, including claims about the independent 'physical properties and physiological effects' of drugs (Fraser and Moore, 2011, p. 6). Crucially, Fraser and Moore (2011, p. 5) argue that Barad's observations compel us to rethink our approach to: 'All things, such as physicists, measuring equipment and light – or, we can add, policy-makers, drug treatment services and drugs – [because all] are necessarily the product of their encounters with each other and with other phenomena.' Overall, the ontological turn in AOD scholarship has resulted in the problematisation of many foundational concepts in the field, studied across a wide range of topic areas, settings and 'problems'. Scholars have examined AOD policy (Moore et al., 2015; Fraser, 2016), service provision (Moore & Fraser, 2013) including online counselling (Savic et al., 2018), health promotion (Fraser and Seear, 2011), drug education (Farrugia, 2017), addiction screening tools (Dwyer & Fraser, 2016a), the use of social media (Dwyer & Fraser, 2016b), autobiographical (Fraser, 2015) and other personal accounts of 'addiction' (Moore et al., 2017; Pienaar et al., 2017), medical interventions (Rhodes et al., 2016), reports on 'recovery' (Lancaster et al., 2015) and drug consumption events and practices (Demant, 2013; Fitzgerald, 2015; Dilkes-Frayne, 2016; Dilkes-Frayne & Duff, 2017; Malins, 2017). They have studied issues in policy and service provision, including in methadone maintenance treatment (Fraser, 2006) and for people affected by hepatitis C (Fraser & Seear, 2011), as well as addiction (Fraser et al., 2014). Such work questions claims about the biological properties and 'effects' of drugs as ontologically singular, stable or fixed (see Fraser & Moore,

2011; Fraser & Seear, 2011; Duff, 2013; Dwyer & Moore, 2013; Seear & Moore, 2014). As we explain in the next section, however, there has been less work considering how these kinds of theoretical approaches and tools might be extended to the study of the law itself.

Troubling Judgments: Critical Approaches to the Law

There has been surprisingly little work that incorporates or applies these various critical approaches to a centrally important institutional context: the law. Indeed, beyond a few examples, including our own work (Flacks, 2012, 2018, 2019a, 2019b, 2021; Seear & Fraser, 2014a, 2014b, 2016; Seear, 2015, 2017, 2020) and a handful of other studies (e.g., Race, 2012; Vrecko, 2009; Bunn, 2019), it is rare for these theoretical approaches to be extended to the law, or for in-depth analyses of legal processes and practices to be undertaken. This is a missed opportunity, especially as there is a rich and growing tradition of critical legal scholarship that uses STS approaches, New Materialism and/or posthumanism, to name just a few, applied to a wide range of legal issues and problems (e.g., Cloatre, 2008; Rooke et al., 2012; Philippopoulos-Mihalopoulos, 2015; Davies, 2017; Gandorfer, 2020; Gandorfer & Ayub, 2021). Put simply, there is much to be gained from bringing these fields – of critical AOD scholarship, critical legal scholarship and critical theory – together. One of the best-known STS scholars, Bruno Latour, began his career studying scientific processes, including the workings of laboratories (Latour & Woolgar, 1986) but studied legal processes and practices in later years (Latour, 2013, 2009). Approaching the law as an anthropologist, Latour was keen to understand what it means when people say that they are going to 'speak legally', but he was also concerned with how the law produces 'truth' (Latour, 2009, p. ix). Based on ethnographic work in France, Latour concluded that the essence of law 'does not lie in a definition *but in a practice*' (2009, p. x; emphasis added). To make this point, Latour (2009, p. 264; original emphasis) compares law with other entities and modes of inquiry, including science, finding that:

> Law is not made 'of law' any more than a gas pipe is made *of* gas or science *of* science. On the contrary, it is by means of steel, pipes, regulators, meters, inspectors and control rooms that gas ends up flowing uninterruptedly across Europe; and yet it is well and truly gas that circulates, and not the land, nor steel.

Latour's work on law was concerned with exploring the various processes by which the content of law is made, and stabilised, as well as how uniquely legal versions of 'truth' and 'facts' are generated. He concluded that the law was a 'highly distinctive world' (Latour, 2013, p. 54), with its own processes of 'veridiction' – or truth making, which differ from processes of truth making underway in other institutions, such as science. Importantly, 'modes of connecting' (Matthews & Veitch, 2016, p. 355) are central to law and the realities it constitutes. As the legal scholar Kyle McGee (2015, pp. 62–63; original emphasis) explains, studying these connections requires us to carefully and methodically examine how legal practices and apparatuses forge links and constitute realities:

> To track the slow composition of a unique trajectory of legal truth; to register the specific processes and techniques deployed to fuse a continuous pathway out of scattered elements of uncertain relevance and to thus achieve an order that is witnessably legal; to map the decisive yet easily overlooked transformations of volatile value-objects into disciplined obligations or the multiple transfers of agency implicated in the fabrication of a legal statement; none of these 'earthbound' jurisprudential phenomena are accessible without a dogged insistence on a kind of casuistry that places a premium on the actions occurring in courts of first instance. The conceptual point of this casuistic method is that, when we bypass the radically uncertain, tenuous, hesitant production of judgments, we carelessly afford a set of pricey values – neutrality, objectivity, certainty, integrity, *sécurité juridique* even the rule of law – to wonky artifacts that perhaps do not deserve them or, more interestingly, that have in fact acquired alternative versions of some of these values in ways quite different than we had imagined.

In what follows, our contributors approach the law, as does Latour, from the point of view that it is a 'highly distinctive world' with its own unique processes for generating 'facts' and 'truths'. In examining each case, our authors 'track' how the law constitutes truths about AOD, consider what these truths mean and do and whether other truths or realities might be emerging or be being made possible. The contributions to this collection bring a variety of perspectives and conceptual approaches to bear on exploring these issues, including insights from the broad range of theoretical perspectives we have described in the preceding sections, often attending to questions of gender, sexuality, race, class, discourse and materiality. Different scholars approached their topic in different ways, but all were advised to select a case of interest to them, and to explain why that case raised issues of broader interest. Each chapter includes a summary of that case, followed by an explanation of the author's theoretical, methodological, conceptual or critical approach. The remainder of the chapter is, in each circumstance, dedicated to a discussion of the ways in which this approach illuminates or resolves key issues in the case concerned. Contributors were encouraged to think about 'how things might be otherwise', and future directions for critical enquiry/ legal reform.

A series of themes emerge across the cases studied. These include the centrality of AOD in the making and stabilisation of normative, gendered, sexualised and racialised subjects; the relationship between the governance of drugs and drug-using subjects in the contemporary geopolitical world order; and the role of AOD, law and legal practices in stabilising ideas about the origins and nature of harms, and of 'proper' subjecthood, agency, responsibility and comportment. Across the chapters, our contributors also make important arguments about the ways in which the law stabilises and sustains itself, shapes and enables forms of harm associated with drugs, or can (and might) ameliorate such harms, including through engagement with human rights frameworks and logics that generate sometimes opposing results. Of course, additional or alternative readings of these cases are also possible, including readings that emphasise distinct issues or implications to the ones our contributors have chosen to emphasise here. But the possibility of alternative readings tells us something vital about the law, reminding us of the law's simultaneous power and fragility (see also Seear, 2020), its immanent capacity for rupture and renewal, and the possibility that cases could have been decided otherwise. In this sense, we see the collection as aligned with a growing trend in sociolegal scholarship towards 'prefigurative' thinking (see Cooper, 2022), including through the emergence of a series of critical judgments projects around the world (e.g., Majury, 2006; Hunter et al., 2010; Douglas et al., 2014; Stanchi et al., 2016; McDonald et al., 2017; Ferreira et al., 2020; Chandra et al., 2021; Watson & Douglas, 2021). In these critical judgments projects, contributors also selected real court cases decided in different fields (e.g., family law), critiqued and then rewrote them from critical perspectives, including feminist, Indigenous and queer perspectives. In rewriting real cases, these critical projects aimed to bring 'to the surface the embodied subjectivities of all judicial officers' and reveal how the law is 'composed of *doings*: active subjects, with their own experiences, interpretations, and narratives' as opposed to a singular, true or objective law (Davies, 2017, p. 120; original emphasis). More recently, these critical judgments projects have been joined by a critical legislation project, where legislation is rewritten from feminist perspectives (Batagol et al., 2023). Although the contributors to our edited collection did not rewrite court cases or legislation, we see ourselves as collectively engaged in a kind of 'prefigurative' thinking, insofar as the collection sheds light on how the law is done and how AOD are held together as objects of concern and apparent significance, and considers how these cases might have unfolded differently if new or different ideas were brought into play (see also Seear & Mulcahy, 2024). Overall, we hope that the collection will help us better understand how the law 'works', holds together and comes under pressure, sparking new ideas, opportunities and interventions in the complex global landscape in which drugs and those who use them are judged.

Structure

In Chapter 1, Helen Keane addresses the Australian case of *Van Heerden v Hawkins* (2016) WASCA 42, which effectively made the sale of electronic cigarettes illegal in Western Australia. The case was an unsuccessful appeal by an e-cigarette vendor against a conviction for selling 'products designed to resemble a tobacco product'. The question at the heart of the Supreme Court of Western Australia case was one of resemblance and therefore comparison: to what extent is one object (an e-cigarette) like another object (a conventional cigarette)? In dismissing the appeal, the court asserted that the phrase 'designed to resemble' referred to more than physical similarity but also that considerations of 'use after sale' were irrelevant. Significantly, the vendor had first been acquitted of the offence by a magistrate who concluded that resemblance was not proven, based on the appearance, smell and feel of the specific e-cigarette models offered for sale. Keane draws on two main theoretical resources to critically read this case. The first is an ontological politics approach which understands realities as made and remade through practices and processes of repetition, including in the law (Seear, 2020). The second is recent critical examination of the notion and practice of comparison (Krause, 2016; Fraser & Ekendahl, 2018). The chapter explores the opposing realities of e-cigarettes enacted in the case, one in which e-cigarettes are *not like* conventional cigarettes and therefore reduce tobacco-related harm and one in which e-cigarettes are *like* conventional cigarettes and therefore undermine tobacco control. Keane's analysis is located in a broader discussion of the ontological politics of tobacco control in which new products challenge the regulatory categories and practices of smoking and its elimination.

In Chapter 2, Kate Seear considers findings from the landmark inquest into the death of Veronica Nelson, who was a thirty-seven-year-old Gunditjmara, Dja Dja Wurrung, Wiradjuri and Yorta Yorta woman who died in police custody in Victoria, Australia. The *Inquest into the death of Veronica Nelson* (2023) was a complex and wide-ranging coronial decision that explored the circumstances leading up to Veronica's death in the early hours of the morning on 2 January 2020. Veronica was an Aboriginal woman with complex medical conditions, and a history of injecting drug use. She experienced severe withdrawal in custody, for which she repeatedly sought medical care. The case considered the adequacy of this care and the causes of Veronica's death. The coroner made fifty-one findings and thirty-nine recommendations across a wide range of areas, including matters related to bail, policing, legal advice and representation, court processes and systems, legal education, custodial health care and health care policy, corrections policy and practice and human rights. In this chapter, Seear examines the finding that Veronica's treatment was 'inhumane, cruel and degrading', that 'drug-related' stigma had shaped the nature of care she received and that it had contributed to her death, and the significance of the conclusion that drug-related stigma is a human rights issue. Drawing on critical approaches to human rights 'habits' (Seear & Mulcahy, 2024, following Sedgwick, 1993), and feminist approaches to concepts of 'suffering' in human rights (Sifris, 2013), this chapter considers both what the court's reading of stigma as a human rights issue opens up and makes possible, and whether the court could have gone further. In particular, Seear asks whether the case paves the way to argue that criminalisation is itself 'inhumane, cruel and degrading', and what such a reading could do for people who use drugs into the future.

In Chapter 3, Simon Flacks considers the 2018 UK case of *R v Taj* using John Law's ontological work on collateral realities (Law, 2011). The case was well publicised. It was based on the actions of a defendant who, mistakenly believing a person who had stopped his car on the side of the road to be a terrorist, beat him unconscious with a tyre lever. Taj was experiencing paranoia and psychosis at the time and, in a significant departure from existing legal principles, a set of Court of Appeal judges agreed that he was fully responsible for the crime since his psychosis had been brought on by a bout of drinking in the previous days. He was not intoxicated at the time of the incident. The case has largely been analysed on the basis that it unduly extended the notion of 'prior fault', but Flacks takes a different approach. Instead of attempting to understand the ruling as the (ir)rational or reasonable application of objective rules or precedent, he draws attention to the ways in which the judgment produced knowledge about violence, intoxication and responsibility.

In Chapter 4, Alexandra Dmitrieva and Vladimir Stepanov examine the case of *Abdyusheva and others v Russia*, which was brought before the European Court of Human Rights (ECHR) in 2011. In this case, three individuals argued that Russia's ban on opioid agonist therapy (OAT) programmes violated their rights to freedom from torture, to private and family life, and to non-discrimination, as guaranteed by the European Convention on Human Rights. The case is considered to comprise a set of public political utterances that frame discourses on people who use drugs, OAT, and human rights in Russia, Ukraine and the 'West', as all three parties have been involved in the case, albeit not in equal proportions. Dmitrieva and Stepanov argue that the ECHR served as a platform for Russia to showcase its performance aimed at influencing the international legal order, while the ECHR seemed to accept Russia's terms of engagement. Ukraine, bound to Russia by its Soviet past and at the same time occupied by it, while also aspiring to be part of 'the West', became a place of 'constant engagement' (Fournier, 2012), located within a post-Soviet limbo where the violence against people who use drugs leaves a 'mark that is no mark' (Butler, 2004). Then the mark of these people is less than mark; it exists somewhere between traces of opiates in urine tests and amounts of HIV viral load in blood tests, between the number of criminal records and those that were made in the drug registry. While drug policy itself becomes both the cause and effect of occupation, embodying not only discursive difference but also asserting geopolitical claims within which human lives in general are of little value.

In Chapter 5, Shana Harris discusses a case in which the United States government sued the provider of a supervised consumption site (SCS) to prevent its opening. SCSs are spaces where drug use takes place under the supervision of trained staff who monitor for overdose and administer needed medical assistance. Coupled with the provision of sterile drug use equipment and referrals to services, SCSs are vital apparatuses for reducing overdose, transmission of blood-borne infections, and other harms associated with drug use. At present, only three authorised SCSs operate in the United States; two opened in New York City in 2021 and one opened in Rhode Island in 2024. Another SCS was poised to open years earlier in Philadelphia, Pennsylvania, until the organisation managing it, Safehouse, was sued by the federal government. The resulting lawsuit, *United States v Safehouse*, claims that the establishment of the SCS would violate a provision of the *Controlled Substances Act* known colloquially as the 'crack house statute', which prohibits owning or operating a facility for the purpose of drug use or sales. The lawsuit argued that Safehouse would knowingly provide a place for people to use controlled substances unlawfully if it operated a SCS, which the government saw as equivalent to a 'crack house'. Harris examines this court case and the ongoing litigation against Safehouse to discuss the effects of equating SCS – an established harm reduction intervention – with the pejorative 'crack house' at the heart of the moral panic around crack cocaine in the late twentieth century. She argues that the US government weaponises drug policy against SCS by engaging in a politics of (false) equivalency. By illustrating how this politics is an extension of the war on drugs, she demonstrates the high stakes of this false equivalency on overdose prevention in the United States.

In Chapter 6, Nancy Campbell critically examines a recent turn in the contestation of maintenance therapies in the United States. Long before methadone maintenance arose as a treatment for opiate addiction in the mid 1960s, morphine maintenance was a contested treatment modality, continually constructed not as treatment but as condoning drug use, being 'soft on addicts', or 'substituting' one addiction for another. Metabolic researcher Vincent Dole, a progenitor of methadone maintenance therapy (MMT), presciently asked, 'What kind of disablement does a drug produce?' Although US antidiscrimination and disability rights law did not refer to opioid use disorder (OUD) or medication for opioid use disorder (MOUD) until 2022, since then the United States Department of Justice has brought suit against counties, municipalities, and states in order to counter unlawful discrimination and retaliation on the basis of OUD and MOUD in violation of the 1990 Americans with Disabilities Act (ADA). When lawfully prescribed medications for opioid use disorder are withheld from individuals under court supervision or public employment, there is now a legal basis for remedy. This chapter critically examines the first ADA Title I case, settled by the Department of Justice (DOJ) and the US District Court for the Middle District of Tennessee in January 2023. Reframing opioid use as a disability allowed MOUD to be considered 'reasonable accommodation', the legal standard set by the ADA. This case was the Justice Department's first ADA settlement resolving claims of employment discrimination based on opioid use disorder, and it was clearly designed to send a clear message to employers. The ADA defined disability to include physical or mental impairment[s] that 'substantially limit [...] one or more major life activities', and these have included conditions for which medication is prescribed. Of course, engaging in illegal drug use is clearly defined as falling outside the bounds of protection against discrimination under the ADA – a statement that goes without saying but which is often reiterated in news coverage of these cases. However, policymakers are now encouraged to expand access to treatment with an FDA-approved medication that has been legally prescribed, and to ensure continuity of care for those enrolled in medication-assisted treatment for OUD. The long-standing pro-prohibition and anti-maintenance drug policy of the United States may be shifting, as the DOJ's stance towards these cases heralds the possibility that the weight of the law is now pressuring these long calcified attitudes.

In Chapter 7, Allison Schlosser turns her attention to the issue of drug-induced homicide. She writes that the US continues to struggle with a drug overdose crisis, surpassing 100,000 overdose deaths in 2021. While efforts to frame drug overdose as a public health problem have gained momentum, the criminal legal system remains deeply involved in responding to overdose death punitively. Drug-induced homicide (DIH), a prosecutorial strategy that charges people who sell or deliver drugs to another person who dies of an overdose as manslaughter or homicide, has become a prominent legal response. Criminal legal and public health safety representatives justify this approach by framing people who are charged with DIH as 'kingpin' drug distributors, despite available data suggesting that they are often friends or family of the deceased. Ohio, a state in the Midwestern US hit especially hard by the overdose crisis, pursues more DIH charges than all but one other state in the country. Drug-induced homicide cases are often covered in local news, circulating discourses that define some drug market actors as 'villains' and others as 'victims'. These representations provide opportunities for compassion or derision and social belonging or exclusion. In this chapter, Schlosser examines a 2015 case in which an Ohio woman was charged with involuntary manslaughter and 'corrupting another with drugs' after the overdose death of a friend to whom she delivered drugs. This was considered a 'test case' of the viability of DIH convictions. She draws on Mbembe's theory of necropolitics to examine the influence of local drug overdose prevention organisations and news reporting about the case and explore its implications for the co-construction of life and death in the overdose crisis. Specifically, she argues that DIH cases create what Mbembe calls 'death-worlds' that aim to redeem the social belonging of the deceased as they confer upon the accused the status of the living dead, creating new forms of social life and death.

In Chapter 8, Mats Ekendahl explores one aspect of Sweden's long history of prohibitionist drug policy. Politicians and law enforcement officials show pride in being tough on drugs but also in providing legal certainty and treatment to so-called 'drug abusers'. Those who ignore the illegality of drugs (through producing, trafficking, selling, buying, possessing or using) are considered to choose deviance, and must accept consequences such as prosecution and stigmatisation. Since personal motives for interacting with drugs are plentiful, with blurred boundaries between them (e.g., compulsion versus voluntariness, recreation versus medication), prohibition can be expected to produce different effects in different contexts and lives. Research is scarce, however, on how Swedish case law addresses extenuating circumstances in drug offences. In the light of recent years' political focus on how all illegal drug use feeds gang criminality and violence, thus instigating drugs as inherently bad, it is important to study legal proceedings that deal with situations that could challenge the prohibitionist consensus prevailing in policy, practice and not least law. In this chapter, Ekendahl scrutinises contemporary legal claims related to states of emergency (*nödsituation* in Swedish); one legal case about cannabis trafficking (Swedish Supreme Court, 2012, p. 535) and one about production and use (Swedish Supreme Court, 2017, p. 872). Drawing on Ben Anderson's (2017) work, he reads the cases as illustrating two conflicting invocations of emergency, as governance in a 'state of exception' (prosecutor) and as a 'spark of hope' in a defence of necessity (prosecuted). Results are discussed in relation to Swedish authorities' neglect of the 'slow emergencies' that drug users encounter under prohibition, which include ordinary lives of marginalisation, secrecy, liability, poverty and poor health. The cannabis offence cases studied here could perhaps have been, but were not, treated juridically as legitimate opportunities to let civil rights, social justice and personal well-being transcend the long arm of the law.

In Chapter 9, Renae Fomiatti, Kiran Pienaar and Gemma Nourse explore the question of consent in relation to intoxication. They consider the ways in which the principle of consent, rooted in a social contract model that prioritises individual, liberal personhood in Western legal settings, interacts with concerns relating to the consumption of AOD. They point out that the concept of intoxication and how it is understood and mobilised in the law has significance for assumptions and ideals underpinning sexual consent and, they argue, for sexual politics more broadly. The authors consider how the appellate court case *Still v The Queen* [2010] NSWCCA 131 (23 June 2010) works to reinforce gendered standards of consent. By drawing on theorisations of performativity (Race, 2017) and STS scholarship on standards and standardisation (Bowker & Star, 1999), they track how the law consistently performs intoxication as a non-ideal condition for the exercise of consent. This is achieved by the law's reliance on a conventional account of intoxication as impairment and disorder, one that is sustained and stabilised through the gendering of consent standards. However, they argue that, far from being a non-ideal condition of consent, for example, a situational factor that undermines the full autonomy required for consent – intoxication *preserves* a liberal notion of consent in the law – as rational, orderly and autonomous. As such, it functions as an *ideal* condition (e.g., a normative standard) for the creation of consent. To conclude, they consider the implications of intoxication and consent for the sexual subject in the law, and for the law itself.

In Chapter 10, Aysel Sultan considers the famous case of Maximilian Schmidt, who was accused of setting up Germany's largest digital drug shop under the alias Shiny Flakes, becoming the subject of media stories and Netflix productions. The case provided an opportunity to explore how the move to digitally mediated drug supply has altered the ways in which phenomena such as the 'dealer' and 'dealing' are constituted in socio-technical and legal contexts. The chapter contributes to drug scholarship that identifies the need for novel theoretical frameworks to aid in the study of digitalised drug dealing. Sultan also raises questions about the suitability of the criminal law as the prime means of addressing the use and supply of psychoactive drugs, and particularly the ways in which we attribute 'harm' to contexts with no apparently visible victim.

References

Anderson, B. (2017). Emergency futures: Exception, urgency, interval, hope. *The Sociological Review*, 65(3), 463–477.

Backhouse, C. (1999). *Colour-coded: A legal history of racism in Canada, 1900–1950*. University of Toronto Press.

Barad, K. (2003). Posthuman performativity: Toward an understanding of how matter comes to matter. *Signs Journal of Women in Culture and Society*, 28(3), 801–831.

Batagol, B., Seear, K., Askola, H. & Walvisch, W. (Eds.). (2023). *The feminist legislation project: Rewriting laws for gender-based justice*. Routledge.

Barnard, M., & Barlow, J. (2003). Discovering parental drug dependence: Silence and disclosure. *Children and Society*, 17(1), 45–56.

Bean, P. (2014). *Drugs and crime*. Routledge.

Becker, H. S. (1973). Consciousness, power and drug effects. *Social Science and Modern Society*, 10, 26–31.

Benoit, C., Stengel, C., Marcellus, L., Hallgrimsdottir, H., Anderson, J., MacKinnon, K., Phillips, R., Zazueta, P. & Charbonneau, S. (2014). Providers' constructions of pregnant and early parenting women who use substances. *Sociology of Health & Illness*, 36(2), 252–263.

Berridge, V., & Edwards, G. (1981). *Opium and the people: Opiate use in nineteenth-century England*. Allen Lane.

Bewley-Taylor, D., Blickman, T. & Jelsma, M. (2014). *The rise and decline of cannabis prohibition: The history of cannabis in the UN drug control system and options for reform*. Global Drug Policy Observatory.

Bone, M. (2019). *Human rights and drug control*. Routledge.

Boyd, S. (2019). Gendered drug policy: Motherisk and the regulation of mothering in Canada. *International Journal of Drug Policy*, 68, 109–116.

Bowker, G. C., & Star, S. L. (1999). *Sorting things out: Classification and its consequences*. The MIT Press.

Bunn, R. (2019). Conceptualizing addiction as disability in discrimination law: A situated comparison. *Contemporary Drug Problems*, 46(1), 58–77.

Butler, J. (1990). *Gender trouble: Feminism and the subversion of identity*. Routledge.

Butler, J. (1993). *Bodies that matter*. Routledge.

Butler, J. (2004). *Precarious life: The powers of mourning and violence*. Verso.

Campbell, N. D. (2000). *Using women: Gender, drug policy, and social justice*. Routledge.

Campbell, N. D. (2025). Policing maintenance: Judicial restrictions on medication for opioid use disorder (MOUD) as a violation of the Americans with Disability Act (ADA). In S. Flacks & K. Seear (Eds.), *Judging drugs* (pp. 123–143). Cambridge University Press.

Campbell, N. D., & Ettorre, R. (2011). *Gendering addiction: The politics of drug treatment in a neurochemical world*. Palgrave Macmillan.

Chandra, A., Sen, J. & Chaudhary, R. (2021). Introduction: The Indian feminist judgments project. *Indian Law Review*, 5(3), 261.

Cloatre, E. (2008). TRIPS and pharmaceutical patents in Djibouti: An ANT analysis of socio-legal objects. *Social and Legal Studies*, 17, 263–281.

Cooper, D. (2022). Decertification: Researching a prefigurative law reform proposal. *Legalities*, 2(2), 133–149.

Courtwright, D. (2001). *Forces of habit: Drugs and the making of the modern world*. Harvard University Press.

Davies, M. (2017). *Law unlimited: Materialism, pluralism and legal theory*. Routledge.

Demant, J. (2013). Affected in the nightclub: A case study of regular clubbers' conflictual practices in nightclubs. *International Journal of Drug Policy*, 24(3), 196–202.

Dennis, F., Pienaar, K. & Rosengarten, M. (Eds.). (2023). *Narcofeminisms: Revisioning drug use*. SAGE Publications.

Derrida, J. (1993). The rhetoric of drugs: An interview (M. Israel, Trans.). In A. Alexander & M. S. Roberts (Eds.), *High culture: Reflections on addiction and modernity* (pp. 19–44). SUNY Press.

Dilkes-Frayne, E. (2016). Drugs at the campsite: Socio-spatial relations and drug use at music festivals. *International Journal of Drug Policy*, 33, 27–35.

Dilkes-Frayne, E., & Duff, C. (2017). Tendencies and trajectories: The production of subjectivity in an event of drug consumption. *Environment and Planning D: Society and Space*, 35(5), 951–967.

Dmitrieva, A., & Stepanov, V. (2025). The undeclared war on drugs in the post-Soviet limbo. In S. Flacks & K. Seear (Eds.), *Judging drugs* (pp. 87–105). Cambridge University Press.

Douglas, H., Bartlett, F., Luker, T. & Hunter, R. (Eds.). (2014). *Australian feminist judgments: Righting and rewriting law*. Hart Publishing.

Duff, C. (2013). The social life of drugs. *International Journal of Drug Policy*, 24(3), 167–172.

Dwyer, R., & Fraser, S. (2016a). Addicting via hashtags: How is Twitter making addiction? *Contemporary Drug Problems*, 43(1), 79–97.

Dwyer, R., & Fraser, S. (2016b). Making addictions in standardised screening and diagnostic tools. *Health Sociology Review*, 25(3), 223–239.

Dwyer, R., & Moore, D. (2013). Enacting multiple methamphetamines: The ontological politics of public discourse and consumer accounts of a drug and its effects. *International Journal of Drug Policy*, 24(3), 203–211.

Ekendahl, M. (2025). 'Speaking legally' to rule out emergency in Swedish cannabis cases. In S. Flacks & K. Seear (Eds.), *Judging drugs* (pp. 165–182). Cambridge University Press.

Farrugia, A. (2017). Gender, reputation and regret: The ontological politics of Australian drug education. *Gender and Education*, 29(3), 281–298.

Ferreira, N., Moscati, M. F. & Raj, S. S. (Eds.). (2020). *Queer judgments: Lesbian, gay, bisexual, transgender and queer judges on the importance of LGBTQI+ rights in law and society*. CounterPress.

Fitzgerald, J. (2015). *Framing drug use: Bodies, space, economy and crime*. Palgrave Macmillan.

Flacks, S. (2012). Deviant disabilities: The exclusion of drug and alcohol addiction from the Equality Act 2010. *Social and Legal Studies*, 21(3), 395–415.

Flacks, S. (2018). Making drug harms: Punishments for drug offenders who pose risks to children. *European Journal of Criminology*, 15(5), 561–579.

Flacks, S. (2019a). Dangerous drugs, dangerous mothers: Gender, responsibility and the problematisation of parental substance use. *Critical Social Policy*, 39(3), 477–497.

Flacks, S. (2019b). Substance misuse and parenting: Making drugs and gender in the family court. *International Journal of Law in Context*, 15(4), 424–441.
Flacks, S. (2021). *Law, drugs and the politics of childhood: From protection to punishment*. Routledge.
Flacks, S. (2023). Who is the addict-offender? A historical ontology. *Social & Legal Studies*, 32(1), 85–103.
Flacks, S. (2025). Violence, alcohol and the making of psychosis. In S. Flacks & K. Seear (Eds.), *Judging drugs* (pp. 68–86). Cambridge University Press.
Fomiatti, R., Pienaar, K. & Nourse, G. (2025). Rethinking the sexual subject: Assembling intoxication, gender and consent in the law. In S. Flacks & K. Seear (Eds.), *Judging drugs* (pp. 183–202). Cambridge University Press.
Fournier, A. (2012). *Forging rights in a new democracy: Ukrainian students between freedom and justice*. University of Pennsylvania Press.
Fraser, S. (2006). The chronotope of the queue: Methadone maintenance treatmentand the production of time, space and subjects. *International Journal of Drug Policy*, 17, 192–202.
Fraser, S. (2015). A thousand contradictory ways: Addiction, neuroscience and expert autobiography. *Contemporary Drug Problems*, 42(1), 38–59.
Fraser, S. (2016). Articulating addiction in alcohol and other drug policy: A multiverse of habits. *International Journal of Drug Policy*, 31, 6–14.
Fraser, S., & Ekendahl, M. (2018). 'Getting better': The politics of comparison in addiction treatment and research. *Contemporary Drug Problems: An Interdisciplinary Quarterly*, 45(2), 87–106.
Fraser, S., & Seear, K. (2011). *Making disease, making citizens: The politics of hepatitis C*. Ashgate.
Fraser, S., & Moore, D. (2011). Governing through problems: The formulation of policy on amphetamine-type stimulants (ATS) in Australia. *International Journal of Drug Policy*, 22, 498–506.
Fraser, S., Moore, D. & Keane, H. (2014). *Habits: Remaking addiction*. Palgrave.
Fraser, S., & valentine, K. (2008). *Substance and substitution: Methadone subjects in liberal societies*. Palgrave Macmillan.
Gandorfer, D. (2020). *Matterphorics: On the laws of theory* (Doctoral dissertation). Princeton University.
Gandorfer, D., & Ayub, Z. (2021). Introduction: Matterphorical. *Theory and Event*, 24(1), 2–13.
Ghiabi, M. (2019). *Drugs politics: Managing disorder in the Islamic Republic of Iran*. Cambridge University Press.
Gomart, E. (2002). Towards a generous constraint: Freedom and coercion in French addiction treatment. *Sociology of Health & Illness*, 24, 517–549.
Harris, S. (2025). From crack house to supervised consumption site: Overdose and the politics of (false) equivalency in the United States. In S. Flacks & K. Seear (Eds.), *Judging drugs* (pp. 106–122). Cambridge University Press.

Hunter, R., McGlynn, C. & Rackley, E. (Eds.). (2010). *Feminist judgments: From theory to practice*. Hart Publishing.

Kendell, R. (2003). Cannabis condemned: The proscription of Indian hemp. *Addiction*, 98(2), 143–151.

Kohn, M. (1992). *Dope girls: The birth of the British drug underground*. Lawrence & Wishart.

Koram, K. (Ed.). (2019). *The war on drugs and the global colour line*. Pluto Press.

Krause, M. (2016). Comparative research: Beyond linear-causal explanation. In J. Deville, M. Guggenheim & Z. Hrdličková (Eds.), *Practising comparison: Logics, relations, collaborations* (pp. 85–104). Mattering Press.

Kroll, B., & Taylor, A. (2003). *Parental substance misuse and child welfare*. Jessica Kingsley Publishers.

Lancaster, K., Duke, K. & Ritter, A. (2015). Producing the 'problem of drugs': A cross-national comparison of 'recovery' discourse in two Australian and British reports. *International Journal of Drug Policy*, 26, 617–625.

Latour, B. (2004). Why has critique run out of steam? From matters of fact to matters of concern. *Critical Inquiry*, 30, 225–248.

Latour, B. (2009). *The making of law: An ethnography of the Conseil d'État* (M. Brilman & A. Pottage, Trans.). Polity.

Latour, B. (2013). *An inquiry into modes of existence: An anthropology of the moderns* (C. Porter, Trans.). Harvard University Press.

Latour, B., & Woolgar, S. (1986). *Laboratory life: The construction of scientific facts*. Princeton University Press.

Law, J. (2011). Collateral realities. In F. Rubio & P. Baert (Eds.), *The politics of knowledge* (pp. 156–178). Routledge.

Majury, D. (2006). Introducing the Women's Court of Canada. *Canadian Journal of Women and the Law*, 18, 1–19.

Malins, P. (2017). Desiring assemblages: A case for desire over pleasure in critical drug studies. *International Journal of Drug Policy*, 49, 126–132.

Matthews, D., & Veitch, S. (2016). The limits of critique and the forces of law. *Law and Critique*, 27(3), 349–361.

McDonald, E., Powell, R., Stephens, M. & Hunter, R. (2017). *Feminist judgments of Aotearoa New Zealand: Te Rino: A two-stranded rope*. Bloomsbury Publishing.

McGee, K. (Ed.). (2015). *Latour and the passage of law*. Edinburgh University Press.

Mol, A. (1999). Ontological politics: A word and some questions. *The Sociological Review*, 47(1), 74–89.

Mol, A. (2002). *The body multiple: Ontology in medical practice*. Duke University Press.

Møller, K., & Hakim, J. (2023). Critical chemsex studies: Interrogating cultures of sexualized drug use beyond the risk paradigm. *Sexualities*, 26(5–6), 547–555.

Moore, D., & Fraser, S. (2013). Producing the 'problem' of addiction in drug treatment. *Qualitative Health Research*, 23(7), 916–923.
Moore, D., Fraser, S., Törrönen, J. & Tinghög, M. E. (2015). Sameness and difference: Metaphor and politics in the constitution of addiction social exclusion, and gender in Australian and Swedish drug policy. *International Journal of Drug Policy*, 26(4), 420–428.
Moore, D., Pienaar, K., Dilkes-Frayne, E. & Fraser, S. (2017). Challenging the addiction/health binary with assemblage thinking: An analysis of consumer accounts. *International Journal of Drug Policy*, 44, 155–163.
Musto, D. (1973). *The American disease: Origins of narcotic controls*. Yale University Press.
Oltermann, P. (2022, 12 September). Germany's move to legalise cannabis slows over fears of clash with EU laws. *The Guardian*. www.theguardian.com/world/2022/sep/12/germany-coalition-legalise-cannabis-laws-eu-european-court-justice.
Philippopoulos-Mihalopoulos, A. (2015). *Spatial justice: Body, lawscape, atmosphere*. Routledge.
Pienaar, K., Moore, D., Fraser, S., Kokanovic, R., Treloar, C. & Dilkes-Frayne, E. (2017). Diffracting addicting binaries: An analysis of personal accounts of alcohol and other drug 'addiction'. *Health: An Interdisciplinary Journal for the Social Study of Health, Illness and Medicine*, 21(5), 519–537.
Pienaar, K., Murphy, D. A., Race, K. & Lea, T. (2020). Drugs as technologies of the self: Enhancement and transformation in LGBTQ cultures. *International Journal of Drug Policy*, 78, 102695.
Queirolo, R., Rossel, C., Álvarez, E. & Repetto, L. (2019). Why Uruguay legalized marijuana? The open window of public insecurity. *Addiction*, 114(7), 1313–1321.
Race, K. (2009). *Pleasure consuming medicine: The queer politics of drugs*. Routledge.
Race, K. (2012). Framing responsibility: HIV, biomedical prevention, and the performativity of the law. *Bioethical Inquiry*, 9, 327–339.
Race, K. (2017). *The gay science: Intimate experiments with the problem of HIV*. Routledge.
Reith, G. (2004). Consumption and its discontents: Addiction, identity, and the problems of freedom. *British Journal of Sociology*, 55(2), 283–300.
Rhodes, T., Closson, E., Paparini, S., Guise, A. & Strathdee, S. (2016). Towards 'evidence-making intervention' approaches in the social science of implementation science: The making of methadone in East Africa. *International Journal of Drug Policy*, 30, 17–26.
Rooke, C., Cloatre, E. & Dingwall, R. (2012). The regulation of nicotine in the United Kingdom: How nicotine gum came to be a medicine, but not a drug. *Journal of Law and Society*, 39(1), 39–57.

Room, R. (2006). The dangerousness of drugs. *Addiction*, 101(2), 166–168.

Savic, M., Dilkes-Frayne, E., Carter, A., Kokanovic, R., Manning, V., Rodda, S. N. & Lubman, D. I. (2018). Making multiple 'online counsellings' through policy practice: An evidence-making intervention approach. *International Journal of Drug Policy*, 53, 73–82.

Schlosser, A. V. (2025). 'This is only the beginning': Drug induced homicide, a test case, and the construction of death-worlds in the U.S. overdose crisis. In S. Flacks & K. Seear (Eds.), *Judging drugs* (pp. 144–164). Cambridge University Press.

Seddon, T. (2010). *A history of drugs*. Routledge.

Seddon, T. (2020). Immoral in principle, unworkable in practice: Cannabis law reform, the Beatles, and the Wootton Report. *The British Journal of Criminology*, 60, 1567–1584.

Seddon, T., Williams, L. & Ralphs, R. (2012). *Tough choices: Risk, security and the criminalisation of drug policy*. Oxford University Press.

Sedgwick, E. (1993). Epidemics of the will. In E. Sedgwick (Ed.), *Tendencies*. Duke University Press, 130–142.

Seear, K. (2013). What do we really know about doping 'effects'? An argument for doping effects as co-constituted 'phenomena'. *Performance Enhancement and Health*, 2(4), 201–209.

Seear, K. (2015). Making addiction, making gender: A feminist performativity analysis of Kakavas v Crown Melbourne Limited. *Australian Feminist Law Journal*, 41(1), 65–85.

Seear, K. (2017). The emerging role of lawyers as addiction 'quasi-experts'. *International Journal of Drug Policy*, 44, 183–191.

Seear, K. (2020). *Law, drugs and the making of addiction: Just habits*. Routledge.

Seear, K. (2025). Remembering Poccum: Stigma, suffering, torture and rupture after the death of Veronica Nelson. In S. Flacks & K. Seear (Eds.), *Judging drugs* (pp. 49–67). Cambridge University Press.

Seear, K., & Fraser, S. (2014a). Beyond criminal law: The multiple constitution of addiction in Australian legislation. *Addiction Research and Theory*, 22(5), 438–450.

Seear, K., & Fraser, S. (2014b). The addict as victim: Producing the 'problem' of addiction in Australian victims of crime compensation laws. *International Journal of Drug Policy*, 25(5), 826–835.

Seear, K., & Fraser, S. (2016). The addict as victim: Producing the 'problem' of addiction in Australian victims of crime compensation laws. *International Journal of Drug Policy*, 25(5), 826–835.

Seear, K., & Moore, D. (Eds.). (2014). Complexity: Researching alcohol and other drugs in a multiple world (Conference Special Issue). *Contemporary Drug Problems*, 41(3), 293–484.

Seear, K., & Mulcahy, S. (2025). Troubling drug law, political participation and human rights: A dope sick ontology. *Contemporary Drug Problems*, 52(4), 450–466.

Seear, K., & Mulcahy, S. (2024). Forging new habits: Critical drugs scholarship as an otherwise to rights. *International Journal of Human Rights*, 8–9, 1329–1352.

Sifris, R. (2009). *Reproductive freedom and torture in international human rights*. Routledge.

Stanchi, K., Berger, L. L. & Crawford, B. J. (2016). *Feminist judgments: Rewritten opinions of the United States Supreme Court*. Cambridge University Press.

Stevens, A. (2011). *Drugs, crime and public health*. Routledge.

Swedish Supreme Court. (2012). *NJA 2012 s. 535* [Cannabis trafficking case].

Swedish Supreme Court. (2017). *NJA 2017 s. 872* [Production and use of cannabis case].

valentine, K., & Seear, K. (2020; early online). Commentary on Alex Stevens (2020) Critical realism and the 'ontological politics of drug policy'. *International Journal of Drug Policy*, 84.

Valverde, M. (1998). *Diseases of the will: Alcohol and the dilemmas of freedom*. Cambridge University Press.

Vrecko, S. (2009). Therapeutic justice in drug courts: Crime, punishment and societies of control. *Science as Culture*, 18(2), 217–232.

Watson, N., & Douglas, H. (2021). *Indigenous legal judgments: Bringing Indigenous voices into judicial decision making*. Routledge.

Weinberg, D. (2002). On the embodiment of addiction. *Body & Society*, 8(4), 1–19.

1

What Is an E-cigarette?

Comparison and Resemblance in Tobacco Control

HELEN KEANE

Introduction

'What is an e-cigarette?' This ostensibly simple question is central to the classification and regulation of these popular and contested devices. From their first development, e-cigarettes, which deliver nicotine via vaporisation of a liquid solution, were marketed and presented as *like* conventional cigarettes in crucial ways. Not only were they called electronic cigarettes, that is, a type of cigarette, but early models were designed to look like conventional cigarettes, including a tip which lit up when inhaled (Ozga et al., 2022). Moreover, the clouds of vapour they produced resembled smoke. Public health and tobacco control organisations quickly identified e-cigarettes as a threat to individual and population health. They emphasised the devices' capacity to produce nicotine addiction (just like cigarettes), to undermine the denormalisation of smoking and to enable tobacco industry expansion (Bell & Keane, 2012; Berridge et al., 2023). The rapid rise of e-cigarette use (or vaping as it is now known) among young people has solidified and intensified this emphasis on harm. In contrast, supporters of their harm reduction potential highlight the fundamental difference of e-cigarettes from cigarettes: there is no combustion of tobacco involved in their use. Therefore, they represent a significantly safer form of nicotine consumption and a valid and effective smoking cessation option (Mendelsohn et al., 2023). From the harm reduction perspective, the similarities between vaping and smoking are a crucial beneficial feature as they underpin the appeal of vaping to smokers who are unable or reluctant to quit using other less cigarette-like methods (Keane et al., 2017).

Dramatic changes in product design have taken place since the early days of e-cigarettes, and the disposable pods and tank models which currently dominate the market no longer look like cigarettes. Alongside these product changes has been the rise and proliferation of the language of vapes and vaping, and the adoption of 'electronic nicotine delivery system' (ENDS) or 'nicotine vaping products' (NVP) as accepted terminology in scientific and academic research (although e-cigarette is still also used in academic publications) (O'Connor et al., 2021). Vaping is now established as a practice independent from smoking and smoking cessation, especially among young people (McCausland et al., 2020; Tokle, 2020). Most obviously, many young vapers have never been smokers of conventional cigarettes. A recent Australian survey found that curiosity rather than a pre-existing relationship with smoking was the most common reason for using cigarettes among fifteen- to twenty-four-year-olds (Australian Institute of Health and Welfare, 2024a). The automatic coupling of conventional cigarettes and electronic devices has loosened in academic research, public discourse and daily life. However 'dual use' (combining e-cigarettes use with smoking) is common among adult vapers (Brown et al., 2020; Smith et al., 2021; Australian Institute of Health and Welfare, 2024b).

Despite the increasing independence of vaping from smoking, the relationship of e-cigarettes to conventional cigarettes and the extent of their similarity remains central to the devices' legal and regulatory categorisation. Jurisdictions classify e-cigarettes in different ways: as tobacco products, as medicines, as consumer products and as unique products requiring new legislation. Some jurisdictions use multiple classifications to regulate these products (Campus et al., 2021). Nicotine is also subject to different forms of classification depending on form, for example, it may be controlled as a poison or made available as a therapeutic good. Regulation as a 'tobacco product' groups e-cigarettes with cigarettes and enables their inclusion in existing tobacco control legislation, such as bans on smoking in public places (Campus et al., 2021). Categorisation as a medical product enables e-cigarettes to be constituted as therapeutic smoking cessation devices, similar to existing nicotine replacement therapies, but if they are regulated *solely* as medicinal devices, accessibility is restricted, especially if they are prescription only (Morphett et al., 2019). This restrictive medical classification is currently in place in Australia, although in practice there is 'widespread non-compliance' (Gailberger cited in Gartner, 2023, p. 1298). Crucially, different classifications not only effect levels of availability but also produce different practices and meanings of use (Lempert et al., 2016).

Summary of the Cases

This chapter analyses a series of Australian court cases which wrestled with the identity and legal status of e-cigarettes as non-tobacco cigarette-like products. More specifically, the question at the heart of the cases was one of resemblance. The key case is *Van Heerden v Hawkins* (2016) WASCA 42, which effectively made the sale of e-cigarettes illegal in Western Australia (including nicotine-free devices). *Van Heerden v Hawkins* was an unsuccessful appeal in the Western Australia Supreme Court by the owner of an online e-cigarette business following his conviction under the Western Australia Tobacco Products Control Act 2006 (henceforth referred to as the Act). The case includes forensic and detailed legal discourse about the kind of object an e-cigarette is, what resemblance means in the context of tobacco legislation, and how broadly or narrowly resemblance should be defined. My discussion also includes the preceding cases on the same matter as these are referred to and extensively quoted in *Van Heerden v Hawkins*. These preceding cases are the cigarette vendor's original acquittal in the magistrates' court, the successful Supreme Court appeal against the acquittal which convicted the vendor (*Hawkins v Van Heerden WASC 127*, 2014), and the consequent sentencing of the vendor (*Hawkins v Van Heerden [No.2] WASC 226*, 2014).

The timeline begins in 2011, when sixty-nine packages of e-cigarettes were seized by the Western Australia health department after being found at the home of Vincent Van Heerden, operator of the Heavenly Vapours website. Van Heerden was charged under section 106 (henceforth s. 106) of the Act, which prohibits selling 'any food, toy or other product that is not a tobacco product' but is 'designed to resemble a tobacco product or a package' (2006, part 7, div. 2, p. 51). He pleaded not guilty. At the magistrates' court trial, the prosecutor tendered as evidence the two models of e-cigarettes that were seized, the 510-T and the eGo-T, both with user manuals, as well as a printout of text and images from the Heavenly Vapours website (*Van Heerden v Hawkins*, p. 11).

The magistrate concluded that these devices were within the category of 'other product' in the Act and therefore were subject to its provisions. She then interpreted resemblance to be properly limited to 'the physical appearance of the product' (*Van Heerden v Hawkins*, p. 13). On this basis she acquitted Van Heerden, outlining the tangible material differences between the e-cigarettes and conventional cigarettes in some detail. She further asserted that even if use were to be taken into account as well as appearance, the products did not resemble tobacco products. In opposition, the prosecution witness, a compliance officer with the Western Australia Department of Health, stated that someone who is smoking an e-cigarette looks exactly like someone who is smoking a normal cigarette. The product is similar in shape, the hand and mouth actions are very similar and some features of e-cigarettes such as the vapour and the LED light at the end were designed to simulate the burning of a cigarette (*Van Heerden v Hawkins*, p. 12).

Van Heerden's acquittal was successfully appealed in the Western Australia Supreme Court by the health department in 2014, and a fine of $1,750 imposed (*Hawkins v Van Heerden*; *Hawkins v Van Heerden [No. 2]*). In its judgment in favour of the health department, the court stated that 'designed to resemble' should be interpreted broadly to mean 'intended to have a likeness or similarity to, or to have some feature in common with, a tobacco product' (*Hawkins v Van Heerden*, p. 20). Thus the comparison should *not* be restricted to physical appearance. The court therefore considered the similarity between using an e-cigarette and smoking, rather than exclusively considering the features of the devices themselves, as the magistrate had done. The court accepted the health department's position that e-cigarette users 'are seen to be engaging in a practice which resembles the smoking of tobacco products' (*Hawkins v Van Heerden [No. 2]*, p. 8). In dismissing Van Heerden's subsequent appeal against conviction, the Supreme Court similarly ruled that e-cigarettes (even if free of nicotine) were subject to the relevant section of the Act and did resemble tobacco products, thereby rendering their sale prohibited.

Approach

I draw on two main theoretical resources to read these cases and to explore what they reveal about tobacco control and tobacco harm reduction. The first is an ontological politics approach which understands realities as made and remade through practices and processes of repetition, including in the law (Mol, 2002; Law, 2011; Seear, 2020). This approach is a radical challenge to the idea that objects, such as e-cigarettes, have a singular and fixed identity that can be independently observed. Instead, as noted in the introduction to this volume, maintaining an object's stable identity as it moves between sites requires ongoing effort, and this identity is a fragile effect of processes and practices rather than an inherent essence. As science and technology studies scholar John Law argues, 'if reality *appears* (as it usually does) to be independent, prior, definite, singular or coherent this is because it is being *done* that way' (Law, 2011, p. 156, emphasis in original). In his analysis of a PowerPoint lecture on animal welfare, Law (2011) identifies key processes of selection, juxtaposition, deletion, ranking and framing which enable the performance of a coherent reality.

Anthropologist Rebecca Lynch has recently used this ontological approach to analyse the multiple constructions of e-cigarettes in public health debates about their benefits, risks and harms (Lynch, 2018). As she observes, 'e-cigarettes are not one thing, separate from space and time, but rather are objects that emerge relationally from particular circumstances' (Lynch, 2018, p. 195). Therefore the opposing 'sides' in the public health commentary about vaping are talking about different things, and the 'e-cigarette objects' that emerge in these debates may not be recognisable to users. Her account demonstrates the value of attending to the dynamic qualities of objects in contested evaluations of risk.

Legal practices provide compelling examples of the enactment of multiple realities because the law is designed to be performative, to have a capacity to 'provoke transformations and change worlds' (Seear, 2020, p. 172). While this capacity is perhaps more obvious in grand moments of proclamation and prohibition, the cases I examine are examples of small-scale and mundane constitutive power which nevertheless contribute to the stabilisation of reality within a highly politicised and high stakes field. In the magistrates' court in 2013, e-cigarettes were enacted as *not like* cigarettes, leaving open their capacity to reduce tobacco harm. In the Supreme Court in 2014 and 2016, they were enacted as *like* cigarettes, thereby closing down this capacity while also making them prohibited items. These decisions changed the local worlds of tobacco control and nicotine consumption. Despite the specificity of these cases, they have implications for the management and regulation of drugs and other forms of risky consumption. However, in this chapter my analysis will focus on the ontological and comparative politics of tobacco control (in particular strategies of denormalisation) and tobacco harm reduction.

The second theoretical resource I draw on is recent critical examination of the notion and practice of comparison (Krause, 2016; Fraser & Ekendahl, 2018; Seear et al., 2020). Comparison, alongside other practices already mentioned such as framing, selection and ranking, is a taken-for-granted and ubiquitous technique in knowledge-making (Stengers, 2011). As a tool in the enactment of realities, comparison is not neutral but is rather a political process which can produce and reinforce normalising hierarchies (Seear et al., 2020). Comparison is a common device in drug policy and law, as substances and practices are evaluated and stabilised in terms of their differences from and similarities to each other. In the case of e-cigarettes, the comparison and ranking of different forms of risk and harm are central to debates about classification and regulation. In what follows I examine the enactment, mobilisation and participation of e-cigarettes in contemporary tobacco control, focusing on two material-discursive sites where questions of comparison and resemblance are both significant and contentious. These are smoking denormalisation and tobacco harm reduction.

Smoking Denormalisation and Ontologies of (Non-)resemblance

Van Heerden v Hawkins cannot be understood without some knowledge of tobacco control, and in particular, the strategy of smoking denormalisation. The transformation of cigarette smoking from a widespread, routine and socially valued practice to an abject and stigmatised addiction inseparable from disease and death is one of the most lauded triumphs of modern public health (Brandt 2004; Bell, 2011; Keane, 2014). The decline in adult smoking rates from the 1970s to the present in countries like Australia is in large part attributed to the tobacco control strategy of denormalisation (Voigt, 2013).

Denormalisation seeks to make smoking 'less desirable, less acceptable, and less accessible' by reinforcing 'the fact that tobacco use is not a mainstream or normal activity in our society' (California Department of Public Health cited in Sanders et al., 2020, p. 497). The goal is to erode community tolerance for smoking (Hanley-Jones et al., 2023). The types of action which promote denormalisation include advertising and marketing bans, sales restrictions, smoke-free legislation and public health campaigns which reinforce the idea of smoking as repulsive, dirty and antisocial. As Sanders and colleagues (2020) and others (e.g., Bell et al., 2010) have observed, smoking denormalisation is unusual in contemporary public health because it effectively increases substance-related stigma, within a field that otherwise views stigma as an obstacle to health and social justice.

Denormalisation expands the category of smoking-related harm, from the direct effects of the practice on individuals to its influence on social and cultural norms. This expansion is perhaps most apparent in relation to location restrictions on smoking outdoors, for example the prohibiting of smoking on beaches, near playgrounds and at outdoor events (Greenhalgh et al., 2024). While the original justification for indoor smoke-free areas was the health harms of passive smoking, these kinds of outdoor restrictions are as much about making smoking less convenient and visible as they are about exposure to second-hand smoke (Painter, 2019). They also reproduce the idea of cigarettes, especially the sight and smell of smoke, as contaminating even at minimal levels and from a distant source (Dennis, 2016). In particular, the removal of smoking from public areas likely to be used by children, or associated with children, has both a safety and a symbolic value (see also Nancy Campbell, Chapter 6).

The Act exemplifies denormalisation as a public health strategy. In particular it demonstrates the regulatory expansion that is characteristic of tobacco denormalisation. In the second reading of the bill which became the 2006 Act, the then state minister for health, James McGinty, stressed its progression from existing legislation, with new restrictions related to advertising, sponsorships, packaging and labelling, and sales to minors. In s. 106 the new Act would also extend 'coverage to non-tobacco products, such as herbal cigarettes and confectionary and toys that resemble tobacco products' (Western Australia, 2005). By including non-tobacco products in tobacco control measures, s. 106 reveals that the concern with visibility in denormalisation strategies extends beyond the observable presence of actual smoking and actual cigarettes to include issues of imitation, simulation, meaning and symbolic value. The section specifically mentions food or toys which look like cigarettes, highlighting the aim of protecting children from the belief that smoking is a normal and fun activity and an everyday practice to be emulated in play.

However, as the cases this chapter discusses demonstrate, the rise of e-cigarettes has given s. 106 and the issue of resemblance a potentially much wider and more significant application. In these court cases, the determination of resemblance is tied to a crucial question about e-cigarettes and their status: whether their availability 'is capable of creating or contributing to the perception that smoking is a commonly pursued and desirable activity' (*Hawkins v Van Heerden [No.2]*, p. 8). In their diverse comparative enactments of e-cigarettes, the courts are doing (at least) two things. Firstly, they are making these devices and their use more or less like a notoriously harmful practice and long-standing, wicked global health problem. Secondly, they are forecasting the impact of these devices on health at a societal or population level, independent of benefits or risks to individual users. To put this another way, the court cases are involved in the transformation of the seized e-cigarettes and their effects.

As outlined earlier, the 2013 magistrates' court case enacted the e-cigarettes as not like cigarettes and therefore not prohibited. This reality was established through what the magistrate framed as an objective assessment of the two seized models based on their physical appearance (*Van Heerden v Hawkins*, p. 13). She first described the 510-T model:

> [It is] made up of two components, one measuring 6 cm in length the other approximately 2 cm in length and when screwed together measured 8 cm. The 510-T is metallic to the touch and at one end there is a grey plastic rounded end.
>
> (cited in *Van Heerden v Hawkins*, p. 11)

Then the eGo-T model:

> [It is] black greyish in colour, with a silver end and a band in the middle. The eGo-T is metallic to touch and comprises three components (including a clear plastic end or mouth piece) which, when assembled, measure approximately 13 cm in length.
>
> (cited in *Van Heerden v Hawkins*, p. 11)

Here objective evaluation is a process of disaggregation into separate parts and qualities, followed by the selection of specific parts (such as the mouthpiece) and qualities (such as metallic feel). It is this disaggregation and selection which renders the devices un-cigarette-like, in part because of their colour and material, in part because a fundamental quality of manufactured cigarettes is their monolithic rather than modular design. That is, cigarettes cannot be disassembled in the way the 510-T and the eGo-T can. Cigarettes are also characterised by their generic form, so the very existence of two distinct models of e-cigarette also acts to highlight difference (Keane, 2014).

Later in her judgment, the magistrate employs an additional mode of comparison which further reinforces the non-resemblance between the e-cigarettes and tobacco products. She states:

> Both products are sold in a black box lacking any reference to cigarettes or cigars. They are not white or brown in colour as might be expected with a cigarette or cigar. Further the products are metallic to the touch. They are not surrounded by paper or a material designed to look like a tobacco leaf or the leaf of another plant. Nor do either have an area designed to resemble the butt of a cigarette delineated by a different colour. The products lack a smell similar to that of tobacco.
>
> (cited in *Van Heerden v Hawkins*, p. 13)

She goes on to note that both models require assembly before use and incorporate a push button (for activation) rather than being ignited by a match or lighter. Overall, 'they appear to resemble a fountain pen or metal writing pen because of their shape, size and metallic feel' (cited in *Van Heerden v Hawkins*, p. 14).

This enactment reiterates some already-mentioned differences but also invokes some new comparisons. Firstly, the products are identified as not emulating the outer material of a cigarette (paper), secondly, the smell of tobacco is introduced as a relevant feature and thirdly, there is a juxtaposition with other familiar and harmless non-cigarette-like objects. By asserting their resemblance to pens, the magistrate installs a new vision of the devices which removes them from the concerns of the Act.

This enactment of the contested e-cigarettes turned out to be fragile and precarious, despite the careful selection and listing of objective differences. It was dismantled by the successful appeal brought by the health department and the subsequent unsuccessful appeal by the vendor. These Supreme Court cases stabilised and made real the resemblance of e-cigarettes to cigarettes, thereby enacting their potential to renormalise smoking and undermine tobacco control. How was this reality of resemblance done? The most obvious process involved giving the 'manner of use' of the devices a much higher ranking in the assessment of resemblance, in line with the health department's assertion that a person vaping looks very much like a person smoking (*Hawkins v Van Heerden*, p. 15). In its deliberations about manner of use, the court effectively produces a new reality, a device-user assemblage, which performs e-cigarette use as an emulation of smoking.

This reality is supported by statement, repetition and comparison of the 'facts' about how the devices are used. First the 'notorious facts' about tobacco products:

> The cigarette or cigar is held in the user's hand. The cigarette or cigar is lit, the user places the cigarette or cigar into his or her mouth, and inhales through the cigarette or cigar so as to take the tobacco smoke into his or her body, and then exhales that smoke upon breathing out.
>
> (*Hawkins v Van Heerden*, p. 25; also cited in *Van Heerden v Hawkins*, p. 19)

These 'notorious facts' are juxtaposed and compared with the 'agreed facts' about e-cigarettes:

> the conveyance of the electronic cigarette to the mouth by hand, the inhalation of the vapour through the cigarette and into the user's mouth, and the exhalation of that vapour out of the body.
>
> (*Hawkins v Van Heerden*, pp. 22–3; also cited in *Van Heerden v Hawkins*, p. 18)

The seized e-cigarette user manuals' references to 'puffs' is also selected by the court as relevant to the determination of resemblance (*Hawkins v Van Heerden*, p. 25; cited in *Van Heerden v Hawkins*, p. 20). In contrast, the difference between the composition of vapour and smoke, stressed by the vendor, is deleted in this representation of facts.

As well as the specific enactment of the device-user assemblage, *Van Heerden v Hawkins* authorised an expansive practice of comparison which brought a relationship of resemblance into being. Three elements were key to this process. The first was the judgment that in assessing resemblance, *all* the attributes and features of the product should be taken into account including 'use' and 'the manner in which the product is ordinarily used', not just appearance (*Van Heerden v Hawkins*, p. 43, emphasis added). As already discussed, this interpretation of resemblance shifts the issue from a restricted concern with the static and fixed surface features of an object, to a more fluid and dynamic evaluation of practices. The second element was the assertion that comparison should involve a consideration of whether products share common features or characteristics, rather than a process of selecting individual features to assess similarity (*Van Heerden v Hawkins*, p.16). This was an endorsement of the related point that the term 'resemble' does not require that the 'offending products' are identical to cigarettes (*Hawkins v Van Heerden*, p. 14). Finally, the court also addressed the significance of intention versus actual resemblance. While s. 106 of the Act does not mention intention, the court's interpretation was that 'designed to resemble' connotes a product which has been produced and manufactured '*with the intention* that it should be like, or have a likeness or similarity to, a tobacco product or a package' (*Van Heerden v Hawkins*, p. 36, emphasis in original). Therefore it found that the prohibition in s. 106 actually refers to the intention, as distinct from whether the product 'is *in fact* like' a tobacco product (emphasis in original). However, it adds that the judgment of intention will necessarily be informed by what the product is in fact like. In this circular logic, intention and factual likeness are distinguished but then reconnected as the latter is taken to be evidence of the former.

So far I have not discussed the vendor Vincent Van Heerden's grounds for appeal against conviction. This omission is because he did not directly dispute the Supreme Court's finding of resemblance, at least in terms of the physical features or manner of use of the devices. Rather his claim was that 'designed to resemble' should properly include not just intention but purpose. He argued that while there may be similarities with tobacco products, the primary purpose of e-cigarettes was to 'minimise the harm of smoking by weaning smokers away from "tobacco products"' in favour of a device without the risks of smoke and tar. The intention evident in their design is 'diametrically opposite, and antithetical, to "tobacco products"' (*Van Heerden v Hawkins*, p. 30). Therefore the e-cigarettes promoted rather than undermined the aims of the Act.

Van Heerden's claims performed e-cigarettes as *anti-tobacco* products, which should be embraced by the health department. His framing attempted to delete or reduce the significance of tobacco denormalisation, instead highlighting potential positive effects of his devices on the health of users. The Supreme Court rejected his framing, stating bluntly that s. 106 was strictly concerned with resemblance, not with whether the products were designed to maintain, promote, reduce or eliminate tobacco smoking. Therefore, it was entirely possible for a product to be prohibited under the Act while also being harm-reducing (*Van Heerden v Hawkins*, p. 45). What this judgment demonstrates is that a prioritisation of resemblance in tobacco control can act to bring smoking denormalisation into direct conflict with harm reduction. The production or reduction of harm is rendered irrelevant to the status of a new technology if it is adjudged to be too similar to smoking.

There is a notable absence in the enactments of e-cigarettes I have outlined so far: nicotine and nicotine addiction. On the one hand this absence can be obviously explained. The e-juice sold by Van Heerden and seized by the health department did not contain nicotine. Moreover, nicotine is outside the realm of resemblance: it is not a visible feature of cigarettes, neither is it observable when tobacco products are used. However, it is still striking that the multiple comparisons of the seized e-cigarettes and conventional cigarettes do not mention the absence and presence of nicotine, given its role in the perpetuation of smoking and the production of smoking-related harm. In the next section, I move from the specific court cases to examine e-cigarettes more broadly in relation to tobacco harm reduction. In this context, nicotine is foregrounded as a crucial element of the e-cigarette device-user assemblage.

E-cigarettes, Nicotine and Tobacco Harm Reduction

Van Heerden v Hawkins can be interpreted as a failed attempt to mobilise e-cigarettes as a form of anti-smoking tobacco harm reduction. In the years since this case, the discourse of tobacco harm reduction has become well established and formalised in research literature and expert debate.

E-cigarettes and vaping are central participants in this field, deployed to both make the case for harm reduction and to demonstrate its inadequacies and risks (Berridge et al., 2023). Indeed the development of electronic vaping technology in the early twenty-first century was crucial to the revitalisation of the idea of tobacco harm reduction. In public health, tobacco harm reduction had been utterly discredited by the failed 'safer smoking' low tar and nicotine strategies of the 1970s (Klein et al., 2022). E-cigarettes and vaping have had the effect of dividing tobacco control, previously unified against smoking and the tobacco industry, into what can be roughly characterised as opposing camps on harm reduction (Carroll et al., 2021; Klein et al., 2022). Governments have also diverged on this question, with the UK health system adopting e-cigarettes as a form of harm reduction, while Australia has imposed increasingly strict restrictions based on what the Department of Health calls 'a precautionary approach' (Hall et al., 2021, p. S325; Berridge et al., 2023).

As I stated in the Introduction, for tobacco harm reduction advocates, the similarity between e-cigarettes and conventional cigarettes are crucial to the devices' potential value and positive impact. This similarity is not about resemblance or emulation, rather it is a matter of substitution, specifically the delivery of substitute nicotine. For supporters, vaping is a useful harm reduction option because it could help smokers who have been unable or unwilling to quit using the methods already on offer (Thirlway et al., 2019; Erku et al., 2020). Unlike nicotine gum or patches, it replaces enough of the pleasures and effects of smoking to be an appealing substitute for this category of 'entrenched' smokers who are disproportionately likely to be from disadvantaged or marginalised groups (Bonevski et al., 2017; Keane et al., 2017; Notley et al., 2018). E-cigarettes could therefore hasten the obsolescence of smoking, allowing tobacco control to achieve its ultimate goal. Unsurprisingly, comparison is central to this enactment of e-cigarettes as harm reduction devices. The comparison to conventional cigarettes highlights their greater safety. The comparison to nicotine replacement therapies such as gum and patches highlights both their legitimacy and unique efficacy as quit aids.

This positive version of e-cigarettes as health-promoting relies on the enactment of some other related realities which together produce a device-user assemblage quite different from the one assembled in *Van Heerden v Hawkins*. Firstly, the user is constituted as a habituated adult smoker who already has a fully established nicotine addiction. Their use of the device is fundamentally a form of replacement – it is enabling them to forgo or at least reduce a notoriously lethal practice in favour of a less harmful one. Secondly, nicotine is framed as a relatively benign substance with a solid track record as a medically endorsed and widely available smoking-cessation aid (Klein et al., 2022). Therefore while not ideal, nicotine dependence can be consistent with health improvement (Berridge et al., 2023, p. 129). E-cigarettes are a modern and cleaner smoke-free method of nicotine delivery, a rational choice for people who are desperate to quit smoking. In this reality, addiction is deleted or at least ranked low as a harm in itself, quite unlike most public health messaging about drugs and drug use.

In Australia this e-cigarette harm reduction device-user assemblage has not been successfully stabilised or translated into policy. The Australian government has imposed a contrasting vision of e-cigarettes as an urgent threat to public health and children's welfare (Butler, 2023). In 2021 all e-cigarettes containing nicotine were designated as prescription-only medications. In 2023 the government acted against 'the growing black market in illegal vaping' by prohibiting the importation and sale of e-cigarettes, including nicotine-free devices. All disposable vaping devices were banned (Butler, 2023; Cohen et al., 2023). It remained possible to access e-cigarettes through medical prescription, prescribed devices must conform to strict packaging, nicotine concentration and flavouring rules which would make them very different from the consumer products which have dominated the market (Butler, 2023; Mendelsohn et al., 2023). In 2024 the regulations were changed to allow adults to purchase vapes with a nicotine concentration of 20 mg/ml or less from a 'participating pharmacy' without a prescription (where state and territory laws allow). Consultation with a pharmacist is required and the devices must be for therapeutic use (Department of Health and Aged Care, 2024). It is not yet clear how this federal regulation will interact with prohibition under s. 106 of the Tobacco Control Act in Western Australia (Greenhalgh et al., 2024).

The dominant Australian reality of e-cigarettes as a dangerous resurgence of the tobacco epidemic depends on a transformation in the figure of the vaper, from an experienced adult smoker to an unsuspecting vulnerable child (Flacks, 2021). The appeal and accessibility of e-cigarettes to children and teenagers became the central matter of concern as evidence mounted of a dramatic rise in youth vaping (Gartner, 2023). Announcing the 2023 reforms, federal health minister Mark Butler framed the government's action as a child protection response. He stated that vaping had become the 'No 1 behavioural issue in high schools.' He accused the tobacco industry of trying to create a 'new generation of nicotine addicts' by targeting children with products 'sold alongside lollies and chocolate bars' (Davey, 2023). Rather than an adult smoker trying to quit (as in the harm reduction assemblage), the typical vaper was now a young non-smoker being exposed to a toxic, addictive drug, and an increased risk of future smoking (Stockings et al., 2024). In addition, a sudden outbreak of serious lung injuries associated with e-cigarette use in young men in the United States further reinforced the harm-producing assemblage (Centers for Disease Control, 2020). The potential of e-cigarettes as smoking cessation devices became irrelevant in this vision of an escalating epidemic of harm.

Material changes in e-cigarettes have also weakened the harm reduction assemblage. Colourful easy to use pod-type vapes with an array of sweet and fruity flavour resist therapeutic or medical categorisation as they connote pleasure, leisure and fun (Keane et al., 2017). These are not the only types of vaping devices available or in use, but they have come to dominate the public health and policy imaginary. To apply the logic of *Van Heerden v Hawkins*, their product design reveals an intention which seems antithetical to smoking cessation and health improvement. As consumer commodities, they are designed to attract and entice customers and to promote both impulse and repeat purchasing.

Conclusion

Juxtaposing *Van Heerden v Hawkins* with the current Australian response to e-cigarettes, as I have done in this chapter, reveals some of the challenges which face tobacco harm reduction as a strategy. In both juridical and policy sites, e-cigarettes are established as risky harm-producing technologies and any health-promoting potential is set aside as irrelevant or illusory. In *Van Heerden v Hawkins* it is the way e-cigarette use resembles smoking and its effect on tobacco denormalisation which is the basis of this enactment (and consequent prohibition). In current Australian policy and public discourse, resemblance is no longer a significant part of the justification for prohibition. Vaping is instead framed as a novel practice, a new form of nicotine consumption which is independently and uniquely harmful due to its appeal to young people. However, the history of smoking, especially tobacco industry malfeasance, remains important to the enactment of vaping as a public health emergency (Butler, 2023; Chapman, 2023). In this account of vaping, centred around concern for children and teenagers, addiction is reinstalled as a national, moral, and health crisis, and any connection to nicotine replacement therapy is severed.

Despite the Australian government's consistently restrictive approach to e-cigarettes, the regulatory classification and control of nicotine products remains complex, arguably incoherent, and open to challenge. Tobacco denormalisation coexists with the legal sale of combustible cigarettes and about 10 per cent of Australian adults still smoke (Greenhalgh et al., 2024). Therapeutic nicotine products, including 'inhalators' advertised as replicating the 'hand to mouth action' of smoking, can be easily purchased in supermarkets and online. The evidence on the long-term effects of nicotine vaping is unclear and health professionals report confusion about the prescription pathway for vaping products (Morphett et al., 2024). Adults who have switched from smoking to vaping feel strongly about its benefits and actively promote it to others (Keane et al., 2017; Morphett et al., 2019).

In this situation of heterogeneous forces, actors and elements, it is not surprising that facts and realities are generated, assembled, and dismantled in multiple sites, including in the law. In *Van Heerden v Hawkins* two models of e-cigarettes were determined to resemble cigarettes, overturning an earlier determination of non-resemblance. Both legal realities required work to be brought into being, specifically the construction of distinct e-cigarette device-user assemblages. Another quite different device-user assemblage is currently dominant in Australia, centred on children and nicotine, and supported by a prohibitionist policy. However, this situation could be disrupted by changes in the materiality of vaping, in the profile and practices of users, and in the broader landscape of tobacco and nicotine consumption.

References

Australian Institute of Health and Welfare. (2024a). Young people's use of vapes and e-cigarettes. www.aihw.gov.au/reports/smoking/young-peoples-vapes-e-cigarettes.

Australian Institute of Health and Welfare. (2024b). Vaping and e-cigarette use in the NDSHS. https://www.aihw.gov.au/reports/smoking/vaping-e-cigarette-use.

Bell, K. (2011). Legislating abjection? Secondhand smoke, tobacco control policy and the public's health. *Critical Public Health*, 21(1), 49–62.

Bell, K., & Keane, H. (2012). Nicotine control: E-cigarettes, smoking and addiction. *International Journal of Drug Policy*, 23(3), 242–247.

Bell, K., McCullough, L., Salmon, A. & Bell, J. (2010). 'Every space is claimed': Smokers' experiences of tobacco denormalisation. *Sociology of Health & Illness*, 32(6), 914–929.

Berridge, V., Bayer, R., Fairchild, A. L. & Hall, W. (2023). *E-cigarettes and the comparative politics of harm reduction: History, evidence, and policy*. Palgrave Macmillan.

Bonevski, B., Borland, R., Paul, C. L. et al. (2017). No smoker left behind: It's time to tackle tobacco in Australian priority populations. *Medical Journal of Australia*, 207(4), 141–142.

Brandt, A. (2004). From nicotine to Nicotrol: Addiction, cigarettes and American culture. In S. Tracy & C. Acker (Eds.), *Altering American consciousness* (pp. 383–402). University of Massachusetts Press.

Brown, R., Bauld, L., de Lacy, E. et al. (2020). A qualitative study of e-cigarette emergence and the potential for renormalisation of smoking in UK youth. *International Journal of Drug Policy*, 75, 102598.

Butler, M. (2023, 2 May). Taking action on smoking and vaping (media release, Commonwealth of Australia Dept. of Health and Aged Care). www.health.gov .au/ministers/the-hon-mark-butler-mp/media/taking-action-on-smoking-and-vaping.

Campus, B., Fafard, P., Pierre, J. S. & Hoffman, S. J. (2021). Comparing the regulation and incentivization of e-cigarettes across 97 countries. *Social Science & Medicine*, 291, 114187.

Carroll, D., Denlinger-Apte, R. L., Dermody, S. S. et al. (2021). Polarization within the field of tobacco and nicotine science and its potential impact on trainees. *Nicotine and Tobacco Research*, 23(1), 36–39.

Centers for Disease Control. (2020). *Outbreak of lung injury associated with the use of e-cigarette, or vaping, products*. US Department of Health and Human Services. www.cdc.gov/tobacco/basic_information/e-cigarettes/severe-lung-dis ease.html.

Chapman, S. (2023, 6 March). A potted history of smoking, and how we're making the same mistakes with vaping. *The Conversation*. https://theconversation.com/ a-potted-history-of-smoking-and-how-were-making-the-same-mistakes-with-vaping-200708.

Cohen, J. E., Gartner, C., Edwards, R. & Hammond, D. (2023). Australia tightens its prescription-only regulation of e-cigarettes. *The British Medical Journal*, 381, 1216.

Davey, M. (2023, 1 May). Australia to ban non-prescription vapes in biggest smoking reforms in a decade. *The Guardian*. www.theguardian.com/australia-news/2023/may/01/australia-to-ban-non-prescription-vapes-in-biggest-smok ing-reforms-in-a-decade.

Dennis, S. (2016). A touching analysis: Of thirdhand smoke, family, publics, and touch. *Contemporary Drug Problems*, 43(2), 154–168.

Department of Health and Aged Care. (2024). *Changes to vaping in Australia from 1 October 2024 – Information for people who vape*. Australian Government.

www.health.gov.au/sites/default/files/2024-09/changes-to-vaping-in-australia-from-1-october-2024-fact-sheet-for-people-who-vape.pdf.

Erku, D., Gartner, C. E., Morphett, K. et al. (2020). Nicotine vaping products as a harm reduction tool among smokers: Review of evidence and implications for pharmacy practice. *Research in Social and Administrative Pharmacy*, 16(9), 1272–1278.

Flacks, S. (2021). *Law, drugs and the politics of childhood: From protection to punishment*. Routledge.

Fraser, S. & Ekendahl, M. (2018). 'Getting better': The politics of comparison in addiction treatment and research. *Contemporary Drug Problems*, 45(2), 87–106.

Gartner, C. (2023). How do you solve a problem like youth vaping? *Drug and Alcohol Review*, 42, 1298–1300.

Greenhalgh, E., Scollo, M. & Winstanley, M. (2024). *Tobacco in Australia: Facts and issues*. Cancer Council Victoria. www.tobaccoinaustralia.org.au.

Hall, W., Morphett, K. & Gartner, C. (2021). A critical analysis of Australia's ban on the sale of electronic nicotine delivery systems. *Neuroethics*, 14, 323–331.

Hanley-Jones, S., Letcher, T. & Wood, L. (2023). The profound effects of the denormalisation of smoking. In E. Greenhalgh, M. Scollo & M. Winstanley (Eds.), *Tobacco in Australia: Facts and issues*. Cancer Council Victoria. www.tobaccoinaustralia.org.au/chapter-5-uptake/5-24-denormalising-smoking.

Hawkins v Van Heerden [2014] *WASC 127*. Supreme Court of Western Australia.

Hawkins v Van Heerden [No. 2] [2014] *WASC 226*. Supreme Court of Western Australia.

Keane, H. (2014). Cigarettes are no longer sublime. *Australian Humanities Review*, 57, 1–20.

Keane, H., Weier, M., Fraser, D. & Gartner, C. (2017). 'Anytime, anywhere': Vaping as social practice. *Critical Public Health*, 27(4), 465–476.

Klein, D. E., Hawkins, B. & Schwartz, R. (2022). Understanding experts' conflicting perspectives on tobacco harm reduction and e-cigarettes. *SSM-Qualitative Research in Health*, 2, 100197.

Krause, M. (2016). Comparative research: Beyond linear-causal explanation. In J. Deville, M. Guggenheim & Z. Hrdličková (Eds.), *Practising comparison* (pp. 45–67). Mattering Press.

Law, J. (2011). Collateral realities. In P. Baert & F. Rubio (Eds.), *The politics of knowledge* (pp. 156–178). Routledge.

Lempert, L. K., Grana, R. & Glantz, S. A. (2016). The importance of product definitions in US e-cigarette laws and regulations. *Tobacco Control*, 25, e44–e51.

Lynch, R. (2018). Slippery slopes and Trojan horses: The construction of e-cigarettes as risky objects in public health debate. In R. Lynch & C. Farrington (Eds.), *Quantified lives and vital data: Exploring health and technology through personal medical devices* (pp. 179–200). Palgrave.

McCausland, K., Jancey, J., Leaver, T., Wolf, K., Freeman, B. & Maycock, B. (2020). Motivations for use, identity and the vaper subculture: A qualitative study of the experiences of Western Australian vapers. *BMC Public Health*, 20, 1–14.

Mendelsohn, C., Wodak, A. & Hall, W. (2023). How should nicotine vaping be regulated in Australia? *Drug and Alcohol Review*, 42(5), 1288–1294.

Mol, A. (2002). *The body multiple*. Duke University Press.

Morphett, K., Holland, A., Ward, S. et al. (2024). Evaluating the implementation of a prescription-only regulatory model for nicotine vaping products: A qualitative study on the experiences and views of healthcare professionals. *International Journal of Drug Policy*, 125, 104353.

Morphett, K., Weier, M., Borland, R. et al. (2019). Barriers and facilitators to switching from smoking to vaping: Advice from vapers. *Drug and Alcohol Review*, 38(3), 234–243.

Notley, C., Ward, E., Dawkins, L. & Holland, R. (2018). The unique contribution of e-cigarettes for tobacco harm reduction in supporting smoking relapse prevention. *Harm Reduction Journal*, 15(1), 1–12.

O'Connor, R., Durkin, S. J., Cohen, J. E., Barnoya, J., Henriksen, L., Hill, S. E. & Malone, R. E. (2021). Thoughts on neologisms and pleonasm in scientific discourse and tobacco control. *Tobacco Control*, 30(4), 359–360.

Ozga, J. E., Felicione, N. J., Douglas, A., Childers, M. & Blank, M. D. (2022). Electronic cigarette terminology: Where does one generation end and the next begin? *Nicotine and Tobacco Research*, 24(3), 421–424.

Painter, K. (2019). Outdoor smoking: Fair or foul? *The British Medical Journal*, 366. https://doi.org/10.1136/bmj.l5754.

Sanders, E., Antin, T., Hunt, G. & Young, M. (2020). Is smoking queer? Implications of California tobacco denormalization strategies for queer current and former smokers. *Deviant Behavior*, 41(4), 497–511.

Seear, K. (2020). *Law, drugs and the making of addiction: Just habits*. Routledge.

Seear, K., Moore, D., Fraser, S. et al. (2020). Consumption in contrast: The politics of comparison in healthcare practitioners' accounts of men who inject performance and image-enhancing drugs. *International Journal of Drug Policy*, 85, 102883.

Singh, S., Windle, S. B., Filion, K. B., Thombs, B. D., O'Loughlin, J. L., Grad, R. & Eisenberg, M. J. (2020). E-cigarettes and youth: Patterns of use, potential harms, and recommendations. *Preventive Medicine*, 133, 106009.

Smith, H., Lucherini, M., Amos, A. & Hill, S. (2021). The emerging norms of e-cigarette use among adolescents: A meta-ethnography of qualitative evidence. *International Journal of Drug Policy*, 94, 103227.

Stengers, I. (2011). Comparison as a matter of concern. *Common Knowledge*, 17(1), 48–63.

Stockings, E. A., Gardner, L. A. & Newton, N. C. (2024). Vaping among young people: Our best defence is self-defence. *Drug and Alcohol Review*, 43(2), 355–358.

Thirlway, F., Bauld, L., McNeill, A. & Notley, C. (2019). Tobacco smoking and vulnerable groups: Overcoming the barriers to harm reduction. *Addictive Behaviors*, 90, 134–135.

Tokle, R. (2020). 'Vaping and fidget-spinners': A qualitative, longitudinal study of e-cigarettes in adolescence. *International Journal of Drug Policy*, 82, 102791.

Van Heerden v Hawkins [2016] WASCA 42.

Voigt, K. (2013). 'If you smoke, you stink': Denormalisation strategies for the improvement of health-related behaviours – The case of tobacco. In D. Strech, I. Hirschberg & G. Marckmann (Eds.), *Ethics in public health and health policy: Concepts, methods, case studies* (pp. 47–61). Springer.

Western Australia (2006). Tobacco Products Control Act 2006 (Western Australia).

Western Australia (2005, 29 June). *Parliamentary debates, Legislative Assembly.*

2

Remembering Poccum

Stigma, Suffering, Torture and Rupture after the Death of Veronica Nelson

KATE SEEAR

Introduction: Enduring Connections

The research for this chapter was undertaken on the lands of the Wurundjeri people of the Kulin Nations. As is customary in the country in which I live and work, or so-called 'Australia' (see Watego, 2021), I acknowledge them as the traditional owners of country, as well as elders past and present. I acknowledge that sovereignty over these lands was never ceded, and that Aboriginal and Torres Strait Islander peoples remain strong in their enduring connections to land, sky, water and culture.

I make these acknowledgements here, first and foremost, as a sincere gesture of recognition and respect. Such acknowledgements also matter in the context of work on drug policy, given the many important connections between drug policy and colonialism. These connections are central to the issues I will examine in this chapter. Many have written about the links between colonialism, imperialism, racism and the war on drugs. Prohibition has both sexist and racist origins (Manderson, 1994; Courtwright, 2002; Zieger, 2008; Cruz, 2017), and racially asymmetrical impacts (Koram, 2019), including in terms of policing and incarceration. The impact of prohibition has fallen 'hardest upon the poorest and most vulnerable populations of the world, especially groups already social [*sic*] constructed as racially other' (Koram, 2019, p. 18). Various drugs have therapeutic, spiritual and cultural uses spanning millennia, including among Indigenous and First Nations populations, but these populations have had to confront these ancient ancestral practices being reclassified as 'criminal' through invasion, colonisation and imperialism, and endure resulting punishments (e.g., Shah, 2004; Stolberg, 2011; Tupper, 2012).

Writing about these various connections between drug policy and race, Dertadian (2024) argues that a key critique of postcolonial studies is its tendency at times to present colonisation 'as having occurred in the past', a practice that 'then determines its analysis of the *effects* of colonial *legacies*' (Dertadian, 2024, p. 2; original emphasis). Drawing on the work of scholars such as Moreton-Robinson (2016, 2015), Nakata (2007) and Wolfe (1999), he instead argues that colonisation is 'an active and ongoing part of how the settler-state continues to impose itself, and how it maintains a colonial ordering of society' (Dertadian 2024, p. 2). Dertadian (2024, p. 1) argues that prohibition 'is not just one of the tools of post-colonial governance, but is instead a key arm of the settler-colonial state, and a significant way in which coloniality is maintained and continues to assert itself in contemporary settler societies'. Aboriginal and Torres Strait Islander people have occupied the territory that came to be known as 'Australia' for an estimated 65,000 years (Clarkson et al., 2017). Representatives of the British Empire arrived in 1788, claiming the land as their own and establishing a colony for convicts. In 1992, the Australian High Court handed down a landmark decision in the case of *Mabo and Others v Queensland (No. 2)* [1992] HCA 23. The British had claimed Australia as their own by virtue of a logical fallacy. In particular, they had incorrectly asserted that the land was *terra nullius* – or that it belonged to no one – and could therefore be claimed under international law. Their assertion depended on them overlooking the inhabitants of the land, in part based on the assumption that Aboriginal and Torres Strait Islander people were not politically organised and had no customs or laws. The case allowed for a limited recognition of native title rights for some Aboriginal and Torres Strait Islander peoples. Beyond this, however, the effects of colonisation remain far-reaching and ongoing, including in terms of relatively poor literacy, reduced health outcomes and lower life expectancies for Aboriginal and Torres Strait Islander people (Commonwealth of Australia, 2024).

Also, and relevant to the argument I make in this chapter, Aboriginal and Torres Strait Islander people experience very high rates of arrest and incarceration, and shockingly high numbers have (and continue to) die in custody. In 1987, the historic Royal Commission into Aboriginal Deaths in Custody was established, exploring the nature and circumstances of these deaths, along with ways to prevent them. The Commission's final report was released in 1991 and produced 339 recommendations (Royal Commission into Aboriginal Deaths in Custody, 1991). The Commission found, among other things, that most

Aboriginal people were in custody due to public drunkenness and theft-related offences, or for fine default-related offences (Royal Commission into Aboriginal Deaths in Custody, 1991). The recommendations were wide-ranging. They included a call for prison to be used only as a last resort, and a call that the standard of health care provided to people in custody be equivalent to that which is available to the general public (a concept separately enshrined in Principle 9 of the United Nations Basic Principles for the Treatment of Prisoners, known colloquially as the Mandela Rules). Although work has been done to implement some of these recommendations, including reforms in the aftermath of other Aboriginal deaths in custody such as that of the Victorian woman Tanya Day in 2017, after she was taken into police custody for a public drunkenness offence (see Pennay et al., 2020; Human Rights Law Centre, 2023; Dertadian, 2024), several of the Royal Commission's recommendations are yet to be implemented (Department of Prime Minister and Cabinet, 2018). Equivalence of care in custody is an ongoing problem for people who use drugs – with many gaps in policy and practice being evident, including in terms of available health care (see Walker et al., 2023). Since the Royal Commission released its report, there have been 569 further deaths in custody, as at the time of writing (Australian Institute of Criminology, 2024). The failure to prevent deaths in custody remains one of the nation's most sustained public policy failures. It is in this context of ongoing colonisation and the racialised war on drugs that I now turn to the case I will examine in this chapter. I also provide a caution to Aboriginal and Torres Strait Islander readers that, in what follows, I use the real name of an Aboriginal person who has passed away.

The Death of Veronica Nelson

Veronica Nelson was a thirty-seven-year-old Gunditjmara, Dja Dja Wurrung, Wiradjuri and Yorta Yorta woman who died in custody (on remand) in Victoria, Australia. She was affectionately known as 'Poccum'. The circumstances of her arrest and death in the early hours of the morning on 2 January 2020 are tragic and confronting. On the afternoon of 30 December 2019, Veronica was with her brother at a train station in central Melbourne. She was stopped and arrested by Victoria Police on outstanding warrants for minor offences, having been accused of thefts from shops in the two months prior. She was arrested, taken to the local police cells, interviewed and then transferred to a custody centre below Melbourne Magistrates' Court. She was remanded overnight in custody. Representing herself in court the next morning, Veronica applied to the magistrate for bail but was refused. This is partly due to a controversial and narrow test for bail in place at the time that imposed a presumption against bail and required someone to demonstrate 'exceptional circumstances' if they were to be bailed. She was then transferred in a van to the local women's prison. She became unwell in the van and vomited multiple times in transit. She arrived at the prison at about 4:35 p.m. on 31 December 2019. Over the next thirty-six hours or so, Veronica used an intercom forty-nine times to request assistance. She vomited on numerous occasions, experienced severe cramping and was left to lie in her own vomit for hours. She was given some help. There was evidence that Veronica's complaints were ignored on several occasions. After asking to see a doctor, she was told by one staffer that 'it's not an emergency, stop asking' (Coroners Court of Victoria 2023, p. 7). When wailing in her cells, she was told by a guard on duty to 'try and stop 'cause you're keeping the other prisoners awake' (Coroners Court of Victoria 2023, p. 255). Another woman also on remand, but located in an adjacent cell, used the intercom to reiterate the call for help. Veronica's last call for help was made on the intercom at 3:58 a.m. on the morning of 2 January 2020. She was not heard from again and was found dead on the concrete floor of her cell at 7:55 a.m. on 2 January 2020.

The *Finding into death with inquest of Veronica Nelson* (2023) was a complex and extensive coronial decision that explored the circumstances leading up to her death. The presiding coroner, Simon McGregor, made fifty-one findings and thirty-nine recommendations across a wide range of areas, including matters related to bail, policing, legal advice and representation, court processes and systems, legal education, custodial health care and health care policy, corrections policy and practice and human rights. His key finding was that: 'Veronica died on 2 January 2020 at [the prison] of complications of withdrawal from chronic opiate use and Wilkie Syndrome in the setting of malnutrition' (Coroners Court of Victoria, 2023, p. 73). My interest is in a related key finding: that some staff had, in the words of the coroner, failed to 'take seriously their obligations to Veronica' and that this was 'linked to an assumption that suffering and unwellness was "normal" for a prisoner experiencing withdrawal'. At the inquest into her death, one doctor said that she was withdrawing from heroin and that although 'I'm sure that's incredibly uncomfortable [. . .] that's not very sick' (Coroners Court of Victoria, 2023, p. 178). A nurse gave evidence that people experiencing withdrawal symptoms are 'just withdrawing' as opposed to being sick.

The implication of some of this evidence was that such symptoms are an inevitable and perhaps even necessary part of withdrawal as opposed to a medical problem in and of themselves. The coroner went on to find that the 'normalisation of the suffering of women experiencing drug withdrawal results in the desensitisation' of relevant staff to withdrawal and that such desensitisation rendered some staff 'virtually unresponsive to Veronica's persistent pleas for assistance and blind to her clinical deterioration' (Coroners Court of Victoria, 2023, p. 232). He concluded that this was 'evidence of pervasive stigma' (Coroners Court of Victoria, 2023, p. 232), and that this stigma 'causally contributed to Veronica's passing' (p. 235). The coroner concluded that stigma was 'inherent' in some policies and practices governing Veronica's care. This included: that relevant policies permitted no clinical discretion regarding the dosage or type of opiate substitution therapy/pharmacotherapy that treating medical practitioners could provide to prisoners, instead offering prisoners a 'standard withdrawal pack' (Coroners Court of Victoria, 2023, p. 146; see also Coroners Court of Victoria, 2023, p. 179). The coroner also found it inherently stigmatising that prisoners 'are inhumanely not afforded the suite of pharmacotherapy that would otherwise be available to them in the community' (Coroners Court of Victoria, 2023, p. 179), such that they might be 'forced into involuntary withdrawal', and that 'prisoners who do access substitution therapy may be removed from the program for non-compliance' (Coroners Court of Victoria, 2023, p. 179). Although lawyers and experts in the case argued that the intermingling of racism and drug-related stigma shaped Veronica's care, the coroner made no findings on racism (see Schwartz, 2023). Importantly, the coroner found that Veronica's treatment was 'inhumane, cruel and degrading', that 'drug-related stigma' had shaped the nature of care she received and contributed to her death, and that these were human rights violations.

In what follows, I focus on the finding that Veronica's treatment was 'inhumane, cruel and degrading', that 'drug-related' stigma had shaped the nature of care she received and that it had contributed to her death, and the significance of the conclusion that drug-related stigma is a human rights issue. Drawing on critical approaches to 'habits' (Sedgwick, 1993; Latour, 2009, 2013; Seear, 2020; Seear and Mulcahy, in press) and feminist approaches to the gender of law and concepts of 'suffering' in human rights (Charlesworth, 2002; Sifris, 2014), this chapter considers both what the court's reading of stigma as a human rights issue opens up and makes possible, and whether the court could have gone further. I also ask whether the decision might pave the way for more radical ruptures in drug law, policy and practice into the future. To set the scene, I first provide an overview of the legal framework within which the coroner was operating.

The Legal Context

Australia is unique among Western liberal democracies in that it is the only country to not have a national bill or charter of human rights. In Australia, rights protections are very limited, with a few found in our national constitution, and others spread across laws at the Commonwealth, state and territory level. In the absence of a national charter or bill of human rights, a few jurisdictions have struck out on their own, introducing laws that are designed to promote and protect human rights. These laws are known collectively as 'the Charters' and can be found in the states of Victoria and Queensland, as well as the Australian Capital Territory. There is also a bill at the federal level that gives some limited recognition to rights. Both the charters and the federal Act enshrine some rights, but in ways that fall short of rights protections that can be found in other countries, such as Canada. The charters do not give Australian courts the power to strike down laws that are inconsistent with human rights, for example. One thing they do, however, is impose human rights obligations on 'public authorities'. The Victorian Charter recognises twenty human rights, including: the right to recognition and equality before the law (s. 8); the right to life (s. 9); the right to protection from torture and cruel, inhuman or degrading treatment (s. 10); and the right to privacy and reputation (s. 13). Section 38(1) of the Charter states that it is 'unlawful for a public authority to act in a way that is incompatible with a human right, or in making a decision, to fail to give proper consideration to a relevant human right'. The Charter recognises two types of public authority. 'Core' public authorities are defined in section 4 of the Act and include: Victoria Police, local councils, Ministers, and other 'public officials' within the meaning of the Public Administration Act 2004. Public officials include employees of the public service, heads of government departments or administrative offices, and the Victorian Public Sector Commissioner. It does not include judges, magistrates, coroners, members of the Victorian Civil and Administrative Tribunal, the Governor of Victoria and some others. 'Functional' public authorities are those 'whose functions are or include functions of a public nature, when it is exercising those functions on behalf of the State or a public authority' – per section 4(1)(c).

The various rights listed in the Charter are adopted from international law, including treaties and conventions to which Australia is a signatory. Section 10 of the Charter – which recognises a right to protection from torture and cruel, inhuman or degrading treatment – reflects rights articulated in, for example, the *International convention on civil and political rights*, the *Universal declaration of human rights*, and the *Convention against torture and other cruel, inhuman or degrading treatment or punishment*. The Charter's approach to torture was modelled on Article 7 of the *International convention on civil and political rights* (Parliament of Victoria, 2006), which states: No one shall be subjected to torture or to cruel, inhuman or degrading treatment or punishment. In particular, no one shall be subjected without his [*sic*] free consent to medical or scientific experimentation.

Importantly, these terms (torture, cruel, inhuman, degrading) are not defined. As the United Nations Human Rights Committee (2003) has noted, in a discussion of the *Convention against torture and other cruel, inhuman or degrading treatment or punishment*:

> The Covenant does not contain any definition of the concepts covered by article 7, nor does the Committee consider it necessary to draw up a list of prohibited acts or to establish sharp distinctions between the different kinds of punishment or treatment; the distinctions depend on the nature, purpose and severity of the treatment applied.

We know from international jurisprudence that 'cruel' and 'inhuman' are essentially considered as interchangeable and that 'degrading' treatment equates to humiliating treatment (see Sifris, 2014). The international approach overall establishes a hierarchy of wrongful acts, where torture is the most grave, followed by cruel or inhuman acts, followed by degrading ones. This hierarchy matters for various legal and political reasons. Notably, the *Convention against torture* contains a requirement that states hold the perpetrators of torture criminally responsible, unlike the perpetrators of cruel, inhuman or degrading treatment or punishment. Also, it has been argued that torture attracts a 'special stigma' (Nowak, 2010, cited in Sifris, 2014, p. 229) for governments such that characterisation of something as torture carries greater political and moral weight. Although the coroner's decision in the inquest into Veronica Nelson's death was made under domestic law, it is a finding that links back to how torture is understood more broadly and could conceivably be mobilised by people in other parts of the world. In other words, although the coroner's decision involved a finding under the Victorian Charter, it has implications for how people who use drugs are treated more broadly. Perhaps most importantly, and as I explain in the next section, it may offer new language and concepts for people who use drugs to work with when advocating for reforms to drug law, policy and practice, or when advocating for more caring and compassionate approaches to drug use.

Recognition and Rupture

Many scholars have debated whether activities related to drugs might ever constitute torture under international law (e.g., Lines, 2017; Takahashi, 2019; Bone, 2020). Much of this work centres on mandatory alcohol or other drug treatment. The Open Society Foundation (2011) has argued that involuntary or mandated treatment could fit the definition of torture in a few senses, including because it is often imposed by or on behalf of the state, with a punitive intention or objective to intimidate. This argument is controversial, however, and considered by at least one analyst to be 'extremely bold' (Takahashi, 2019, p. 159). In debates about the possible application of international conventions dealing with torture to people who use drugs, we find ourselves in the weeds of legal argumentation about the proper scope of the doctrine, the nature and extent of state power in dealing with apparently 'problem' populations, debates about purpose and intentionality, and the proper aims of mandated treatment. Is mandated treatment designed to treat and heal, or intended to hurt and punish? Is it possible that its aims and effects are at odds with one another (i.e., that it is both therapeutic and harmful at the same time)? In exploring these questions, we are of course working within existing legal frameworks and definitions, including arguably narrow, problematic definitions and approaches. In other words, in considering the relationship between one kind of drug policy practice, we may find ourselves butting up against the apparent limits of the law, including the potential parameters and flaws of human rights law more broadly. I take a different view of law here, however, drawing on insights from Bruno Latour (2013, 2009; see also McGee, 2015). Latour argues that the essence of law 'does not lie in a definition *but in a practice*' (2009, p. x; emphasis added). Notably, his approach emphasises 'modes of connecting' as the essence of law (Matthews & Veitch, 2016, p. 355), underscoring the ontological function of habits of thought and practice, in which legal and non-legal concepts are produced, reproduced and connected to produce legal 'truths'. As I have argued elsewhere (Seear, 2020), taking up these ideas, habits of thought and practice *are law*, and although habits have great force and power, they (and thus law) are also fragile, with an immanent capacity for rupture. I think of this possibility (for rupture) in part through Eve Sedgwick's work on habit (1993) as an otherwise to 'addiction'. Sedgwick argued that habits are repetitive but not rigid, and thus always already open to rupture. I think of the decision in the Veronica Nelson case as a kind of rupture in precisely this sense.

As I noted earlier, the coroner did not find that the treatment of Veronica had risen to the level of torture. This appears to be because of his interpretation of intentionality – specifically that torture is an *intentional* act whereas cruel, inhuman or degrading treatment need only be negligent or reckless. But he did find, as I noted earlier, that her treatment was stigmatising, and that this was cruel, inhuman and degrading. There are three broad reasons why this finding matters. The first is that it sidesteps debates of the kind that are commonplace in drug law – such as those I mentioned earlier – which focus on the nature and scope of the 'torture' doctrine. It does so in part by moving around questions about the aims of drug law and policy to focus on the effects of practices, including, in particular, the way practices can generate stigma. In this sense, it involves new habits of thought and practice, and new modes of connection in the Latourian sense, rupturing ideas about what stigma is, means and can do, politically and legally. This brings me to the second reason why the case matters, and this is for its radical politics of recognition. It recognises drug-related stigma as both a properly legal object and a wrong in and of itself. This matters because drug-related stigma is often naturalised, treated as inevitable, or as a kind of 'good' that is needed to deter people who use drugs from their ostensibly delinquent ways. In the Nelson case, however, the coroner found, first, *as a matter of fact*, that various acts and omissions in the course of managing someone who use drugs can be stigmatising and second, *as a matter of law*, that stigma can be unlawful, as a form of cruel, inhuman or degrading treatment. This is an important departure from logics that so often operate in drug law, policy and practice, including in settings as diverse as: opioid substitution therapy; voluntary and involuntary drug treatment; and in drug courts. In all of these settings (as well as others), shame, humiliation and other kinds of cruelty are assumed not only to be lawful, but to be *necessary and productive*: a means of initiating change, abstinence or 'recovery', and of fixing apparently 'disordered' subjects (see, for example: Moore, 2007;

Fitzgerald, 2008; Vrecko, 2009; Murphy, 2011; Fomiatti et al., 2019; Sarmiento et al., 2019), or for protecting others such as children (Flacks, 2021). In this sense the decision also breaks with certain long-standing habits in law and legal thinking including those that 'naturalise' or normalise drug-related harms and drug-related suffering. The decision constitutes such suffering as neither deserved nor acceptable, natural nor inevitable, and instead positions it as preventable and cruel. In doing so, the coroner's finding opens up the possibility that other practices pertaining to drugs, including in law, might be unlawful and in need of remedying. These include drug treatment practices of the kind I mentioned earlier, such as involuntary treatment. Embedded within the decision are important *affective dynamics*, insofar as the coroner centred the affective dynamics of drug policy and practice – such as the possibility for degradation, embarrassment and humiliation – and rendered them as properly legal objects of concern. This is a radical reading in many respects.

The third reason why the case matters is for its finding that people who use drugs can in fact be treated inhumanely because of their drug use. This renders people who use drugs, by implication, as intrinsically human (or at least human in the context of instances of their mistreatment). This might seem like an inconsequential point, but it is one with a kind of tragically ironic significance. People who use drugs are frequently constituted as compulsive, irrational, duplicitous, chaotic and less-than-fully-human (e.g., Levine, 1978; Room, 1985; Sedgwick, 1993; Valverde, 1998; Keane, 2002; Reinarman, 2005; Fraser & valentine, 2008; Fraser & Moore, 2011; Fraser & Seear, 2011). The lives of people who use drugs are often viewed as less valid, valuable and 'grieveable' than others, in Judith Butler's (2006) terms (Fraser et al., 2018). Legal contexts often work to concretise this positioning, sustaining stigma and abjection (Seear & Fraser, 2014; Seear, 2020; Flacks, 2021). Somewhat paradoxically, human rights law can also do this, despite the fact that human rights frameworks are supposed to protect people against rights violations by the state (Seear, 2020). I have previously explained (Seear, 2020) the way this works: first, the state proposes measures – such as mandatory drug treatment or the quarantining and control of welfare payments – that affect people who use drugs. Then, these measures attract criticism on the basis that they are violating human rights such as the right to bodily autonomy or privacy. But governments often then successfully push back against these criticisms, arguing not only that such infringements on rights are legal but that they are legal because they are *necessary to help restore people who use drugs to full functioning or to a life of dignity* (Seear, 2020, 2024). In other words, various kinds of interventions are said to be *necessary* in order to advance people's human rights, defined as the right to live a 'productive' life of 'dignity'. Here, human rights become a way for making people who use drugs differently, as more 'fully' or 'properly' human in normative terms (Seear, 2020; see also Keane, 2003). The rights of others also shape these approaches, because alcohol and other drugs are often said to pose a risk to the safety of others, especially women, children and families, and thus a risk to other people's rights to health, and to life (Seear & Mulcahy, 2022). But the inquest into Veronica Nelson's case disrupts these logics by forging different connections between humans, rights and drugs. Access to rights does not depend on normative compunctions about what it means to be 'properly' human, nor does the case neatly reproduce such normative logics. It does not mobilise rights in order to remake or 'repair' people who use drugs. It does not rely on ideas of 'productivity' or 'dignity' (normatively defined). It does not require the drug-using subject to enact subjecthood in normative terms. And it does not, as I noted earlier, reproduce the idea that people who use drugs are disordered and in need of fixing as a precursor to their humanisation. It centres other, more fundamental, concerns, including the importance of avoiding stereotypes and assumptions about what people who use drugs 'need', or what they should have to endure, through hierarchical and paternalistic logics of care. In every respect this is a more capacious account of 'the human' and a rupture of rights; a way of 'generating new and more generous realities regarding what it means to be human' (Seear & Mulcahy, in press). Of course, the tragic irony of the case is that the coroner was only able to enact Veronica Nelson as intrinsically human in the event of her death.

Despite its rupture to drug policy logics and practices, the decision left as untouched one vital question. Given that criminalisation is *itself* stigmatising, the question arises: might criminalisation, too, be thought of as cruel, inhuman and degrading? Coroner McGregor's decision was about both the formal instruments of law and the law's effects, including what it enables, such as detention, incarceration, policing. Where such effects are cruel, inhuman and degrading, might the conditions of possibility that gave rise to it come to be viewed as themselves unlawful? In the next section, I consider this issue, and whether another rupture might lie ahead.

Rupturing Criminalisation Itself

To help us understand the possibility of further ruptures to drug law, policy and practice, I turn to feminist critiques of international law in general and the law of torture in particular. Feminists have, of course, long critiqued law's normative dimensions and effects and challenged and expanded the contours of law in ways broadly compatible with the logics of rupture I described in the previous section. Many feminist scholars have contributed to this endeavour, but I want to start with Hilary Charlesworth's (2002, p. 94) well-known argument on the 'hidden gender of international law' (after Graycar & Morgan, 1990), in which she argues that 'international law has a gender' and that its gender is male. As Charlesworth (2002, p. 96) has explained, applying critiques of binary logic to law: 'Law, as we know it, represents a very limited aspect of human experience. The language and imagery of the law underscore its maleness; it lays claim to rationality, objectiveness, and abstraction, characteristics traditionally associated with men, and is defined in contrast to emotion, subjectivity, and contextualized thinking.' A key argument made by feminists is that international law 'is a system prioritising issues that concern men such that issues that disproportionately concern women are largely neglected' (Sifris, 2014, p. 11). As Hilary Charlesworth and Christine Chinkin (2000, p. 17) put it, the international legal regime was 'constructed upon particular male assumptions and experiences of life where "man" is taken to represent the "human"'. These critiques extend to the doctrine of torture. As Ronli Sifris (2014, p. 7) has explained, writing about torture from a feminist perspective, feminists generally take issue with the 'male-centric orientation' of torture discourse. Put another way, torture discourse is viewed by many feminists as flawed because it was originally defined in narrow, masculinist terms, with the most grave kind of wrongdoing imaginable being something that 'only takes place within the traditional paradigm of interrogation, punishment or intimidation of a detainee' (Sifris, 2014, p. 10). This rendered it largely relevant, initially, only to men at war, unmoored from the lived experiences of women. In addition, the approach to torture reproduces a private/public dichotomy within law which has long been critiqued by feminists, particularly through its emphasis on the acts or omissions of public officials or other people acting in an official capacity, thereby excluding torture from the domestic sphere or home within which severe kinds of pain and suffering – such as family violence – might be being perpetrated. Over time, however, a more expansive interpretation of torture under international law has developed, with the private/public dichotomy being challenged, for instance, and more and more activities being interpreted as forms of torture, through being tied to public officials or the state. This includes various kinds of wrongs, such as the failure to investigate rape or family violence allegations and the failure to protect women from female genital mutilation and trafficking. In any event, the key point of feminist critiques is that torture was never designed with the interests of marginalised groups such as women in mind, and that although the category has been slowly developing over time, much more work is needed to expand – or rupture – its contours.

In her analysis of reproductive freedom and the torture doctrine, Sifris (2014) carefully explains how and why certain practices, such as legal and policy restrictions on access to abortion, might nevertheless be seen as a form of either torture or cruel, inhuman and degrading treatment. Central to her argument are the various effects – on both physical and mental health – of restrictions on access to abortion. This includes the way that restrictions can generate or exacerbate stigma, or produce various harms to physical health, by, for instance, putting women at risk of sepsis, haemorrhage, peritonitis, renal failure, bowel injury, infertility and chronic pelvic pain. As Sifris reminds us, laws can be lawful while nevertheless generating effects that are cruel, inhuman and degrading, as well, at times, as fatal. Feminist analyses of this kind are especially important and valuable for drug policy because they ask vital, searching questions of policy effects and legal logics, urging us to consider ways the law's contours might be disrupted, ruptured and expanded from within. There are, I suggest, obvious analogies between laws that restrict access to (or criminalise) abortion and laws that criminalise drugs. A huge literature establishes the many adverse effects of drug criminalisation on both the physical and mental health of people who use drugs, including through putting people at risk of harms such as fatal and non-fatal overdose, blood-borne viruses such as hepatitis C and HIV, needlestick injuries, injecting-related infections and abscesses (Global Commission on Drug Policy, 2021, 2023). These are sometimes described as stigmatising effects, made possible through processes of labelling, differentiation and segregation, but criminalisation often manifests in more deliberately violent ways, including through state-sanctioned violence and killing (Rafael, 2020; Harm Reduction International, 2022). There can be no doubt that many people who use drugs experience criminalisation as profoundly harmful, cruel, inhuman, degrading, demeaning, embarrassing, shameful, a source of indignity and informed by ableism (e.g., Russell, 2021). Such effects are significant and often lifelong (Lloyd, 2010, 2013). Of course, many would argue that these effects are positive, in the sense that singling out attributes or behaviours and punishing people who use drugs is productive: a means of discouraging purportedly 'difficult' behaviours and encouraging change. But this so-called 'positive stigma' approach is problematic in at least three senses. First, it overlooks the many obvious failings of drug policy stigma, including its failure to prevent drug use. Second, and relatedly, it overlooks the fact that criminalisation generates harms, including the very harms it sets out to prevent, through the deployment of counterproductive and harmful practices and logics. This includes a dogged insistence that people's behaviour will improve if only they are made to feel shame, embarrassment or discomfort. In drug policy contexts, such logics are increasingly coming under pressure, and we are being pushed to rethink how we do things. This brings me to the third problem with the 'positive stigma' approach: it is arguably at odds with the torture doctrine itself, or the direction in which it is has expanded over time following feminist critiques and interventions. Feminist critiques have helped sensitise us to cruelty, suffering and degradation in law and policy, paving the way for a radical rupture to drug law and policy itself. Feminist work reminds us that the normalisation of suffering and the reproduction of indignity in law can be cruel, inhuman and degrading and thus a legal wrong. The criminal law is at the centre of inhumanity and degradation in this sense, helping to generate and sustain suffering. It is not beyond the realms of possibility, therefore, that criminalisation will eventually come to be seen as cruel, inhuman and degrading in a legal sense. The decision in Veronica Nelson's case may have helped pave the way for that reading. In this sense, the most profound rupture of all may still lie ahead.

Conclusion: Remembering Poccum

This chapter has been about the past, present and future of drug law, policy and practice, its rupture and remaking, through one case that unfolded in Victoria, Australia. Although the case has lessons for drug law, policy and practice broadly, it was also a case about one woman's tragic and preventable death, and the ways in which carceral logics, drug prohibition, race, gender and pain were entangled and mutually reinforcing, with devastating, fatal effects. I want to close by remembering that woman, Veronica Nelson, or 'Poccum' to those who knew her. I acknowledge her. I also acknowledge the considerable courage of her family and friends in pushing for reforms in the midst of such heartbreak. I want to also recognise the hard work of many lawyers, researchers and advocates, including Aboriginal and Torres Strait Islander cultural experts, stigma and harm reduction experts (including people who use drugs), who pressed the case before Coroner Simon McGregor. The coroner in turn embraced the immanent possibilities for rupture from within the law itself. In remembering Poccum, the coroner explained:

> Veronica was 37 years old at the time of her passing. She was the eldest child of Aunty Donna Nelson, and the second child of her late father, Uncle Russell Walker. She was a sister to Belinda, Russell, Dwayne, Trisha, Richard and Jodie, and shared a long loving relationship with Percy Lovett, which began in her teenage years. Veronica was loved and respected by those who knew her.

In statements released after the inquest was finalised, Veronica's partner Uncle Percy Lovett described her as 'a kind and loving girl, who would always help people, no matter who they were' and as someone who 'taught me everything I know about Aboriginal culture' (Victorian Aboriginal Legal Service, 2023). Additionally, 'she loved [the rock band] AC/DC, was clever, would speak her mind, and had a big personality and beautiful laugh' (Schwartz, 2023). Her mother Aunty Donna Nelson described Veronica as 'kind, caring and compassionate', someone 'loved by her family, her community, and her friends', and 'a proud Aboriginal woman who loved her culture. She never harmed a soul other than her own' (Victorian Aboriginal Legal Service, 2023). Their hope is that she will not be forgotten.

References

Australian Institute of Criminology. (2024). *Dashboard: Quarterly reporting of deaths in custody*. Australian Institute of Criminology. www.aic.gov.au/statistics/deaths-custody-australia.

Bone, M. (2020). *Human rights and drug control: A new perspective*. Routledge.

Butler, J. (2006). *Precarious life: The powers of mourning and violence*. Verso.

Charlesworth, C. (2002). The hidden gender of international law. *Temple International and Comparative Law Journal*, 16(1), 93–102.

Charlesworth, H., & Chinkin, C. (2000). *The boundaries of international law*. Manchester University Press.

Clarkson, C., Jacobs, Z., Marwick, B., Fullagar, R., Wallis, L. & Smith, M. (2017). Human occupation of northern Australia by 65,000 years ago. *Nature*, 547, 306–310.

Commonwealth of Australia. (2024). *Commonwealth Closing the Gap 2023 Annual Report and Commonwealth Closing the Gap 2024 Implementation Plan*. National Indigenous Australians Agency.

Coroners Court of Victoria. (2023). *Finding into death with inquest of Veronica Nelson* (COR 2020 0021). VicCorC 28312 (30 January).

Courtwright, D. (2002). *Forces of habit: Drugs and the making of the modern world*. Harvard University Press.

Cruz, G. M. (2017). A view from the South: The global war on drugs. *Contexto Internacional*, 39(3), 635–655.

Department of Prime Minister and Cabinet. (2018). *Review of the implementation of the recommendations of the Royal Commission into Aboriginal deaths in custody*. Department of Prime Minister and Cabinet.

Dertadian, G. C. (2024). The coloniality of drug prohibition. *International Journal of Drug Policy*, 126, 104368.

Fitzgerald, J. (2008). Drug diversion: An intersection between law enforcement and the public health approaches to the control of illicit drug use. In P. Dietze & D. Moore (Eds.), *Drugs and public health: Australian perspectives on policy and practice* (pp. 103–113). Oxford University Press.

Flacks, S. (2021). *Law, drugs and the politics of childhood*. Routledge.

Fomiatti, R., Moore, D. & Fraser, S. (2019). The improvable self: Enacting model citizenship and sociality in research on 'new recovery'. *Addiction Research and Theory*, 27(6), 527–538.

Fraser, S., Farrugia, A. & Dwyer, A. (2018). Grievable lives? Death by opioid overdose in Australian newspaper coverage. *International Journal of Drug Policy*, 59, 28–35.

Fraser, S., & Moore, D. (Eds.). (2011). *The drug effect: Health, crime and society*. Cambridge University Press.

Fraser, S., Moore, D. & Keane, H. (2014). *Habits: Remaking addiction*. Palgrave Macmillan.

Fraser, S., & Seear, K. (2011). *Making disease, making citizens: The politics of hepatitis C*. Ashgate.

Fraser, S., & valentine, K. (2008). *Substance and substitution: Methadone subjects in liberal societies*. Palgrave.

Global Commission on Drug Policy. (2021). *Time to end prohibition*. Global Commission on Drug Policy.

Global Commission on Drug Policy. (2023). *HIV, hepatitis and drug policy reform*. Global Commission on Drug Policy.

Graycar, R., & Morgan, J. (1990). *The hidden gender of law*. Federation Press.

Harm Reduction International. (2022). The death penalty for drug offences: *Global overview 2022*. Harm Reduction International.
Human Rights Law Centre. (2023, January 17). *No further police powers once public drunkenness is decriminalised: Day family statement*. www.hrlc.org.au/news/2023/1/16/day-family-statement.
Keane, H. (2002). *What's wrong with addiction?* Melbourne University Press.
Keane, H. (2003). Critiques of harm reduction, morality and the promise of human rights. *International Journal of Drug Policy*, 14(3), 227–232.
Koram, K. (Ed.). (2019). *The war on drugs and the global colour line*. Pluto Press.
Latour, B. (2009). *The making of law: An ethnography of the Conseil d'État*. Polity Press.
Latour, B. (2013). *An inquiry into modes of existence: An anthropology of the moderns*. Harvard University Press.
Levine, H. (1978). The discovery of addiction: Changing conceptions of habitual drunkenness in America. *Journal of Studies on Alcohol*, 39, 143–174.
Lines, R. (2017). *Drug control and human rights in international law*. Cambridge University Press.
Lloyd, C. (2010). *Sinning and sinned against: The stigmatization of problem drug users*. UK Drug Policy Commission.
Lloyd, C. (2013). The stigmatization of problem drug users: A narrative literature review. *Drugs: Education, Prevention, and Policy*, 20(2), 85–95.
Lyons, T. (2014). Simultaneously treatable and punishable: Implications of the production of addicted subjects in a drug treatment court. *Addiction Research and Theory*, 22(4), 286–293.
Manderson, D. (1994). *From Mr Sin to Mr Big: A history of Australian drug laws*. Oxford University Press.
Matthews, D., & Veitch, S. (2016). The limits of critique and the forces of law. *Law Critique*, 27, 349–361.
McGee, K. (2015). *Latour and the passage of law*. Edinburgh University Press.
Moore, D. (2007). *Criminal artefacts: Governing drugs and users*. University of British Columbia Press.
Moreton-Robinson, A. (2016). *Critical indigenous studies: Engagements in first world locations*. University of Arizona Press.
Moreton-Robinson, A. (2015). *The white possessive: Property, power, and indigenous sovereignty*. University of Minnesota Press.
Murphy, J. (2011). Drug court as both a legal and medical authority. *Deviant Behavior*, 32(3), 257–291.
Nakata, M. N. (2007). *Disciplining the savages, savaging the disciplines*. Aboriginal Studies Press.
Open Society Foundation. (2011). *Treatment or torture? Applying international human rights standards to drug detention centers*. Open Society Foundation.

Parliament of Victoria. (2006). *Explanatory memorandum, Charter of Human Rights and Responsibilities Bill*. https://content.legislation.vic.gov.au/sites/default/files/c511c353-78b4-35c0-bccf-06bf896af3b6_551406exi1.pdf.

Pennay, A., Savic, M., Seear, K., Volpe, I., Manning, V. & Room, R. (2020). Decriminalising public drunkenness: Accountability and monitoring needed in the ongoing and evolving management of public intoxication. *Drug and Alcohol Review*, 40(2), 205–209.

Rafael, V. (2020). Photography and the biopolitics of fear: Witnessing the Philippine drug war. *Positions: Asia critique*, 28(4), 905–933.

Reinarman, C. (2005). Addiction as accomplishment: The discursive construction of disease. *Addiction Research and Theory*, 13(4), 307–320.

Room, R. (1985). Dependence and society. *British Journal of Addiction*, 80, 133–139.

Royal Commission into Aboriginal Deaths in Custody. (1991). *Final report. Royal Commission.*

Russell, D. (2021). In/dignity. *International Journal of Drug Policy*, 98, 103365.

Sarmiento, E., Seear, K. & Fraser, S. (2019). Enacting alcohol and other drug (testing)-related harms in an Australian drug court. *Contemporary Drug Problems*, 46(3), 282–303.

Schwartz, S. (2023). Prison healthcare as punishment: The killing of Veronica Nelson. *Overland Literary Journal*, 253, Summer, 42–51.

Sedgwick, E. (1993). Epidemics of the will. In E. Sedgwick (Ed.), *Tendencies* (pp. 130–142). Routledge.

Seear, K. (2020). *Law, drugs and the making of addiction: Just habits*. Routledge.

Seear, K. (2024). Shifting solutions: Tracking transformations of drugs, health and the 'human' through human rights processes in Australia. *Health Sociology Review*, 33(3): 257–272.

Seear, K., & Fraser, S. (2014). The addict as victim: Producing the 'problem' of addiction in Australian victims of crime compensation. *International Journal of Drug Policy*, 25(5), 826–835.

Seear, K., & Mulcahy, S. (2022). Enacting safety and omitting gender: Australian human rights scrutiny processes concerning alcohol and other drug laws. *Contemporary Drug Problems*, 49(3), 258–277.

Seear, K., & Mulcahy, S. (in press). Forging new habits: Critical drugs scholarship as an otherwise to rights. *International Journal of Human Rights.*

Shah, N. C. (2004). Indigenous uses and ethnobotany of *Cannabis sativa* L. (hemp) in Uttaranchal (India). *Journal of Industrial Hemp*, 9(1), 69–77.

Sifris, R. (2014). *Reproductive freedom, torture and international human rights: Challenging the masculinisation of torture*. Routledge.

Stolberg, V. B. (2011). The use of coca: Prehistory, history, and ethnography. *Journal of Ethnicity in Substance Abuse*, 10(2), 126–146.

Takahashi, S. (2019). *Human rights and drug control: The false dichotomy.* Bloomsbury Publishing.
Tupper, K. (2012). Psychoactive substances and the English language: 'Drugs', discourses, and public policy. *Contemporary Drug Problems*, 39(3), 461–492.
United Nations. (1984). *Convention against torture and other cruel, inhuman or degrading treatment or punishment*, adopted 10 December 1984. www.ohchr.org/en/professionalinterest/pages/cat.aspx.
United Nations Human Rights Committee. (2003). General comment 20: Article 7 (*Prohibition of torture or cruel, inhuman or degrading treatment or punishment*), In *Compilation of general comments and general recommendations adopted by human rights treaty bodies*, U.N. Doc. HRI/GEN/1/Rev.6 at 151.
United Nations. (2015). Standard minimum rules for the treatment of prisoners (the Nelson Mandela Rules), adopted 17 December 2015. www.unodc.org/documents/justice-and-prison-reform/SMRs_2015/SMR_ENG.pdf.
United Nations. (2010). Rules for the treatment of women prisoners (the Bangkok Rules), adopted 21 December 2010. www.unodc.org/documents/justice-and-prison-reform/Bangkok_Rules.pdf.
Valverde, M. (1998). *Diseases of the will: Alcohol and the dilemmas of freedom.* Cambridge University Press.
Victorian Aboriginal Legal Service. (2023). Statements from Veronica Nelson's family. www.vals.org.au/statements-from-veronica-nelsons-family/.
Vrecko, S. (2009). Therapeutic justice in drug courts: Crime, punishment and societies of control. *Science as Culture*, 18(2), 217–232.
Walker, S., Wilson, M., Seear, K. et al. (2023). Police custody in Australia: A call for transparency and accountability. *Australia New Zealand Journal of Public Health*, 47(2), 100040.
Watego, C. (2021). *Another day in the colony.* University of Queensland Press.
Wolfe, P. (1999). *Settler colonialism and the transformation of anthropology: The politics and poetics of an ethnographic event.* Cassell.
Zieger, S. (2008). *Inventing the addict: Drugs, race, and sexuality in nineteenth-century British and American literature.* University of Massachusetts Press.

3

Violence, Alcohol and the Making of Psychosis

SIMON FLACKS

Alcohol and other drug use (AOD) use tends to hold a privileged position within legal decision-making (Seear, 2020; Flacks, 2023), and the criminal case of *R v Taj* (2018) was no exception. The defendant, who was – it was agreed by all parties – experiencing paranoia and psychosis, launched a violent attack on a man he suspected of being a terrorist. Mr Taj had been drinking on eve of the incident, and the night before that, but tests on the day found no trace of alcohol in his bloodstream. He was nevertheless unable to plead self-defence on the basis that he honestly believed there was a risk to life and limb because, successive courts argued, he was already at fault for drinking alcohol, which led to the psychotic thoughts. There were some significant and potentially far-reaching claims in the case, including that intoxication-related behaviour does not require the presence of alcohol in the body, and that psychosis can be caused by alcohol alone. This allowed the court to conclude that Mr Taj was wholly responsible for his actions and so could not claim excuse or mitigation. I analyse the judgment using John Law's innovative work on 'collateral realities' in order to understand the ways in which the law asserts truths about drugs, violence and responsibility. This analysis is important, I suggest, for understanding the law not only in terms of its normative consequences but also its function as a producer of knowledge about AOD and intoxication.

Introduction

The victim in *Taj*, Mr Awain, an electrician, had stopped his car on the side of the road on a Sunday afternoon in central London, in 2016, because it was emitting smoke. Mr Taj came across the car and asked if he could do anything to help. Taj became suspicious and, when out of earshot, called the emergency services about a possible bomb scare threat. Under the impression Taj, who was wearing a high visibility jacket, was a local security officer, Awain allowed him to look inside the car boot, which contained electrical equipment and wires. Taj, believing Awain to be intent on detonating a bomb, beat him with a tyre lever. Taj pleaded self-defence to the charge of attempted murder. He claimed that he had honestly believed he, and others, were at risk so did not have the requisite specific intent either for attempted murder or for causing grievous bodily harm with intent contrary to section 18 of the Offences Against the Person Act 1861. The case turned on his mental state. The key question for the court was in relation to Taj's heavy drinking in the days prior to the attack, which had in the past brought on episodes of psychosis and aggression beyond the period of intoxication. Although it was agreed that he was not intoxicated on the day in question, the judge in the lower court ruled that he was nevertheless 'disordered' in thinking due to the prior consumption of alcohol. This meant that the jury were prevented from considering whether the act was committed in self-defence, which could have led to Taj's acquittal. Taj appealed.

The discussion that follows focuses on the Court of Appeal case, where judges agreed with the lower court judgment that Taj's mistaken belief was 'attributable to' voluntary intoxication. Although there was no chemical trace of alcohol or other drugs in the defendant's system on the day of the attack, it was found that he remained subject to the *effects* of intoxication. This meant that the role of alcohol was not only privileged but nominated as the prime causal element in the attack. The court referred to the principle that if a person is drunk or experiencing the effects of drugs, they should not escape conviction for an offence even if they did not intend to commit the act (*DPP v Majewski*, 1977). Taj was sentenced to an extended sentence of nineteen years, comprising a custodial term of fourteen years with five years on probation. The case generated some publicity, with headlines suggesting that Taj's appeal was based on the claim that he was 'hungover' at the time of the attack (Keay, 2018; Parker, 2018).

Criticism of the decision has centred on the selective use of evidence by judges (Crombag et al., 2020), as well as the decision to break with the principle that a defendant's conduct must be understood with reference to their mental state, and causation of harm, at a specific point in time (Dsouza, 2018; Child et al., 2020). However, the main purpose of this chapter is not to critique the decision on normative grounds but to examine the ways in which intoxication and its relationship with psychosis and violence were established as judges sought to assign responsibility for the attack. In line with the critical perspectives outlined in the introduction to this volume, I draw on Science and Technology Studies (STS), and particularly the work of John Law (2009, 2011), to consider how 'collateral realities' about drugs such as alcohol, and their effects, were made during the process of judicial deliberation. It adds to a growing body of work that has sought to critique assumptions about AODs, including the notion, prevalent in policy documents and political decision-making, that alcohol 'causes' violence and other forms of offending behaviour (Fraser, Moore and Keane, 2014; MacLean & Moore, 2014; Seear, 2020). Such claims reflect the tendency to reify and stabilise drugs as having causative and singular effects. The result of this focus on alcohol, for example, is that it can '[foreclose] other ways of understanding the production of violence' (Seear, 2020, p. 115).

I observe that the following 'collateral realities' – made 'along the way' during the process of legal truth-making (Law, 2009, p. 1) – resulted from the decision: (1) some forms of psychosis are *caused* by alcohol (and other drugs); (2) intoxication-related behaviour does not require the presence of AOD; (3) 'alcohol-induced psychosis' is a stable, preventable condition that does not qualify as a 'mental illness'; and (4) intoxication aggravates the responsibility of people with this condition. I go on to discuss the potential consequences of these findings for the ways in which blame is attributed to individuals. The 'reality' that alcohol causes psychosis and therefore violence, for example, 'washed away' (Law, 2011, p. 171) other potential variables that may have contributed to the violent event, including that Taj had experienced paranoid thoughts in the absence of alcohol and therefore had a mental health condition. The claim that intoxication-related behaviour does not require intoxication has significant consequences for attributing legal responsibility, both in criminal and other courts. The presentation of 'alcohol-induced psychosis' as preventable through an individual's power to abstain also has important implications since it limits consideration of the ways in which violent (and other) events are triggered by an assemblage of individual and social/environmental factors (Deleuze & Parnet, 1987). Finally, suggesting that voluntary intoxication aggravates responsibility helps to conceptualise agency as bounded and immutable rather than contingent and fluid.

The work of producing these collateral realities allowed them to seem independent and anterior to the legal practices involved in their constitution. In addition to examining the production and stabilisation of truths in the case, and their future consequences, I also consider the strategic mobilisation of legal precedent and 'common sense' definitions to arrive at this particular understanding of the event. Before discussing these findings, I will outline the law on intoxication and responsibility in order to foreground the subsequent analysis.

The Law on Intoxication and Responsibility

In policy terms, the question of intoxication and criminal liability is contentious. Offenders often appear in criminal courts as a result of offences committed when they were intoxicated (Lightowlers, 2022), and this poses difficult questions for courts. Intoxication – along with other variables – can affect an individual's ability to understand what they are doing, or the consequences of their actions. It may be more difficult to prove, therefore, that someone really intended to do harm (the *mens rea* of the offence, or state of mind). However, legislators and courts want to assure victims that 'justice has been done' and that offenders will not escape criminal responsibility for acts committed when they have voluntarily consumed alcohol or other drugs. In the key case of *DPP v Majewski* (1977), which involved a brawl in a bar, it was found that voluntary intoxication could not deny proof of recklessness in respect of assault. This principle has not always been followed in other common law jurisdictions, for example Australia (*The Queen v O'Connor* (1980) 146 CLR 64) and, as far back as 1993, the Law Commission for England and Wales questioned why the issue of intoxication could not be left to the jury when determining the offender's state of mind. In particular, the Commission wondered 'why it has been thought necessary to establish an elaborate body of law to achieve that end', given that even very intoxicated individuals are usually considered to be at least partly capable (Law Commission, 1993, p. 15).

Importantly for Taj, it is also the case, under section 76(5) of the Criminal Justice and Immigration Act 2008, that a mistaken belief in the need to use force cannot be relied upon to avoid culpability where the person was voluntarily intoxicated at the time. Taj had argued that he was not criminally responsible because he genuinely – albeit mistakenly – believed that he or others were at risk, and so his use of force was necessary. It is not clear why the defence of 'not guilty by reason of insanity' was not invoked during the case, which might have led to compulsory detention in a psychiatric hospital rather than a lengthy prison sentence.

In respect of addiction to alcohol, the courts have taken a different approach, suggesting that in such cases the responsibility of the accused may be attenuated. Judges have thus concluded that at least some of the drinking done by a person with 'alcohol dependence syndrome' may be 'a direct result of [their] illness or disease' and therefore involuntary (Wood [2008] EWCA Crim 1305, [2009] 1 WLR 496 at [41]). The Court of Appeal has suggested that drinking cannot be separated into 'voluntary' and 'involuntary' in such instances, since 'at some levels of severity what may appear to be "voluntary" drinking may be inseparable from the defendant's underlying syndrome' (Stewart [2009] EWCA Crim 593, [2009] 1 WLR 2507 at [28]). When it comes to sentencing, the picture is also somewhat complicated. According to the Sentencing Council for England and Wales, which prescribes how courts should approach sentencing, intoxication is an aggravating factor. However, the question of intoxication may overlap with other issues to consider, including: whether the offender was addicted to AOD (a potential mitigating factor), whether they would benefit from treatment, determining the exact role of intoxication in the offence, and establishing whether consumption was voluntary.

Although the judges at both courts drew on legal principles, as well as other sources, to explain their decisions in respect of both liability and sentencing, they also framed them as a matter of public policy; people who become delusional and dangerous following intoxication, and continue to be so after the effects have worn off, are a risk to the public. The judges favourably cited a passage from another case: 'To accede to the argument on behalf of the appellant would leave the citizen legally unprotected from unprovoked violence where such violence was the consequence of drink or drugs having obliterated the capacity of the perpetrator to know what he was doing or what were its consequences.'[1] This does not entirely explain why the matter could not have been left up to the jury. Even if is accepted that detention was necessary, had he been found insane, the purpose of a psychiatric detention would also have been to protect the public (Criminal Procedure (Insanity) Act 1964). It does point, however, to the different influences on legal decision-making, including policy considerations as well as previous case law (precedent) and the interpretation of evidence.

Approach

Researchers have for some time argued that drug use and intoxication are shaped by the cultural, social and political-economic contexts in which they occur (Becker, 1953; Levine, 1978; Douglas, 1987). More recently,

[1] According to Lord Simon of Glaisdale, p. 476G.

critical drug studies perspectives have interrogated the ways in which alcohol and other drugs, and concepts such as addiction, are 'made' and understood in policy circles, scientific studies and, to some extent, legal discourse (Seear, 2020; Flacks, 2023). Crucially, these analyses rest on the important principle, developed in STS, that knowledge practices do not simply describe pre-existing realities but 'enact' or 'perform' them (Mol, 2002; Latour, 2005; Law, 2011). This body of work thus shares a concern with troubling the notion, common also in social constructionist literature, that pharmacology is 'anterior to its interaction with set and setting' (Moore, 2020, p. 217). A pioneer of such approaches, David Moore (ibid.), thus argues that drug effects 'emerge from – are co-constituted by – the multiple forces and elements in assembled in consumption networks or events', including substances, bodies, gender, spatio-temporalities, technologies and more. In other words, the effects of alcohol and other drugs and the forms of harm associated with them are not inherent to substances, inevitable, unavoidable or natural, but shaped by drug events (e.g., Dilkes-Frayne & Duff, 2017; Dennis, 2019) and assemblages (Deleuze & Parnet, 1987) of various material, human and non-human forces in intra-action (Fraser, 2006; Barad, 2007).

Although intoxication cannot be understood in isolation from its practice, Moore and colleagues (2023, p. 484) write that intoxication and its effects are 'generally presented as a universal and singular state' in policy discourses, and as a 'a threat to health and social order, both a harm in itself and a source of other harms' (see also Ekendahl et al., 2023). The multiplicity of contexts, practices and effects are thus reduced to linear relationships of causality, so that 'preventing intoxication is equated with preventing harm, and other elements related to alcohol consumption tend to be relegated to the background' (Moore et al., 2023, p. 484). In her Australian study of sentencing practices in relation to alcohol, violence and Indigenous populations, Kate Seear (2020, p. 113) draws on assemblage thinking in order to acknowledge the multiplicity of factors involved in violence, and the instability of different contributing factors (including alcohol and other drug effects). In law, in particular, there is resistance to the level of complexity or indeterminacy required for assemblage thinking. Questions of intention and responsibility presuppose that human actors are rational and wholly responsible for the reasonably foreseeable, ordered and linear consequences of their actions (see also Ekendahl et al., 2023).

In this chapter, I take inspiration from these works and, more specifically, use John Law's (2009, p. 1) method of problematising the apparent truths and 'collateral realities' that emerge from the Court of Appeal case transcript. Collateral realities are those meanings that 'get done incidentally, and along the way' (Law, 2009, p. 1) while other truths are being stabilised and made predictable – in this case 'realities' about the supposedly stable relationship between intoxication, psychosis and violence. These realities are made to appear incontestable and commonsensical but are instead 'fragile' and mutable (Seear, 2020). Law (2011) identifies five practices involved in the performance of realities: juxtaposition, ranking, selection, deletion and framing. *Ranking* involves building those hierarchies which are required for guiding the *selection* of phenomena and those that are destined to be *deleted*. *Juxtapositions* concern boundary setting between categories (e.g., human versus non-human objects). All these practices ae subject to *framing* whereby different realities are contextualised for the purpose of a particular, situated performance(s). In court, the process of giving a legal shape to disparate events and features is a particularly powerful means of asserting such realities. In the case, judges made use of 'expert' scientific discourses, and the 'ordinary' dictionary definitions of 'attribute' and 'intoxication', as well as ancient texts, to justify their findings. This process of interlinking, connecting and forging to establish responsibility, among other things, has been described as 'jurimorphing' by the critical legal theorist Kyle McGee (2015; see also Seear, 2020). The legal standard of responsibility, therefore, is created – performed – according to what 'everyone knows or should know' as imagined in court (McGee, 2015, p. 69; Seear, 2020, p. 44).

The concept of collateral realities provides a means of examining the outcomes of these processes, and in particular how legal discourses and practices enact alcohol as an uncontested driver of harm, thus producing other realities about, for example, psychosis and the effects of intoxication along the way. In drawing attention to the 'performative effect of strategic and representational techniques' in the Taj case (Duncan et al., 2022, p. 3), I note how other explanations for the violent event are silenced or ignored entirely, most notably the possibility that Taj was suffering from a long-term mental illness, perhaps triggered by a climate of fear around terrorism and the presence of various non-human entities (wires, cars and equipment) that played a role in the attack.

Analysis

I identify four collateral realities in the case transcript, enacted through practices of juxtaposition, ranking, selection, deletion and framing.

Some Forms of Psychosis Are Caused *by Alcohol (and Other Drugs)*

The first collateral reality concerned the explanation of the relationship between alcohol consumption, psychosis and violence. It was argued in the Court of Appeal that new scientific developments provided a coherent and conclusive explanation of the links between alcohol consumption, psychosis and violence. The finding suggested that Taj would not have behaved violently if he had not consumed alcohol over the course of the two evenings prior. Psychiatric experts employed by both defence and prosecution lawyers agreed that Taj was suffering from a drug or alcohol-induced psychotic disorder at the time of the offence. According to the transcript, they said that 'the use of drugs and alcohol could induce a condition very similar to psychosis and that the effects could last for weeks' (*R v Taj* [2018] EWCA Crim 1743, [18]). They also agreed that there was no evidence of an 'ongoing' psychosis.

Their Lordships went into detail about the nature of the amount of drinking involved, and kinds of beverages consumed in the days before the attack. They noted how Taj drank light ales, lager, Jägerbombs, Quattro, Red Bull, vodka, champagne and Sambuca two evenings prior, and a further four pints of beer on the eve of the attack (*R v Taj* [2018] EWCA Crim 1743, [15]). Importantly, there was no discussion of any independent relationship between psychosis and violence, only of the key contribution of alcohol to Taj's state of mind. They concluded that:

> The fact is that medical science has advanced such that, in the modern age, the longer term sequelae of abusing alcohol or drugs are better known and understood; and, as in the present case, it was agreed that Taj's episode of paranoia which led him to mistake the innocent Mr Awain as a terrorist *was a direct result* of his earlier drink and drug-taking in the previous days and weeks.
>
> (*R v Taj* [2018] EWCA Crim 1743, [57], emphasis added)

The judgment stresses (*R v Taj* [2018] EWCA Crim 1743, [60]) that this conclusion does 'not extend to long term mental illness precipitated (perhaps over a considerable period) by alcohol or drug misuse'. This distinction between 'long-term mental illness' which may have, at one stage, been 'precipitated' by alcohol, and the apparent episodic nature of Taj's mental state which was a 'direct result' of – or caused by – alcohol, is one of a list of claims that have been subject to criticism by Child, Crombag and Sullivan (2020). They argue that there is no scientific basis for the argument that it is possible to identify a specific bout of psychosis as attributable to intoxication, nor for separating one form of psychosis from another, and distinguishing forms of psychoses according to whether an individual is 'mentally ill' or simply intoxicated (Child et al., 2020, p. 312). This, they argue, was reflected in the expert reports submitted to the Court. A subsequent medical report submitted by Dr Reid, acting for the defence, cast doubt on his earlier evidence. Dr Reid visited Taj while in custody and concluded that a diagnosis of bipolar affective disorder was appropriate (*R v Taj* [2018] EWCA Crim 1743, [33]). He also stated that it was 'certainly very possible' that Taj was 'experiencing symptoms of mental illness in the absence of substance or alcohol misuse at the time of the index offence' (*R v Taj* [2018] EWCA Crim 1743, [33]). Their Lordships stated, however, that this conclusion did not break the link between Taj's intoxication and his subsequent violent behaviour, arguing 'that a psychotic episode may have been precipitated without alcohol or drugs says nothing about whether it was (as Taj agreed he knew to be the case) in fact precipitated on this occasion by alcohol and drugs' (*R v Taj* [2018] EWCA Crim 1743, [61]). The judges did not produce any further evidence to support this claim that, even if Taj *did* have an ongoing psychiatric condition, this particular episode was the consequence of a previous bout of intoxication.

The point here is not so much to dispute what is 'real' or 'correct' about the decision, although challenging the court's assertions remains an important endeavour. Rather, the aim is to examine what, and how, truths were made in the judgment, with a view to their contingency and potential consequences, as well as their ability to be 'unmade' (Seear, 2020). In addition to the muting of the question of any ongoing mental illness, there was a climate of fear about terrorism that existed at the time following the attacks in the 2000s in the UK and the US. Members of the public, especially Londoners, were frequently being urged to report anything that might lead to the prevention of an attack.[2] These often racialised campaigns (Hark, 2020) help to normalise distrust towards strangers and encourage anxiety about 'ordinary objects' including parked vans (Larsson, 2016, p. 105). This is not to suggest that this was the prime contributory factor, of course, but it seemed that these conditions helped to trigger a psychotic episode that the court reduced or

[2] The 'See It. Say It. Sorted' campaign run by British Transport still asks us to be ever-vigilant about out-of-the-ordinary incidents that could be signs of terrorist planning. Cinema advertising urges viewers 'look again' in order to 'defeat terrorism'. Visit: https://news.npcc.police.uk/releases/counter-terrorism-policing-launch-cinema-advertising-campaign-to-encourage-reports-from-the-public.

bracketed (Blomley, 2014) to the simple question of intoxication. Other possible explanations, causes and factors (human and non-human) were *deranked* or *deleted* as the court sought to assign responsibility for the attack to Taj's behaviour in the preceding days.

Intoxication-Related Behaviour Does Not Require the Presence of AOD

As discussed at the outset, a crucial and highly consequential aspect of the case was the conclusion that, even if Taj was not 'intoxicated' at the time of the attack, he was still suffering from the effects of alcohol consumption. The Court of Appeal stated that 'There was no evidence to suggest that Taj had taken any drugs or alcohol on the 31 January 2016 itself and nobody spoke of him showing signs of having recently consumed alcohol or drugs *other than his irregular behaviour*' (*R v Taj* [2018] EWCA Crim 1743, [17], emphasis added). Nevertheless, Judge Dodgson decided, in the lower Crown Court, that the phrase 'attributable to intoxication' in section 76(5) of the 2008 Act was not limited to those cases in which alcohol or other drugs were present in the appellant's system. Quoting the Oxford English Dictionary, he argued that intoxication was: 'The action of rendering stupid, insensible, or disordered in intellect, with a drug or alcoholic liquor; the making drunk or inebriated; the condition of being so stupefied or disordered' (*R v Taj* [2018] EWCA Crim 1743, [21]). In the Court of Appeal, Their Lordships also considered the meaning of 'attribute'. They again pointed to the dictionary definition, noting that it means 'Regard as belonging or appropriate to (a poem attributable to Shakespeare) 2. Ascribe to; regard as the effect of a stated cause (the delays were attributable to the heavy traffic) . . . ' (*R v Taj* [2018] EWCA Crim 1743, [59]). Crucially, Their Lordships agreed that that there was nothing to suggest that a person had to be intoxicated at the time of an offence, as long as there was sufficient evidence to suggest that the effect of alcohol or drugs was to render the person disordered. A key passage in the appeal judgment reads:

> In our view, the words 'attributable to intoxication' in s. 76(5) are broad enough to encompass both (a) a mistaken state of mind as a result of being drunk or intoxicated at the time and (b) a mistaken state of mind immediately and proximately consequent upon earlier drink or drug-taking, so that even though the person concerned is not drunk or intoxicated at the time, the short-term effects can be shown to have triggered subsequent episodes

> of e.g., paranoia. This is consistent with common law principles. We repeat that this conclusion does not extend to long term mental illness precipitated (perhaps over a considerable period) by alcohol or drug misuse.
>
> (*R v Taj* [2018] EWCA Crim 1743, [60])

According to Their Lordships, drinking did not need to have taken place the day before, or even several days prior, to an intoxication-related incident. The transcript states that: 'With regards to the *weeks leading up* to the incident he admitted that he had been habitually drinking to excess and had used cocaine' (*R v Taj* [2018] EWCA Crim 1743, [16], emphasis added). It was enough that Taj 'knew' drugs and alcohol had a 'detrimental effect on his mental wellbeing' and could lead to 'feelings of aggression' for him to be responsible (*R v Taj* [2018] EWCA Crim 1743, [16]). Their Lordships later reiterated that:

> a defendant who is suffering the immediate effects of alcohol or drugs in the system is, in truth, not in a different position to a defendant who has triggered or precipitated an immediate psychotic illness as a consequence of proximate ingestion of or drugs in the system whether or not they remain present at the time of the offence.
>
> (*R v Taj* [2018] EWCA Crim 1743, [56])

Once again, this removes or *deletes* the element of mental illness as a potential mediating factor, and particularly how this may have affected the decision to consume alcohol in the first place. A collateral reality of the finding that Taj was still experiencing the *effects* of intoxication, although he was not 'intoxicated', is therefore that alcohol can cause violence even where no traces of the substance are present in an individual's body. Other potential factors that might have led to the violent episode, discussed further in the following section, were downplayed (*deranked*) – in the case of 'psychosis' – or deleted entirely. This also leaves open the possibility that other states of mind or behaviours, besides psychosis-related violence, might be 'attributed' to intoxication even where an individual is no longer intoxicated.

Intoxication (Also) Aggravates the Responsibility of People with 'Alcohol-Induced Psychosis'

In determining whether Taj was fully responsible for his actions, or if he might plead self-defence, the court enacted a further collateral reality: that intoxication renders individuals *more* rather than less responsible. As indicated earlier, this legal truth is not a given, although it does follow legal precedent, but is rather a consequence of how the decision was framed. In some jurisdictions and circumstances, an intoxicated offender may lack the necessary state of mind (*mens rea*) for conviction. In a limited number of sentencing decisions in England and Wales (Lightowlers, 2022), intoxication has also rendered a defendant less culpable. However, the court made reference to legal judgments delivered in the sixteenth century, which in turn pointed to a principle dating back to antiquity:

> And Aristotle says, that such a Man deserves double Punishment, because he has doubly offended, viz. in being drunk to the evil Example of others, and in committing the Crime of Homicide. And this Act is said to be done ignoranter, for that he is the Cause of his own Ignorance.
>
> (*R v Taj* [2018] EWCA Crim 1743, [51])

This seems to suggest that Taj's crime was not just to have committed the violent act, but to have drunk to a disreputable degree – to have 'doubly offended' (aggravating his responsibility). This assumes that the decision to consume alcohol was an active one – an exercise of Taj's unconstrained agency. It does not allow for the possibility that Taj's will or decision-making was attenuated by his mental health difficulties, of which there was little discussion in contrast to the granular focus on intoxication and Taj's use of AOD. Their Lordships observed, for example, that 'Taj had abused drugs and alcohol from a very young age. It appears that he started drinking alcohol and abusing cannabis from as early as the age of 12' (*R v Taj* [2018] EWCA Crim 1743, [15]). The use of the word 'abuse' suggests deliberate or active agency on the part of Taj, despite his age and the constraints on his decision-making capabilities, and there was no further discussion about what may have led to AOD consumption at such a young age.

Nevertheless, the judges in both the Court of Appeal and the lower court emphasised that Taj should have foreseen how he might act and respond by abstaining from alcohol. In sentencing Taj, the judge at the lower court stated:

> had Taj not been fully aware that his state of mind would be affected by consumption of cocaine and alcohol, [the judge] might have had more sympathy. His conduct had created a ticking time bomb . . . I do not regard the fact that you were suffering from the mental disorder as lowering your degree of culpability in this case. This is not a case where someone acted as they did, because of an inability to control their actions. Rather, this is a case where you knew your actions would induce a state of

> mind where you could be a danger both to yourself and others. And, therefore, it does not afford you mitigation.
>
> (*R v Taj* [2018] EWCA Crim 1743, [68])

Their Lordships in the Court of Appeal agreed that, in respect of Taj's culpability, 'he knew that the cocaine and alcohol he took would induce a state of mind that could make him a danger' and so any reduction in sentence – as requested by the defence – was unmerited (*R v Taj* [2018] EWCA Crim 1743, [71]). Moreover,

> Taj knew the effect of consuming alcohol and taking drugs and although he may not have foreseen that he would attack an innocent member of the public with murderous intent, it is beyond argument that his behaviour demonstrated that he created a real risk to the public and was very likely to continue to do so without treatment and a decision to abstain from risks likely to generate a paranoid state.
>
> (*R v Taj* [2018] EWCA Crim 1743, [70])

According to the courts, therefore, Taj was both at fault for the psychotic incident and fully culpable when it came to sentencing. By framing the incident as one where Taj's culpability was aggravated, other potential contributory factors were either ignored, disconnected or *ranked* – in terms of importance – below his decision not to abstain. For example, it does not appear that Taj was taking medication for his psychosis, or that he had received a diagnosis. There is limited mention of any medical history, at least in the appeal judgment, nor why his condition – recognised in sentencing as a 'mental disorder' – appeared to have remained untreated. Taj had a history of mental health problems, and it was not clear that these were reducible to alcohol or other drug consumption; he had, in 2009, been subject to detention under the Mental Health Act 1983. Taj had previous convictions for theft, possessing a bladed article, possessing controlled drugs, criminal damage, threatening behaviour and assault, but nothing on the scale of attempted murder.

'Alcohol-Induced Psychosis' Is a Stable, Self-Induced Condition – and Not a 'Mental Illness'

Although the question of intoxication, and what might be attributed to it, was the subject of considerable discussion in the case, it was notable that the question of Taj's psychosis went largely unexamined. As discussed earlier, psychiatric experts employed by both defence and prosecution lawyers agreed that 'the use of drugs and alcohol could induce a condition very similar to psychosis and that the effects could last for weeks' (*R v Taj* [2018] EWCA Crim 1743, [18]). This appears to suggest that Taj was not in fact 'psychotic' but had a condition akin to psychosis. Indeed, the judgment *juxtaposes* Taj's diagnosis of a short-term mental disorder with a long-term mental illness precipitated by alcohol or other drug use (*R v Taj* [2018] EWCA Crim 1743, [60]). Recall also that neither the scientific literature nor the expert evidence provided to the court were as conclusive about these causal connections and distinctions as Their Lordships suggested (Child et al., 2020, p. 312). The language used in the transcript was not consistent; Taj had experienced a 'psychotic episode' (*R v Taj* [2018] EWCA Crim 1743, [61]), was suffering from a 'psychotic illness' (para. 56) and had a 'psychotic disorder' (*R v Taj* [2018] EWCA Crim 1743, [71]). He was also described as merely 'paranoid' due to his drinking (*R v Taj* [2018] EWCA Crim 1743, [54]). Importantly, none of these terms were explained or defined. This is surprising given that the question of whether Taj's condition was intermittent or 'long-term' appeared crucial to the decision-making. There was limited examination of how Taj's state of mind may have been influenced by an underlying mental illness, or how/whether this might lead to the kind of violence he inflicted upon the victim. The court did find that, because the victim was not armed and did not resist, and as Taj had received reassurances from the police that the victim was not a terrorist, his subsequent actions could not constitute 'reasonable' force (*R v Taj* [2018] EWCA Crim 1743, [64]). However, this assesses Taj's actions as if he were acting rationally or according to the standards of the 'reasonable man', rather than under the influence of a psychiatric condition or episode that all parties agreed he was experiencing.

As the court stabilised truths about the relationship between these objects, suggesting they were predictable and certain, a collateral reality 'made along the way' was therefore that 'alcohol-induced psychosis' was a distinct and temporary (as opposed to 'long-term') condition, and that it could be prevented merely by abstaining from alcohol and other drugs. The court's stabilisation of alcohol effects contrasted with the testimonies of the psychiatrists in the case, and academic commentary on the matter, which instead pointed to the unpredictability, instability and inconsistency of both drug effects and diagnoses of psychosis.

Discussion: Privileging Alcohol

The truths and collateral realities enacted by the court, as it sought to stabilise the relationship between intoxication, violence and responsibility, 'washed away' other variables – notably mental illness – that may have contributed to the incident occurring. Reducing the relationship between alcohol and violence to the question of an unwillingness to abstain simplifies the causal links between the decision to drink, which may be affected by an individual's mental health condition, and subsequent behaviours. Although the court seemed aware of the broader social context in which the attack happened – including the climate of fear about possible terrorist threats, bound up with questions of race, and the apparent historic lack of mental health support for Taj – these issues were disentangled from the final decision-making process as the judges 'bracketed' (Blomley, 2014) the alcohol-violence-responsibility question from other considerations.

My argument here is not that Taj necessarily holds no responsibility for what happened, or that his mental health difficulties were the cause, but that a granular attentiveness to legal decision-making is important for understanding the exact ways in which objects and subjects are made, and responsibility (or any other obligation) is attributed. A considerable amount of academic legal research has been devoted to drawing attention to the social context in which offending occurs. Courts are notoriously minded to reify, perhaps even fetishise, individual agency with the result that defences or mitigation based on disadvantage – for example poverty – rarely find much favour with judges (Roberts, 2011). The law is thus focused on shoring up its borders against incursions from 'messy', social scientific explanations for offending which might trouble a legal edifice founded on liberal principles of individual responsibility and accountability (Rose, 2000). However, for assemblage thinkers and STS scholars, neither social context nor individual agency on their own account for the ways in which 'both subjects and the social lives they participate in are the product of a more fundamental set of relations, affects, events and processes' (Duff, 2016, p. 17). It is necessary to consider full panoply of human and non-human, distal and proximate forces – and power relations – at work (DeLanda, 2006; Duff, 2016). This way of thinking means exploring how events and behaviours may be influenced by non-human factors such as, in this case, alcohol. Yet, despite its centrality to the case, alcohol was a non-human element that was entirely *absent* from the event. On the other hand, the parked car, the presence of electrical wires and other equipment all aroused Taj's suspicions and contributed to his decision to attack Awain.

It is challenging – but not impossible – for the law to better recognise and incorporate an understanding of human agency that is not abstracted – or ontologically separate – from practices and relations, and that is not overridden by policy concerns about deterrence. Kate Seear's (2020) work, for example, involves discussion about the mobilisation of 'onto-advocacy' strategies. These strategies or modes of lawyering/judging acknowledge the profoundly ethical nature of legal truth-making and involve a recognition that the legal constitution of objects, subjects and outcomes is fragile, but also *matters*, and must be subject to careful, critical attention.

The judgment also generated a series of normative questions and concerns. For example, it suggests that vulnerable defendants suffering from mental health problems could be unjustly criminalised (Child et al., 2020, p. 2206), and that individuals could be charged with alcohol-related offences (e.g., drink driving or drunk and disorderly conduct) because they were hungover, or experiencing the 'effects' of other drug consumption, at the time of an incident. Recall also that the court heard evidence about Taj's drinking not only on the evening before the attack, but two days prior. Would his actions have been attributable to intoxication had he been drinking only three days prior? Or perhaps a week? While these questions are key, however, it is important that lawyers, judges and legislators are more engaged not just with what constitutes 'intoxication', or 'immediate' and 'proximate' in relation to it, but how such states are affected by a range of human and non-human forces and power relations.

References

Barad, K. (2007). *Meeting the universe halfway: Quantum physics and the entanglement of matter and meaning*. Duke University Press.

Becker, H. S. (1953). Becoming a marihuana user. *American Journal of Sociology*, 59, 235–242.

Blomley, N. (2014). Disentangling law: The practice of bracketing. *Annual Review of Law and Social Science*, 10, 133–148.

Child, J. J., Crombag, H. S. & Sullivan, G. R. (2020). Defending the delusional, the irrational, and the dangerous. *Criminal Law Review*, 4, 306–324.

Criminal Procedure (Insanity) Act 1964, c. 46.

Crombag, H. S., Child, J. J. & Sullivan, G. R. (2020). Drunk, dangerous and delusional: How legal concept-creep risks overcriminalization. *Addiction*, 115(12), 2200–2207.

DeLanda, M. (2006). *A new philosophy of society: Assemblage theory and social complexity*. Continuum.

Deleuze, G., & Parnet, C. (1987). *Dialogues* (H. Tomlinson & B. Habberjam, Trans.). The Athlone Press.

Dennis, F. (2019). *Injecting bodies in more-than-human worlds*. Routledge.

Dilkes-Frayne, E. and Duff C. (2017). Tendencies and trajectories: The production of subjectivity in an event of drug consumption. *Environment and Planning D: Society and Space*, 35, 474–490.

Douglas, M. (1987). *Constructive drinking: Perspectives on drink from anthropology*. Cambridge University Press.

DPP v Majewski [1977] AC 443.

Dsouza, M. (2018). *R v Taj* – Self-defence, drinking and mental illness. UCL Centre for Criminal Law. www.ucl.ac.uk/criminal-law/sites/criminal-law/files/blogpost_on_taj.pdf.

Duff, C. (2016). Assemblages, territories, contexts. *International Journal of Drug Policy*, 33, 15–20.

Duncan, D., Keane, H., Moore, D., Ekendahl, M. & Graham, K. (2022). Making gender along the way: Women, men, and harm in Australian alcohol policy. *Critical Policy Studies*, 16(1), 1–18.

Ekendahl, M., Keane, H. & Moore, D. (2023). The analytical, the political and the personal: Swedish stakeholder narratives about alcohol policy at football stadiums. *Critical Policy Studies*, 17(2), 258–275.

Flacks, S. (2023). Who is the addict-offender? A historical ontology. *Social & Legal Studies*, 33(2), 149–167.

Fraser, S. (2006). The chronotope of the queue: Methadone maintenance treatment and the production of time, space and subjects. *International Journal of Drug Policy*, 17(3), 192–202.

Fraser, S., Moore, D. & Keane, H. (2014). *Habits: Remaking addiction*. Basingstoke: Palgrave Macmillan.

Hark, S. (2020). 'See it. Say it. Sorted.' Control society and the many faces of care. *Coils of the Serpent*, 5, 90–93.

Hart, A., & Moore, D. (2014). Alcohol and alcohol effects: Constituting causality in alcohol epidemiology. *Contemporary Drug Problems*, 41(3), 393–416.

Keay, L. (2018). Removal man jailed for trying to kill a Muslim claims his hangover made him 'psychotic'. *MailOnline*. www.dailymail.co.uk/news/article-5315487/Westminster-Bridge-attempted-killer-appeals-hangover.html.

Larsson, S. (2016). A first line of defence? Vigilant surveillance, participatory policing, and the reporting of 'suspicious' activity. *Surveillance & Society*, 15(1), 94–107.

Latour, B. (2005). *Reassembling the social: An introduction to actor-network-theory*. Oxford University Press.

Law, J. (2009). *After method: Mess in social science research*. Routledge.

Law, J. (2011). Collateral realities. In F. Dominguez Rubio & P. Baert (Eds.), *The politics of knowledge* (pp. 156–178). Routledge.

Law Commission. (1993). *Consultation Paper No. 127: Intoxication and Criminal Liability*. HMSO. www.lawcom.gov.uk/app/uploads/2015/04/cp127.pdf.

Law Commission. (2009). *Consultation Paper No. 314: Intoxication and Criminal Liability*. HMSO.

Levine, H. G. (1978). The discovery of addiction: Changing conceptions of habitual drunkenness in America. *Journal of Studies on Alcohol*, 39(1), 143–174.

Lightowlers, C. (2022). *Intoxication and sentencing: A review of policy, practice and research*. Sentencing Academy.

MacLean, S., & Moore, D. (2014). 'Hyped up': Assemblages of alcohol, excitement and violence for outer-suburban young adults in the inner-city at night. *International Journal of Drug Policy*, 25(3), 378–385.

McGee, K. (2015). On devices and logics of legal sense: Toward socio-technical legal analysis. In K. McGee (Ed.), *Latour and the passage of law* (pp. 61–92). Edinburgh University Press.

Mol, A.-M. (2002). *The body multiple: Ontology in medical practice*. Duke University Press.

Moore, D. (2017). Making visible the politics and ethics of alcohol policy research. *Addiction*, 112(8), 1490–1494.

Moore, D. (2020). Masculinities and intoxication: Notes towards a co-constitutive approach. In F. Hutton (Ed.), *Cultures of intoxication* (pp. 179–196). Palgrave Macmillan.

Moore, D., Keane, H., Duncan, D. & Lenton, E. (2023). Handling complexity: Constituting the relationship between intoxication and violence in Australian alcohol policy discourse. In G. Hunt, T. Antin & V. Asmussen Frank (Eds.), *Routledge handbook of intoxicants and intoxication* (pp. 484–498). Routledge.

Parker, N. (2018, May 31). 'Killer hangover': Man jailed for attempted murder to appeal 'because he was hungover'. *The Sun*. www.thesun.co.uk/news/5427798/jihadi-attacker-appeal-booze-turned-him-psychotic/.

Regina v Taj [2018] EWCA Crim 1743.

Roberts, J. V. (Ed.). (2011). *Mitigation and aggravation at sentencing*. Cambridge University Press.

Room, R. (2001). Intoxication and bad behaviour: Understanding cultural differences in the link. *Social Science & Medicine*, 53(2), 189–198.

Room, R. (2005). Stigma, social inequality and alcohol and drug use. *Drug and Alcohol Review*, 24(2), 143–155.

Rose, N. (2000). Government and control. *The British Journal of Criminology*, 40(2), 321–339.

Rose, N. (2000). The biology of culpability: Pathological identity and crime control in a biological culture. *Theoretical Criminology*, 4(1), 5–34.

Seear, K. (2020). *Law, drugs and the making of addiction: Just habits*. Routledge.

Sentencing Council. (2019). Aggravating and mitigating factors. *Sentencing Council*. www.sentencingcouncil.org.uk/explanatory-material/magistrates-court/item/aggravating-and-mitigating-factors/.

Stewart [2009] EWCA Crim 593, [2009] 1 WLR 2507 at [28].

Trubek, D. M. (1984). Where the action is: Critical legal studies and empiricism. *Stanford Law Review*, 36(1/2), 575–622.

Wood [2008] EWCA Crim 1305, [2009] 1 WLR 496 at [41].

4

The Undeclared War on Drugs in the Post-Soviet Limbo

ALEXANDRA DMITRIEVA AND VLADIMIR STEPANOV

Introduction

The day after launching a full-scale invasion of Ukraine in 2022, in a public speech addressed to multiple audiences, Putin called for the 'overthrow' of the Ukrainian government, which he labelled a 'gang of *narcomany* ("drug addicts") and neo-Nazis' (Roth, 2022). We will return to the significance of this speech later; here we would add to the picture that after Russia's initial invasion of Ukraine in 2014, in all territories under Russian occupation, opioid agonist therapy (OAT) programmes were immediately shut down, reflecting their status as being also banned in Russia. In annexed Crimea, 10 per cent of OAT patients died from overdose or suicide within six months after the programmes were closed in 2014 (Carroll, 2019a). There is no systematic data on how many people died or struggled to get the necessary treatment while facing the same situation after Russia's full-scale invasion in 2022 and occupation of further Ukrainian territories. However, it is documented that in the first month after the invasion, 'at least 57 state-based OAT programs throughout Ukraine either stopped operating, were destroyed by shelling, or ran out of medicines' (Mazhnaya et al., 2023, p. 2). This led to a risk of treatment interruption for over 6,000 officially registered OAT patients. The real number of patients faced with that risk, including the patients of private-funded programmes, many of whom are not officially registered with the drug user registry, could be many times higher.

In this chapter, we examine the case of *Irina Abdyusheva and Others v Russia*,[1] lodged with the European Court of Human Rights (ECHR) in 2011. The case was considered by the ECHR between 2014 and 2019, when the consequences of Russia's initial invasion of Ukraine were difficult to ignore. In this case, three individuals argued that Russia's

[1] Application no. 58502/11.

ban on OAT violated their rights guaranteed by three articles of the European Convention on Human Rights (hereafter Convention) in respect of freedom from torture, private and family life, and non-discrimination. We consider this case not simply in terms of the human right to access drug treatment, but as a set of public political utterances that frame discourses on people who use drugs, OAT and human rights in Russia, Ukraine and the 'West'. The ECHR provides a platform for Russia to engage in a form of political performance aimed at influencing the international legal order – terms of engagement that the ECHR seems to accept. We argue that Ukraine, bound to Russia by its Soviet past as well as physically occupied by it, at the same time as aspiring to be part of 'the West', becomes a place of 'constant engagement' (Fournier, 2012). It is located within a 'post-Soviet limbo' (Dmitrieva et al., 2022, 2024) where the 'violence against those who are already not quite living, that is, living in a state of suspension between life and death, leaves a mark that is no mark' (Butler, 2004, p. 36). 'The West' here refers to the imaginary 'West', or 'Europe', as the 'space to be entered/reentered', and the 'East', 'Russia' or 'Soviet past' refer to the imaginary 'space to be abandoned' (Kasianov, 2012, p. 171).

The Language of Political Utterance: Dealing with Uncertainty in the (Post-)Soviet States

Although Putin's speech referenced above was labelled 'bizarre' (Roth, 2022) in some media, we suggest that it can be characterised as an 'informal' utterance, embedded within the 'formal' framing of an official political statement. The reference to *narcomany* is addressed to audiences in post-Soviet states and points to recent history – the 1990s – a period marked by the aftermath of the collapse of the Soviet Union. One manifestation of that time was a wave of opioid 'narcomania', which 'was pictured as a "national catastrophe" that constituted a threat to security and the very existence of the Russian state' (Meylakhs, 2009, p. 380). 'Narcomania' is a catch-all term that was originally used by Soviet authorities to encompass any medical diagnosis or type of drug use (Miller, 2015), which later migrated into public discourse about drugs in post-Soviet countries. Moving from formal language rooted in medical jargon to an informal one, it reveals disparaging and offensive attitudes in regard to people who use drugs or are suspected of using drugs. Putin's claim that he brought Russia out of the chaos of the troubled 1990s is one of his most persistent political declarations, which lets him both stress his particular authoritative role as a moral leader and evoke an image of the country that has been 'consistently heroic in the course of its entire history' (Boele et al., 2019, p. 207). The image of the 'great and heroic victory' in the Second World War and the role of the Soviet Union 'as the savior of Europe from the evils of the barbarian Nazis' (Wood, 2011, p. 175) is a key instrument of propaganda and a moral project in Russian politics, promoted both domestically and internationally. By shifting from the formal register of a political statement to the informal one, from the territory of one historical period to another, this statement creates uncertainty about what is being said and manages to engage the audience in 'a performance that simultaneously instils a pervasive atmosphere of danger and offers protection from it' (Dunn & Bobick, 2014, p. 41).

Initially this type of utterance emerged within Soviet society as an informal response to the 'hypernormalization' (Yurchak, 2005) of authoritative discourse of Soviet power in the late Soviet period, also known as the 'Epoch of Stagnation' (*Epokha Zastoya*). That discourse existed within its own temporal and historical framework, with the present that belonged to the Communist future, and the past that preceded the creation of the Soviet Union, that is, the imperial capitalist past, being omitted (Groys, 2009). As a result, the phenomena that did not fit into the Soviet framework were not named, but labelled 'remnants' (*perezhitki*) from the imperial/bourgeois/capitalist past, including individual rights as opposed to the collective rights of workers (Hawkesworth, 1980), private life and private property (Boym, 1994; Groys, 2009), drug use (Miller, 2015; Vasilyev, 2022) and so on. This labelling allowed these phenomena to be defined as both an internal 'remnant' and an 'external' threat from 'the West', as both were associated with capitalism. Being carried out in the regime of 'uncertainty avoidance' (Dmitrieva et al., 2022, 2024), the language itself was an embodiment of Communist ideology, and the Soviet individual both its derivative and (re)producer.

The over-formalisation of this language and constant repetition of wording, combined with the lack of possibility for abandoning its use, 'distanced the authoritative discourse of socialism from its desired intimate connection with the language and thinking of its citizen subjects' (Boyer & Yurchak, 2010, p. 182). Borrowing the official language, but placing particular terms in a context or in combination with something that was not inherent to it, the informal response embodied a 'performative shift' (Yurchak, 2005, p. 250) that created uncertainty about the origin and meaning of this utterance. In other words, that kind of utterance appeared within an overregulated discursive order through the use of 'deterritorialized terms, that is, terms which are torn from their area, in order to reterritorialize another notion' (Deleuze & Parnet, 2007, p. 18). The same prerequisites – excessive regulation not even of drugs themselves, which we have explored elsewhere (Dmitrieva & Kravchenko, 2016; Dmitrieva et al., 2022), but of the everyday life of the Soviet people 'to avoid the uncertainty' regarding the image of 'a real Soviet man' – created conditions for the reproduction of the image of drug use. It was reproduced as a hidden, 'informal' practice, mimicking and being forced to mimic other forms of behaviour so as not to be singled out as a separate form of life (Stepanov & Dmitrieva, 2023), but to be kept 'in secrecy' by both the state and society (Dmitrieva et al., 2024). The war on drugs was thus not officially declared – as to not connect the image of the Soviet people with drug use – but was fought as both an external threat to the socialist moral borders and an internal threat to the collective socialist body.

Managing Uncertainty in the Post-Soviet Limbo

In the post-Soviet period, the official political discourse in Russia inherits and simultaneously appropriates the type of utterance that emerged in Soviet society as an informal response to an overregulated discursive order. At the same time, it goes further, transgressing not only discursive but also geopolitical borders. This involves taking discourse out of context and inserting it into a new one. But this applies not only to (post-)Soviet historical events or terms, but also concepts of the international order, such as non-repetition of genocide, sovereignty of the nation-state, prohibition of the use of force, and human rights. By appropriating these concepts through language, this discourse seeks to create uncertainty and simultaneously 'manage' it (Dmitrieva et al., 2022, 2024), by demonstrating commitment to the international legal order while challenging it (Dunn & Bobick, 2014; Leonaite & Zalimas, 2016). Using various platforms, including the ECHR, as podiums to make political statements, this discourse goes beyond the post-Soviet space. At the local level, after the turbulent but liberating period of the 1990s, this discursive regime has increasingly shifted towards 'uncertainty avoidance' through the state's monopolisation of public discourse on many issues, including drugs. This is achieved by excluding any actors that create uncertainty, be it domestic organisations or individuals labelled 'foreign agents', external organisations labelled 'undesirable', or the ECHR itself (Malinowska-Sempruch & Gallagher, 2004; Bartlett et al., 2014; Lilja, 2021).

In Ukraine's official discourse, along with the 'return to normality' (Kasianov, 2012, p. 172) after the Soviet Union's dissolution, the state-led process of 'nationalization' became another filter to build Ukrainian identity and remove 'Soviet remnants' from history, education and everyday life (Kasianov, 2012; Zhurzhenko, 2022). The moral sovereignty of independent Ukraine was justified through opposition to 'normal' citizens and those who use drugs: 'the collective dehumanization of troublesome *narkomany* was clearly (and frequently) articulated, as it helped define true Ukrainianness' (Carroll, 2019b, p. 136). At the same time, by using human rights language to position itself as being in a profitable relationship with those in power, Ukrainian leadership allowed international actors from 'the West' 'to influence administrative strategies within Ukraine's sovereign borders over which the state would typically have control' (Carroll, 2019b, p. 178). Therefore, the start of internationally funded OAT programmes in Ukraine was formally justified as a measure to counteract HIV, mostly concentrated among people who inject drugs, with an evidence-based approach recommended by the World Health Organization (WHO), an authoritative international agency (LaMonaca et al., 2019). Informally, the introduction of internationally funded OAT programmes also represented a way to oppose Russia as an exceptional state with its disrespect to human rights and prohibitionist drug policies, including the ban of OAT, and to indicate, through the emerging difference between the two states, a 'distinct geopolitical line between the Western and non-Western world' (Zhukova, 2013, p. 146). The resulting discursive regime is based on the repetition of the same words and statements denoting a commitment to the international order. However, omitted from that discourse is how terms like OAT or human rights – de-territorialised from the West – are being re-territorialised in ways that are 'similarly punitive to drug policy in Russia, if not more so' (Ukrainian Network of People who Use Drugs (VOLNA) et al., 2020, p. 7; UNAIDS, 2024). Hence, often using the same means of managing uncertainty, Russia and Ukraine seek to achieve different goals: Russia to be 'active – not passive; a provider – not a receiver' (Sjöstedt, 2008, p. 21), and Ukraine to distance itself from Russia by demonstrating a broad openness to 'the West's' influence. In both cases, the discursive regime that emerges aims to reproduce fixed forms containing approved ideological statements without the need for additional argumentation (Boyer & Yurchak, 2010, p. 186). The absence of this need emphasises that drug policy development and implementation is not necessarily (simply) driven by human rights activism or public health issues (e.g., HIV), but is also a consequence of geopolitical interests and a way of realising them.

The idea we propose is that the previous Soviet discursive regime of 'uncertainty avoidance' has been transformed into a post-Soviet discursive regime of 'uncertainty management'. The two regimes are interrelated to produce and reproduce the state of 'post-Soviet limbo' which is characterised by 'overabundance of the past [that] blocks future advancement' (Kasianov, 2022, p. 10). In this chapter, we note that the post-Soviet limbo transcends its own boundaries. Further to that, if what is identified as 'Western' technologies, values or discourses can be de-territorialised and transmitted into the post-Soviet space, then they can just as well be re-territorialised locally. At this point, they do not remain in their modified form, but go abroad or back to where they came from, for example, to the ECHR as a product of 'the West' in one case, and an embodiment of an imaginary future in the other, in order to push for this local interpretation to be universalised and not the other way around. That is, a local understanding of human rights in a discursive or practical sense can work to actively transform what is perceived as a universal model of human rights, not to emphasise its uniqueness, but to question the original model. Thus, such a model will always differ from the initial version, similar in form but not the same in content, recognisable but not familiar. Following Deleuze, but in regard to Ukraine, Fournier noted that this 'double becoming' has no direction, no 'progress': it represents a 'constant engagement' (Fournier, 2012). In such a case, when universal and local understandings collide, these rights appear to be in a process of being continually made and remade. Or perhaps it is not only that human rights are in the process of being made, but also people themselves. In this case, people who use drugs, as possessors of individual rights, are still in the process of becoming human, that is, in the process of becoming entitled to human rights (Fraser & valentine, 2008; Fraser et al., 2014; Seear, 2020; Seear & Mulcahy, 2023). According to Butler, dehumanisation is related to disenfranchisement: in the process of de-realising the Other (making the Other unreal) as a human who does not fully meet the criteria for inclusion in the concept of a human, the violence that is inflicted upon them may not be seen as violence because these lives are already denied (Butler, 2004). Being lifeless in life, they become deathless in death (Alighieri, 2008) and are frozen in a hopeless wait for change.

Case of Irina *Abdyusheva and Others v Russia*

The following section is based on the analysis of the case *Abdusheva and Others v Russia*.[2] As we stated before, we consider this case as both a set of political utterances and a performance. We structure the section according to the following 'dramatic' elements of a performative act: exposition, rising action, climax, falling action and resolution (Freytag, 1900). Italics were added by the authors to emphasise specific words or wordings which we consider particularly pertinent for the discussion.

Exposition: Application and First Responses

In the period between 2014 and 2019, the ECHR considered a case that originated from three applicants who argued that Russia's ban on OAT violated their rights guaranteed by the Convention in respect to freedom from torture, private and family life and non-discrimination. Of the three, only one, Irina's complaint, was fully analysed by the Court, as the other two applicants were no longer using opioids, nor in active treatment, by the time the case was heard. These conclusions were made based on the Russian government's report, which included data exported from the drug user registry (*narcouchet*), where two other applicants carried out urine tests during their '*outpatient visits*' that revealed an '*absence of traces of opiates*' (*Abdyusheva and Others v Russia*, 2019, ss. 11; 29, FJ; emphasis added). Irina's complaint was declared admissible only in respect to the part based on Article 8 of the Convention's 'Right to respect for private and family life'.

According to the application prepared by Irina's lawyer, she was first diagnosed with 'opiate drug addiction' (*Abdyusheva v Russia*, 2011, s. 14.1, App) in 1984 when she was eighteen and had been on the *narcouchet* since then. She had been imprisoned five times for drug-related offences, in 1989, 1995, 1998, 2001 and 2005, and had spent a total of sixteen years in prison. She was treated first in a psychiatric hospital in 1984 and continued her attempts at treatment in various clinics, both compulsory and voluntarily, in prison and civilian settings. These treatments never led to '*lengthy remissions*' (*Abdyusheva v Russia*, 2011, s. 14.1, App; emphasis added). In 2009, she made her last attempt at treatment in Russia and 'resumed using drugs within less than two weeks

[2] *Abdyusheva v Russia*, Application No 58502/11, 25 August 2011, and *Abdyusheva and Others v Russia*, Application Nos. 58502/11, 62964/10, 55683/13, Chamber/Final Judgment, 26 November 2019/15 April 2020.

after completing treatment' (*Abdyusheva v Russia*, 2011, s. 14.1, App). '*As a result of drug addiction*' (*Abdyusheva v Russia*, 2011, s. 14.3, App; emphasis added), she was diagnosed with hepatitis C in 1989, HIV in 2000, AIDS in 2005 and tuberculosis during her last time in prison before the case was heard.

In relation to Article 8 it was argued that: '*barriers to access to effective treatment for drug dependence adversely affect her private life*' (*Abdyusheva v Russia*, 2011, s. 15.22, App; original emphasis). Evidence was cited that treatment with OAT 'can be provided on an *outpatient basis*, achieving high rates of retention in treatment and increasing the time and opportunity for individuals to tackle major health, psychological, family, housing, employment, financial and legal issues while in contact with a treatment service' (*Abdyusheva v Russia*, 2011, s. 24, App; emphasis added).

Rising Action: Third-Party Arguments

Two medical committees and eleven organisations were authorised to intervene in the case proceedings. International parties were represented by organisations '*who support treatment with OAT*'; domestic parties were represented by rehabilitation centres based in Russia – '*who are unfavorable to it*' (*Abdyusheva and Others v Russia*, 2019, s. 72, FJ; emphasis added).

The key argument presented by the third parties in favour of OAT indicated that methadone and buprenorphine are on the WHO Model List of Essential Medicines (WHO Model List). Referring to the three UN Drug Conventions, they noted that both substances are '*subject to international control*' (*Abdyusheva and Others v Russia*, 2019, s. 73, FJ; emphasis added). Being bound by the drug conventions, 'Russia has a fundamental obligation to find a balance between the control of substances on the list and their accessibility for medical needs' (*Abdyusheva and Others v Russia*, 2019, s. 73, FJ).

A medical committee affiliated with a Ukrainian NGO was invited by Irina's lawyer to take part in the final hearing. Referring to the Order of the Ministry of Health (MoH), the committee stated that OAT is recommended when there is a diagnosis of opiate dependence and especially when there are concurrent diagnoses of HIV and hepatitis C. It emphasised the importance of OAT to exclude: 'the commission of offenses to be able to finance the purchase of illicit drugs and the imprisonment following these offences, which would *ultimately lead to the abandonment of the antiretroviral therapy* followed by the person concerned and, *ultimately, to her death from AIDS*' (*Abdyusheva and Others v Russia*, 2019, s. 23, FJ; emphasis added).

Expert opinion submitted by narcologists from a dispensary in Russia claimed that the OAT, which 'consists of consuming drugs', does not lead '*to the elimination of dependence or to remission*' (*Abdyusheva and Others v Russia*, 2019, s. 25, FJ; emphasis added). The commission recommended treatment based on medico-social rehabilitation for the applicant, namely hospitalisation (for detoxification) at the regional narcological dispensary, followed by systematic visits to an outpatient centre for social rehabilitation. Other rehabilitation centres echoed the presented argument and added that their aim is 'not to achieve remission, even stable, but to completely cure the person' (*Abdyusheva and Others v Russia*, 2019, s. 97, FJ).

Climax: The Government's Reply

The government outlined a number of arguments in its reply.[3] It stated that the prohibition of OAT 'is dictated by the State's *duty to protect the life and health* of persons within its jurisdiction by controlling access to narcotic substances' (*Abdyusheva and Others v Russia*, 2019, s. 55, FJ; emphasis added). Moreover, it adds that OAT poses significant dangers to health, creates another form of dependence and contributes to polydrug use which leads to a high risk of death by overdose (the last point was illustrated by the example of the prescription opioid crisis in the US) (*Abdyusheva and Others v Russia*, 2019, ss. 51–53). It claimed that an absolute prohibition is proportionate to the aforementioned aim, insofar as Russia provides 'access to treatments capable of curing drug dependence' (*Abdyusheva and Others v Russia*, 2019, s. 55, FJ). The applicant's treatment failed because she did not follow it completely, including rehabilitation stages available in Russia – in particular, 'a regular follow-up, known as "outpatient visits", were not regular' (*Abdyusheva and Others v Russia*, 2019, s. 47, FJ). Therefore, the reply stated, it cannot be argued that these methods are ineffective. The opposite, the authorisation of OAT is 'nothing more than *a capitulation to drug dependence* and in no way constitutes its treatment' (*Abdyusheva and Others v Russia*, 2019, s. 57, FJ; emphasis added), and 'must be considered as *a request for the*

[3] This section relies on both direct quotation and closely paraphrases the government's position.

legalization of drugs' (*Abdyusheva and Others v Russia*, 2019, s. 56, FJ; emphasis added).

In regard to its international obligations, the government pointed out that they derive them from the UN Single Convention on Narcotic Drugs of 1961. Being '*faithful to its international obligations*, Russia has incorporated these standards into its national law' (*Abdyusheva and Others v Russia*, 2019, s. 58, FJ; emphasis added) by prohibiting the free circulation of methadone (list I) and buprenorphine (list II) listed in that convention. Regarding the WHO recommendations, the government argued that 'these standards are not binding and do not commit Russia to implement them' (*Abdyusheva and Others v Russia*, 2019, s. 58, FJ). In support of this argument, a disclaimer in the WHO Model List was cited (*Abdyusheva and Others v Russia*, 2019, s. 58, FJ), which states that the responsibility for interpretation and use lies with the reader, and the WHO cannot be held liable for any damages resulting from its use. Therefore, although European consensus seems to support OAT, some countries still prohibit its use, and other countries are reducing their OAT programmes (*Abdyusheva and Others v Russia*, 2019, s. 53, FJ).

Finally, the government stated that the request to lift the ban on OAT '*falls within the government's discretion in matters of public health*' (*Abdyusheva and Others v Russia*, 2019, s. 56, FJ; emphasis added). By referring to the ECHR's case law, the government noted that 'the Court has hitherto been very cautious when dealing with medical issues and that it has granted the Member States a wide margin of appreciation'[4] (*Abdyusheva and Others v Russia*, 2019, s. 59, FJ).

Falling Action and Resolution: The Court's Decision

First of all, the ECHR reiterated that the Convention 'does not guarantee the right to health as such or the right to specific medical treatment sought by the applicant' (*Abdyusheva and Others v Russia*, 2019, s. 111, FJ) but had been considering similar complaints 'which it examined under Article 8 of the Convention, including the concept of "private life" which is underpinned by the concept of *personal autonomy*' (*Abdyusheva and Others v Russia*, 2019, s. 111, FJ; emphasis added). The ECHR then noted that it had dealt with '*a request for access to unauthorized medicines*' (*Abdyusheva and Others v Russia*, 2019, s. 114, FJ; emphasis added) and concluded that therapy with methadone and

[4] A term meaning 'room for manoeuvre' in European human rights law.

buprenorphine, although widespread in the member states, was nevertheless controversial (*Abdyusheva and Others v Russia*, 2019, s. 124, FJ). Referring to the other case, the ECHR held that the health authorities did not exceed their 'margin of appreciation' in refusing access to *experimental medication* for patients suffering from a terminal illness, since their aim was 'to protect the latter from a step that could prove harmful to their health, even fatal, even though they were at the end of their life' (*Abdyusheva and Others v Russia*, 2019, s. 128, FJ; emphasis added).

The ECHR held that 'the risks referred to by the government were not unfounded' (*Abdyusheva and Others v Russia*, 2019, s. 128, FJ). Therefore, Russian authorities, 'inspired' by the duty to protect the health of people under their jurisdiction, 'are therefore well justified in taking measures, sometimes as drastic as the prohibition of certain opiates, in order to minimize the harm caused or likely to be caused by them' (*Abdyusheva and Others v Russia*, 2019, s. 128, FJ). It concluded that 'the Russian authorities are better placed to set policy in such a delicate area as the fight against drug trafficking, the regulation of the drug market and medical care for opiate dependents, given their wide margin of appreciation in matters of public health' (*Abdyusheva and Others v Russia*, 2019, s. 130, FJ). Finally, the ECHR recalled that its role is not to replace health professionals and to judge the effectiveness of dependence treatment methods, and 'noted with satisfaction that conventional medical assistance based on the *progress of science* is available to the applicant in Russian medical establishments' (*Abdyusheva and Others v Russia*, 2019, s. 131, FJ; emphasis added).

A 6–1 judgment was issued in support that Russia had not violated the applicants' rights.

Discussion

The exposition of this performance started with the submission of three applications and first responses of the Russian government and the Court. The data that were presented by the government and used by the ECHR to allow Irina's application to proceed and to reject two other applications demonstrate the way in which the '*narcouchet*', referred to by the government's side as 'visits to an outpatient center', works. These visits are to be made for 'sobriety monitoring', assessed by urine tests whose results are to be recorded in a centralised database. The same data can be used to regulate the private lives of people who use drugs in relation to their rights to pursue certain careers, parenting roles and driving. The onset of 'stable remission', not in a pre-determined period of time, but according to the authoritative assessment of a narcologist, may eventually lead to 'deregistration', which, in the discourse of the Russian side, is equated with 'cure', evidenced by the absence of traces of drugs in the urine test. By accepting this argument, the ECHR not only immediately recognised Russia's approach to 'drug dependence treatment' as evidence-based, but also the authority of this political statement, which was subsequently repeated many times without the need for additional argumentation or/and contextualisation. In particular, the legitimacy of the use of confidential data or the very repressive practice of the registration of individuals for drug use in post-Soviet countries, which has been repeatedly raised by human rights defenders, has not been questioned (Malinowska-Sempruch and Gallagher, 2004; Open Society Foundations, 2009). *Narcouchet* appeared as one of the last orders of the USSR MoH before its dissolution, marking the drug use's 'relocation' from the space of informal existence and regulation to the space of formal recognition and governance through 'narcology', a subspecialty of psychiatry established in the Soviet period, and the police (Dmitrieva et al., 2022). It has survived to the present day, including in Ukraine.

Irina's biography, in the way it was presented by her lawyer, indicated two other significant issues. First, it outlined that it was her 'drug addiction' that led to her further diagnoses. It stressed Irina's lack of autonomy, but not the role of the state's drug policy which affected the way she has had to live her life, in particular, during sixteen years in prison. This may have comprised a typical lawyers' strategy 'to attract sympathy' (Seear, 2020, p. 84) for clients. It is used not to oppose the discursive field their clients are already a part of but to de-territorialise it from within: no matter whether a person who uses drugs is presented as sick or as criminal, 'addiction' creates uncertainty about the ability to control their own life; the only difference is that the illness is positioned as the cause, rather than criminal behaviour per se, and this approach can be sympathetic. Second, a person who has been convicted six times for drug-related offences is unlikely to seek out opportunities for systematic visits to any state-based institution and undertake urine testing for drugs that may be used as evidence of her 'criminal activity'. It is more likely that such a person will look for opportunities to avoid these visits in any possible way. Yet, discursively, *narcouchet*, defined as 'systematic visits to an outpatient center', effectively repeated one of the key arguments of the opposing side. As a term, it was taken out of context and inserted into a new context, demonstrating both compliance with international order and the authority of the speaker. In this way, the utterance transcended the discourse in which it was produced and entered another discourse to modify the concept, in which outpatient visits for OAT admission allow patients to have a private life.

The rising action started with the Ukrainian side entering the scene. By using the formal language of the Order of the MoH, the NGO-based medical committee thereby retransmitted and appropriated the state's authority. Switching to informal language, the committee emphasised the inevitability of the negative consequences of the refusal of OAT. This set of utterances demonstrated the way OAT is positioned within a broader discourse: it is a way to simultaneously keep someone 'diagnosed' in treatment and to keep them from crime, prison and death. Thus, this person represents both a viral carrier who is unable to take treatment on their own and a criminal who cannot be kept from crime without the help of OAT. Therefore, the processes of criminalisation and medicalisation, or rather pathologisation, of people who use opioids, is in constant engagement (Carroll, 2019b). The medical commission on the Russian side did not produce any new message, remaining within the framework of the government's discourse that we have already outlined. Repeating the importance of 'systematic visits to an outpatient center' as a mantra, and reinforcing its authority by referring to the exclusivity of its mission to 'cure' individuals from drug use as the main goal of treatment, the speakers reinforced the approach where judging treatment efficacy is restricted to 'cure' versus 'failure to cure' (Elovich and Drucker, 2008).

This performance reached its climax in the government's response. By jumping from the formal register of a political statement to the informal one, from the territory of one country to another, it presented fixed discursive forms that did not require verification and a succession of anecdotes and scare stories that played on the emotional and moral involvement of all parties in the case. First, the government outlined its moral position, expressed in the need to fulfil its duty to the population and the international community through a total ban on OAT, the 'legalisation' of which is nothing more than a 'capitulation to dependence'. Thus, OAT in this discursive territory becomes a 'weapon' of the enemy against a heroic government that continues to fight back. Consequently, the war on drugs that remains undeclared and unnamed in this discourse appropriates methadone and buprenorphine, tearing it from its initial area in order to re-territorialise the notion of OAT. The goal is to expand the boundaries of this discursive territory beyond its borders, while at the same time creating uncertainty by broadening the spectrum of what or whom this war is being waged against (Dunn & Bobick, 2014; Leonaite & Zalimas, 2016). The government also referred to the 'outpatient visits' that Irina underwent irregularly, but only to emphasise her unwillingness to fulfil her obligations and, thus, to highlight her apparent lack of autonomy. To justify the prohibition of OAT, the government referred to the same conventions that the third parties invoked to urge the government to 'comply with international obligations' – a passage that has been frequently used not only in Russia but in other countries to block similar changes (Bewley-Taylor, 2003; Malinowska-Sempruch & Gallagher, 2004; Bartlett et al., 2014;). By doing so, the government demonstrated both its commitment to international law and yet had the last word, ignoring the context that has changed since the establishment of international drug conventions and the idea of human rights, which provides a rationale for the need for change. By making an anecdotal reference to the opioid crisis in the US, the government sowed in the audience a sense of danger about whether the poly use of OAT and other substances were the cause, with the credibility of these 'facts' going unchecked. Finally, the reference to a disclaimer in the WHO Model List was aimed at diminishing the authority of the list among the audience by demonstrating its ambiguous status, which is 'recognised' by the WHO itself.

In the falling action and resolution, the ECHR not only accepted all the arguments proposed by the Russian government but seemed to adopt the very form of utterance employed by Russia. Following the government's arguments, the object under consideration seemed to change from providing access to a prohibited treatment option to celebrating Russia's efforts to 'cure drug dependence'. Noting that the government was inspired by a duty to protect the health of the Russian population, the ECHR designated the treatment approach used in Russia as 'conventional', while OAT accordingly became a form of 'unconventional' treatment. Then, referring to earlier considered cases, OAT was discursively equated with an 'experimental medication', the authorisation of access to which falls within the government's discretion ('margin of appreciation') in matters of public health. In doing so, a complete re-territorialisation of OAT's notion as an approach to treatment based on scientific evidence, traditionally opposed to abstinence-based treatment for this very reason, was discursively achieved. Concluding with satisfaction that 'conventional medical assistance based on the *progress of science* is available to the applicant', the ECHR displaced OAT from the discursive field of human rights, while admitting the 'conventional' approach 'capable of curing drug dependence' into it. Therefore, in this performance, the ECHR took part as a participant and a co-transformer of the international order and the image of the West in the eyes of the audience represented, in particular, by the Ukrainian side. In the territory of post-Soviet discourse, in both Russia and Ukraine, OAT is indeed an approach of the West. Therefore, in this case, Russia occupied the discursive territory of the West, while the West represented by the ECHR did not seem to be willing to defend the sovereign borders of the discourse under examination.

Previously, we argued that the post-Soviet limbo is a state characterised by the edge (Dmitrieva et al., 2022). Then we noted the shift of this limbo from the edge to the centre (Dmitrieva et al., 2024). In this chapter, we can conclude that the interplay between the 'duty to protect' and 'obligation to comply', in a wide and at the same time reduced range of interpretations of threat and good, external and internal, state sovereignty and borders of one's private life, represents a certain state that no longer fits within the framework of post-Soviet liminality. It becomes a form of post-Soviet 'limbinality', or post-Soviet limbo, that goes beyond the specified geographical space, at least in regard to people who are considered 'less than human' (Seear and Mulcahy, 2023, p. 2). The public sphere is thus shaped by 'what cannot be said and what cannot be shown' (Butler, 2004, p. 17), while the boundaries of speech and visibility restrict political discourse and the representation of certain actors. At the same time, what is said is formed through both habits of thought (in our case, ideas about human rights and people who use drugs that were formed historically) and the practice, for example, of Western nations (Seear and Mulcahy, 2023, p. 17). A constant repetition of the same words and concepts forming the discourse on drugs, OAT, and human rights reveals the way these habits are produced and reproduced to manage the uncertainty that people who use drugs present. De-territorialised terms and concepts multiply metaphors related to drug use but do not change the initial meaning (Fraser & valentine, 2008). As a result, the language of human rights becomes over-formalised, losing its connection to the idea behind their introduction as a universal principle. Therefore, following Butler, the violence against people who use drugs leaves a 'mark that is no mark' (Butler, 2004, p. 36), then the mark of these people is less than mark. It exists somewhere between traces of opiates in urine tests and amounts of HIV viral load in blood tests, between the number of criminal records and those that were made in the drug registry. While drug policy itself becomes both the cause and effect of occupation, embodying not only discursive difference but also asserting geopolitical claims within which human lives in general are of little value.

We noted earlier that 'the impossibility of adequately depicting (Butler, 2005) those who wish to go beyond the frame of the picture (and hence the normative frame of society) suggests that one way of visualising people who use drugs is to capture their receding shadow or "inversion" trace in space' (Stepanov & Dmitrieva, 2023, p. 275). The purpose of this chapter, then, goes beyond that which is outlined in the introduction, and we hope that we will be able to preserve the trace of these people not only in the history of judging drugs, but also in memory: to remember people who were sacrificed in the war on drugs but continued to fight for their right to be considered human. Nine years elapsed between the first application in 2011 and the ECHR's decision at the end of 2019. It can be reasonably assumed that the preparation of the applications, which included applications to the domestic courts and the handling of the cases there, also took considerable time. We would like to express our support and respect to the applicants for their incredible courage.

References

Abdyusheva v Russia, Application No. 58502/11 (Eur. Ct. H.R. Aug. 25, 2011).

Abdyusheva and Others v Russia, Chamber/Final Judgment Application Nos. 58502/11, 62964/10, 55683/13 (Eur. Ct. H.R. Nov. 26, 2019/April 15, 2020).

Alighieri, D. (2008). *Divine Comedy: Inferno*. Josef Nygrin.

Bartlett, N., Garriott, W. & Raikhel, E. (2014). What's in the 'treatment gap'? Ethnographic perspectives on addiction and global mental health from China, Russia, and the United States. *Medical Anthropology: Cross-Cultural Studies in Health and Illness*, 33(5), 457–477.

Bewley-Taylor, D. R. (2003). Challenging the UN drug control conventions: Problems and possibilities. *International Journal of Drug Policy*, 14(2), 171–179.

Boele, O., Noordenbos, B. & Robbe, K. (2019). *Post-Soviet nostalgia: Confronting the empire's legacies*. Routledge.

Boyer, D., & Yurchak, A. (2010). American stiob: Or, what late-socialist aesthetics of parody reveal about contemporary political culture in the West. *Cultural Anthropology*, 25(2), 179–221.

Boym, S. (1994). *Common places: Mythologies of everyday life in Russia*. Harvard University Press.

Butler, J. (2005). *Giving an account of oneself*. Fordham University Press.

Butler, J. (2004). *Precarious life: The powers of mourning and violence*. Verso.

Carroll, J. J. (2019a). Sovereign rules and rearrangements: Banning methadone in occupied Crimea. *Medical Anthropology: Cross-Cultural Studies in Health and Illness*, 38(5), 508–522.

Carroll, J. J. (2019b). *Narkomania: Drugs, HIV, and citizenship in Ukraine*. Cornell University Press.

Deleuze, G., & Parnet, C. (2007). *Dialogues* (revised ed.). Columbia University Press.

Dmitrieva, A., & Kravchenko, Z. (2016). Drug control policies in Russia: Unhealthy, deviant and criminal. *Baltic Worlds*, 4(4), 12–22.

Dmitrieva, A., Stepanov, V. & Mazhnaya, A. (2022). Managing opioid agonist therapy in the post-Soviet limbo. *Contemporary Drug Problems*, 49(2), 148–169.

Dmitrieva, A., Stepanov, V. & Titar, I. (2024). (e)Managing the uncertainty of tuberculosis in the post-Soviet limbo: Tracking prisoners' coerced mobility for treatment in Ukrainian prisons. *Social Science & Medicine*, 349(2), 116894.

Dunn, E. C., & Bobick, M. S. (2014). The empire strikes back: War without war and occupation without occupation in the Russian sphere of influence. *American Ethnologist*, 41(3), 405–413.

Elovich, R., & Drucker, E. (2008). On drug treatment and social control: Russian narcology's great leap backwards. *Harm Reduction Journal*, 5(23), 1–5.

Fournier, A. (2012). *Forging rights in a new democracy: Ukrainian students between freedom and justice*. University of Pennsylvania Press.

Fraser, S., Moore, D. & Keane, H. (2014). *Habits: Remaking addiction*. Palgrave Macmillan.

Fraser, S., & valentine, K. (2008). *Substance and substitution: Methadone subjects in liberal societies*. Palgrave Macmillan.

Freytag, G. (1900). *Freytag's technique of the drama: An exposition of dramatic composition and art*. Scott, Foresman & Company.

Groys, B. (2009). *The communist postscript*. Verso.

Hawkesworth, M. (1980). Ideological immunity: The Soviet response to human rights criticism. *Universitas Human Rights*, 2(1), 67–84.

Kasianov, G. (2022). *Memory crash: The politics of history in and around Ukraine 1980s–2010s*. Central European University Press.

Kasianov, G. (2012). The 'nationalization' of history in Ukraine. In A. Miller & M. Lipman (Eds.), *The convolutions of historical politics* (pp. 1–355). Central European University Press.

LaMonaca, K., Dumchev, K., Dvoriak, S., Azbel, L., Morozova, O. & Altice, F. L. (2019). HIV, drug injection, and harm reduction trends in Eastern Europe and Central Asia: Implications for international and domestic policy. *Current Psychiatry Reports*, 21(7), 1–11.

Leonaite, E., & Zalimas, D. (2016). The annexation of Crimea and attempts to justify it in the context of international law. *Lithuanian Annual Strategic Review*, 14(1), 11–63.

Lilja, M. (2021). Russian political discourse on illegal drugs: A thematic analysis of parliamentary debates. *Substance Use & Misuse*, 56(7), 1010–1017.

Malinowska-Sempruch, K., & Gallagher, S. (Eds.). (2004). *War on drugs, HIV/AIDS and human rights*. International Debate Education Association.

Mazhnaya, A., Meteliuk, A., Pykalo, I. & Altice, F. L. (2023). Qualitative exploration of the early experiences of opioid use disorder patients from private clinics after Russia's invasion of Ukraine in five major cities in Ukraine. *Frontiers in Public Health*, 11(12), 1–9.

Meylakhs, P. (2009). Drugs and symbolic pollution: The work of cultural logic in the Russian press. *Cultural Sociology*, 3(3), 377–395.

Miller, B. G. (2015). The new Soviet "narkoman": Drugs and youth in post-Stalinist Russia. *Region: Regional Studies of Russia, Eastern Europe, and Central Asia*, 4(1), 45–69.

Open Society Foundations. (2009). *Drug policy and human rights: A handbook for parliamentarians* (No. 15). Open Society Foundations. www.opensocietyfoundations.org/uploads/def77bbe-43fd-46ad-9f91-b1b8bd26a221/drugreg_20091001.pdf.

Roth, A. (2022, March 4). 'It's not rational': Putin's bizarre speech wrecks his once pragmatic image. *The Guardian*. www.theguardian.com/world/2022/feb/25/its-not-rational-putins-bizarre-speech-wrecks-his-once-pragmatic-image.

Seear, K. (2020). *Law, drugs and the making of addiction: Just habits*. Routledge.

Seear, K., & Mulcahy, S. (2023). Forging new habits: Critical drugs scholarship as an otherwise to rights. *International Journal of Human Rights*, 28(9), 1329–1352.

Sjöstedt, R. (2008). Exploring the construction of threats: The securitization of HIV/AIDS in Russia. *Security Dialogue*, 39(1), 7–29.

Stepanov, V., & Dmitrieva, A. (2023). Pyatak drifters: The making of social and cultural places in Ukrainian cities. In M. Germes, S. Höhne & L. Klaus (Eds.), *Narcotic cities: Counter cartographies of drugs and space* (pp. 274–285). JOVIS.

Ukrainian Network of People Who Use Drugs, Ukrainian CO '100% Life', Canadian HIV/AIDS Legal Network, & Eurasian Harm Reduction Association. (2020). *Report to the 67th session of the Committee on Economic, Social and Cultural Rights on the implementation by Ukraine of Article 12 of the International Covenant on Economic, Social and Cultural Rights as it relates to access of people who inject drugs to health services*. Committee on Economic, Social and Cultural Rights. www.ecoi.net/en/document/2024183.html.

UNAIDS. (2024). *Regional profile: Eastern Europe and Central Asia: 2024 UNAIDS global AIDS update*. www.unaids.org/sites/default/files/media_asset/2024-unaids-global-aids-update-eeca_en.pdf.

Vasilyev, P. (2022). Modern Russian and Soviet drug suppression. In P. Gootenberg (Ed.), *The Oxford handbook of global drug history* (pp. 373–388). Oxford University Press.

Wood, E. A. (2011). Performing memory: Vladimir Putin and the celebration of World War II in Russia. *Soviet and Post-Soviet Review*, 38(2), 172–200.

Yurchak, A. (2005). *Everything was forever, until it was no more.* Princeton University Press.

Zhukova, V. (2013). *Racializing Europe: Transnational and national dimensions of biopolitics, health, and HIV/AIDS: The case of Ukraine* (Doctoral dissertation). Central European University.

Zhurzhenko, T. (2022). Legislating historical memory in post-Soviet Ukraine. In *Memory laws and historical justice* (pp. 97–130). Springer International Publishing.

5

From Crack House to Supervised Consumption Site

Overdose and the Politics of (False) Equivalency in the United States

SHANA HARRIS

Introduction

Supervised consumption sites (SCS) are spaces where people can use pre-acquired drugs under the supervision of trained staff who monitor for overdose and administer medical assistance, if necessary.[1] By providing sterile drug use supplies, referrals to various services and education about safer injection practices, SCS function as harm reduction apparatuses for reducing overdose and the transmission of blood-borne infections like human immunodeficiency virus (HIV) and hepatitis C (HCV) and other harms associated with drug use such as skin and soft tissue infections.[2] While at least one unsanctioned SCS exists in the United States (Kral & Davidson, 2017), there are currently only three government-authorised sites in the country; two opened in 2021 in New York City and one opened in 2024 in Rhode Island. Another SCS was poised to open years earlier in Philadelphia, Pennsylvania, until the US federal government sued Safehouse, the organisation set to manage the site, to prevent it from opening. The government argued that Safehouse would violate federal law if it opened an SCS because the US Controlled Substances Act (CSA) (1970) prohibits the

[1] Supervised consumption sites are also known as safe consumption sites, supervised injection sites, safe injection sites, safe injection facilities, drug consumption rooms and overdose prevention sites. While these terms are used often interchangeably to refer to the same kinds of spaces, I have chosen to use SCS in this chapter.

[2] Harm reduction is a low-threshold (abstinence not required) service approach aimed at reducing the negative effects of drug use and addressing conditions of use.

operation of places where drugs are made or used illicitly.[3] Pointing to a specific section of the CSA originally prohibiting 'crack houses', the government successfully argued that SCS are equivalent to this 'criminal' space.[4]

In this chapter, I examine the civil lawsuit at the centre of the legal battle over the proposed SCS in Philadelphia, *United States v Safehouse*, as a way to critically analyse how SCS are – or not – recognised and equated with unlawful spaces, specifically the proverbial 'crack house', in the eyes of the law, and to what effect. Focusing on the primary legal documents related to *United States v Safehouse*, including the original lawsuit, district court judgments and an appellate judgment filed between 2019 and 2021, I show how and why comparison comes to matter in the federal government's legal argument against Safehouse. Specifically, I argue that the government engaged in what I call a politics of (false) equivalency against safe drug consumption. Such politics work to extend the criminalisation of drugs in favour of a prohibitionist approach to drug use, a move that has high stakes in a country overwhelmed by the tragedy of overdose.

Philosopher of science Isabelle Stengers (2011, p. 48) tells us that '[c] omparison is an important part of any animal's equipment for dealing with its respective world'. The pervasiveness of this epistemological practice has been analysed by scholars from multiple disciplines (Handler, 2009; Choy, 2011; Candea, 2016; Deville et al., 2016), including in the study of drugs (Fraser & Ekendahl, 2018; Seear et al., 2020). Such scholars have debated its utilities and pitfalls, its foundations and assumptions. What stands out most from this scholarship for me is its recognition that comparison is not objective but rather a political act. Stengers (2011) cautions against viewing comparison as a technique for generating universal truths about what is 'correct' in the world. Instead, we must understand the positions or 'concerns' of those engaged in the comparison. Additionally, sociologist and legal scholar Kate Seear and colleagues (2020) call on scholars to engage in critical examinations of comparative processes to identify and avoid normalising binary logics and flawed hierarchies. As they argue, 'When comparisons are handled uncritically, they risk concretizing or naturalizing differences [. . .] thus

[3] The CSA is Title II of the Comprehensive Drug Abuse Prevention and Control Act of 1970 (91 Pub. L. 513). This statute established federal drug policy to classify and regulate the manufacture, importation, exportation, distribution, possession and use of controlled substances.

[4] 'Crack house' is slang for a place where crack cocaine is bought, sold and/or used.

foreclosing questions about the political contexts that give comparisons their meaning' (Seear et al., 2020, p. 2).

For the purposes of this chapter, I follow these scholars to critically examine how comparison is operationalised for legal ends in *United States v Safehouse*. Conducting such an analysis of this lawsuit illuminates not only how equivalency is made but how engagement in a politics of (false) equivalency around safe consumption can have troubling consequences, including but not limited to negative health outcomes for people who use drugs and the continued proscription of harm reduction interventions in the United States. Therefore, this chapter is an exercise in interrogating the stakes of such a comparative effort in the legal arena.

United States v Safehouse

In 2018, more than 1,100 people died from overdose in Philadelphia, more than triple the number of people who died by homicide in the city that year (Whelan & Feliciano Reyes, 2019). This number was slightly less than the 1,217 people who died from overdose the previous year. In fact, the fatal overdose rate had been increasing steadily in Philadelphia since 2014. The city's mayor launched a task force that made several recommendations to combat the opioid use and overdose epidemic, including the private sector development of comprehensive user engagement sites, which would include SCS to provide emergency lifesaving medical care to people who overdose onsite (Brooks & Kotkin, 2017).[5] In early 2018, a non-profit organisation called Safehouse responded to this call by beginning work to open what would have been the country's first legal SCS. With their mission to 'save lives by providing a range of overdose prevention services' (Safehouse, 2023), the organisation hoped to open the SCS in March 2019, but this did not come to pass.

In February 2019, the federal government, under the direction of US Attorney William McSwain, sued Safehouse to prevent it from opening the SCS. The civil lawsuit, *United States v Safehouse*, sought a declaratory judgment against Safehouse by claiming that the establishment of the SCS – referred to as a 'Consumption Room' in the document – would

[5] Various terms are associated with the increase in and damage wrought by opioid use in the United States, such crisis, epidemic and problem, each arguably with their own assumptions, associations and temporal orientations (Carr 2019). Recognising the importance of deliberate word choice to describe this nuanced phenomenon, I intentionally use 'epidemic' in this chapter because it is the term used by the Philadelphia major's task force who proposed the SCS around which my analysis is based.

violate 21 US Code section 856, a section of the CSA colloquially known as the 'crack house statute'. The section prohibits owning or operating a facility for the purpose of drug use or sales, specifically stating:

[I]t shall be unlawful to –

1. knowingly open, lease, rent, use, or maintain any place, whether permanently or temporarily, for the purpose of manufacturing, distributing, or using any controlled substance
2. manage or control any place, whether permanently or temporarily, either as an owner, lessee, agent, employee, occupant, or mortgagee, and knowingly and intentionally rent, lease, profit from, or make available for use, with or without compensation, the place for the purpose of unlawfully manufacturing, storing, distributing, or using a controlled substance. (21 U.S.C. s. 856)

Enacted as part of the Anti-Drug Abuse Act of 1986 sponsored and co-written by then-Senator Joe Biden, section 856 was meant to strengthen the prosecution of drug-related crime during the crack cocaine 'drug scare' of the late twentieth century (Reinarman & Levine, 1989).[6] The type of 'facility' targeted by section 856 was initially the 'crack house', according to a section-by-section description of the 1986 Act in the Congressional Record (132 Congressional Record 26474).[7] At the time, the 'crack house' held a particular place in the popular imagination with respect to race and crime. More than merely indicating a specific form of drug use, the figure of the 'crack house' conjured up negative ideas about those who how inhabited, frequented or managed such a place based on 'racialized conceptions of threat' associated with crack use and dealing in US cities (Smith, 2022, p. 120). It became 'an avatar of drug related-crime', and individuals who participated in the crack economy were cast as 'irredeemably irresponsible and hostile to social order' (Smith, 2022, p. 120). Therefore, to discourage the operation of such sites, violations of section 856 can result in criminal or civil penalties, the former being

6 The Anti-Drug Abuse Act of 1986 (Public Law 99-570) significantly increased the enforcement of the CSA by adding stricter regulations and expanding the penalties for violations of the CSA.

7 The authors of a handbook to assist federal criminal justice personnel with implementing of the law state that section 856 'appears to be aimed at "crack houses" and "shooting galleries" (Saphos et al., 1987, 106), the latter being places where people can borrow or rent needles or syringes to inject drugs. Importantly, however, the authors acknowledge that 'there is no official legislative history behind Section 856' (Saphos et al., 1987, 106). Also, the section was amended in 2003 with the aim of prosecuting organisers of electronic dance parties, or 'raves', from allowing drug use at these kinds of events.

punishable with up to twenty years in prison and/or a fine of $500,000 for individuals or $2,000,000 for persons other than individuals (e.g., corporations).

In the original lawsuit document, the government argued that Safehouse, if it operated a SCS, would violate the CSA section by knowingly providing a place for people to use drugs unlawfully (e.g., a 'crack house'). It claimed that the organisation would 'disregard the law and override Congress' carefully balanced regulatory scheme by establishing, managing, and controlling sites in Philadelphia that will allow individuals to engage in the illicit use of controlled substances [. . .] [I]t does not matter that Safehouse claims good intentions in fighting the opioid epidemic' (*United States v Safehouse*, 2019a). Safehouse disputed this claim and, in April 2019, sought their own declaratory judgment that its proposed SCS would not violate the section 856 because of the site's proposed healthcare focus. Safehouse asserted, 'Providing lifesaving medical services to individuals who are suffering from substance use disorder does not and constitutionally cannot violate Section 856 [. . .] Section 856 does not address, much less prohibit, the legitimate, multifaceted, medical, and public health intervention that Safehouse intends to provide' (*United States v Safehouse*, 2019b). Safehouse certainly took issue with the government's framing of the SCS as a 'crack house'. Safehouse argued:

> Safehouse is nothing like a 'crack house' or drug-fueled 'rave.' Nor is Safehouse established 'for the purpose' of unlawful drug use. Rather, it is established for the exclusive purpose of providing urgent, lifesaving medical care to those at risk of drug overdose. The CSA does not regulate such a legitimate – indeed, critical – medical and public health intervention.
>
> (*United States v Safehouse*, 2019b)

What would be the first of many rulings in *United States v Safehouse* came in October 2019 when US District Judge Gerald A. McHugh ruled in favour of the defendant (Safehouse). McHugh rejected the government's interpretation of the law in relation to Safehouse's proposed SCS. His decision was based first on what he saw as the 'fundamental underlying reality [. . .] that no credible argument can be made that facilitates such as safe injection sites were within the contemplation of Congress either when it adopted s. 856(a) in 1986, or when it amended the statute in 2003' (*United States v Safehouse*, 2019c). Congress was not thinking about SCS when it enacted section 856 against 'crack houses' because the harm reduction approach undergirding SCS, in the judge's words, 'had not yet entered public discourse' (*United States v Safehouse*, 2019c). As such, McHugh found that 'there is no support for the view that Congress meant to criminalize projects such as that proposed by Safehouse' (*United States v Safehouse*, 2019c).

McHugh further argued that opening a SCS would not violate section 856 because the site's primary purpose is not to facilitate drug use or sales, as the plaintiff contended. Instead, he concluded, 'Safehouse plans to make a place available for the purposes of reducing the harm of drug use, administering medical care, encouraging drug treatment, and connecting participants with social services. None of these purposes can be understood as a purpose to facilitate drug use' (*United States v Safehouse*, 2019c). And, since the CSA does not prohibit providing medical care related to drug use, such as assessing and helping with overdose, section 856 does not apply to a SCS as a facility supplying medical attention. McHugh additionally noted that the government's argument is not against the provision of such medical attention but rather the location where it is delivered. Speaking to the government's concession that it would not be illegal to provide overdose prevention care through mobile units or in public places because of the language of section 856, the judge explained, 'The Government seeks to distinguish consumption rooms from the ways in which other entities currently engage in harm reduction (and ways that they could, such as through use of a mobile van) by observing that in those efforts no real property is used' (*United States v Safehouse*, 2019c). He called this textual interpretation 'myopic' and maintained that 'no credible argument can be made that a constructive lawful purpose is rendered predatory and unlawful simply because it moves indoors' (*United States v Safehouse*, 2019c). In other words, McHugh ruled that the purpose of a SCS is not to facilitate drug use.

The federal government immediately announced its intent to appeal the ruling. They feared that a SCS – like the pejorative 'crack houses' of the 1980s and 1990s – would attract people who use drugs and devastate the city. In a press release issued the same day as McHugh's ruling, McSwain stated, 'We believe that Safehouse's proposed activity threatens to institutionalize the scourge of illegal drug use – and all the problems that come with it – in Philadelphia's neighborhoods' (United States Attorney's Office Eastern District of Pennsylvania, 2020). The move to appeal was supported by other government officials who agreed that the ruling endorsed drug use. For example, US Deputy Attorney General Jeffrey A. Rosen (2020) had strong thoughts on the matter in an opinion article in *The Philadelphia Inquirer* newspaper where he asserted that supporting the SCS was advocating for 'government-sanctioned drug abuse' and that the site would 'normalize drug abuse and put communities at risk'. He also invoked the familiar anti-harm reduction rhetoric of 'enablement', claiming that, by allowing people to use drugs on the premises, a SCS would make it easy for 'those suffering from addiction to go to the brink of death' (Rosen, 2020).

In anticipation of the appeal, Safehouse asked the court for a declaratory judgment in anticipation of the appeal, and, in February 2020, Judge McHugh upheld his October 2019 ruling that Safehouse opening a SCS site in Philadelphia would not violate federal law (*United States v Safehouse*, 2020). As the first federal ruling on the legality of such a facility in the United States, the landmark decision was hailed as a victory for harm reduction by Safehouse and its supporters. The victory, however, was short-lived. In June 2020, Safehouse was prevented from opening SCS when the federal government was granted an Emergency Motion to Stay by McHugh until a ruling was made on their appeal. Then, in January 2021, McHugh's February 2020 ruling was overturned by the Third Circuit Court of Appeals in a two-to-one ruling against Safehouse. The court ruled that, although Safehouse's motives are 'admirable', the organisation 'knows and intends that its visitors will come with a significant purpose of doing drugs' and therefore will break federal law (*United States v Safehouse*, 2021). The court also commented on section 856's scope. Contrary to McHugh's reading of the law, they believed that section 856 applies as much to a SCS as a 'crack house': 'Although Congress passed s. 856 to shut down crack houses, its words reach well beyond them. Safehouse's benevolent motive makes no difference' (*United States v Safehouse*, 2021). And, in a failed attempt to challenge the appeal, the US Supreme Court rejected Safehouse's request to review the case in October 2021. The case was sent back to the lower court where it remains in litigation at the time of writing.

At present, the government could criminally prosecute Safehouse if it opens its proposed SCS. The organisation is currently exploring its options to lawfully operate one in Philadelphia in the future.

Politics of Equivalency

United States v Safehouse showcases two contrasting ideological positions regarding how overdose – and drug use more generally – should be addressed. Safehouse follows a harm reduction approach while the government's stance aligns with the hallmark prohibitionist, zero-tolerance, anti-drug agenda of the war on drugs. This is unsurprising given that harm reduction interventions like SCS have long been politically unpopular in the United States (Burris et al., 2003; Beletsky et al., 2008). When commenting on the lawsuit, McSwain demonstrated this disfavour when he referred to Safehouse's proposed SCS as 'a radical experiment that would invite thousands of people onto its property for the purpose of injecting illegal drugs' (Rosen, 2020). Yet this kind of facility is anything but a 'radical experiment;' hundreds of SCS operate in many parts of the world, including in Canada, Australia, Switzerland, Germany and the Netherlands (Dolan et al., 2000; Boyd, 2013). They have repeatedly proven effective in reducing overdose mortality (Kerr et al., 2006; Marshall et al., 2011; Potier et al., 2014; Ng et al., 2017; Kral et al., 2020; Levengood et al., 2021), reducing HIV and HCV infection (Potier et al., 2014; Ng et al., 2017), reducing syringe sharing and reuse (Kerr et al., 2005; Stoltz et al., 2007; Kinnard et al., 2014), improving public safety (Wood et al., 2006; Kennedy et al., 2017) and increasing access to and utilisation of primary healthcare and drug treatment services (Wood et al., 2007; Potier et al., 2014; Levengood et al., 2021). Furthermore, research has debunked many public safety arguments against SCS, namely that they increase criminal activity (Potier et al., 2014; Davidson et al., 2021; Levengood et al., 2021; Chaflin et al., 2023), disorderly conduct (Chaflin et al., 2023), drug trafficking (Wood et al., 2006; Potier et al., 2014) and improper syringe disposal (Wood et al., 2004; Kinnard et al., 2014; Kral et al., 2021;) in the neighbourhoods where they are located.

Even more consequential is the comparative claim at the heart of the lawsuit: SCS are equivalent to 'crack houses' because they both facilitate drug use. Postcolonial theorist R. Radhakrishnan (2009, p. 454) notes, '[C]omparisons are never neutral: they are inevitably tendentious, didactic, competitive, and prescriptive [. . .] [C]omparisons are never disinterested.' He cautions against accepting comparisons as natural or self-evident and urges us to consider the following: '[W]hich subject is initiating the comparison and why? [. . .] [W]ho will benefit from the comparative performance?' (Radhakrishnan 2009, p. 458). In the case of *United States v Safehouse*, the government's comparative claim is a calculated one because it was the crux of their legal argument. But, even more importantly, it reinforces and advances the government's politically driven, anti-drug agenda while simultaneously disavowing and proscribing the scientifically supported harm reduction intervention of SCS. This point is even more significant in the light of the fact that section 856 – the section upon which the government's whole case is based – is part of the CSA, the primary federal legal mechanism for the criminalisation of drugs in the United States.

The act of equating – not just comparing – is especially significant here. Anthropologist Kate McClellan (2022, p. 138) argues that creating equivalency can be a 'political process to justify particular decisions and to elicit particular outcomes'. In *United States v Safehouse*, the government maintains that SCS are the same as 'crack houses' because they both 'facilitate' drug use. By saying that the sites are comparable, the government is engaged in a politics of (false) equivalency in order to discredit SCS by associating them with the unlawful 'crack house'. Safehouse argues that such an equivalency is false because SCS are about healthcare provision and harm reduction unlike 'crack houses'. However, this kind of argument is problematic because it invites a comparison that frames SCS as clean, life-saving harm reduction spaces while 'crack houses' as dirty, criminal and devoid of mutual support. Yet they can serve as 'safe havens' for people who use drugs, 'places offering some perception of safety or protection from a hostile risk environment', including reducing the risk of arrest by enabling off-street drug use (Rhodes et al., 2006). Harm reduction also can take place at such sites, as research has documented 'crack house' gatekeepers providing harm reduction materials to attract users to the site and drug-using peers utilising social ties and relationships of reciprocity to disseminate harm reduction materials and education at such private drug-using spaces (Weeks et al., 2001; Dickson-Gómez et al., 2004).

Creating equivalency between separate subjects and entities, McClellan explains, also requires 'smoothing differences between them' (McClellan, 2022, p. 135). To be sure, the government did all it could to cast SCS as equivalent to 'crack houses' to apply section 856 to the former. It had to draw enough similarities between the two sites to make their argument stick and to iron out any kinks that would unsettle the equivalency. Indeed, their comparative legal argument was ultimately successful in erasing difference, despite Safehouse's attempt to highlight them. Moreover, both parties arguably erased some of nuances about both SCS and 'crack houses' and what transpires in them. While the government did so to show equivalency, Safehouse disavowed the comparison being operationalised against its proposed SCS. In so doing, Safehouse instantiated the comparative object (the 'crack house') as a problematic other in order to distance itself from it.

Nevertheless, engagement in a politics of (false) equivalency is symbolically important in the lawsuit because it invokes the spectre of the US crack epidemic of the 1980s and 1990s. The full-blown 'moral panic' (Cohen, 2011) over crack at that time revolved around false claims of crack being more potent and addictive than powder cocaine, as well as racialised fears of violence, urban ghettos and the so-called 'crack babies' born to Black mothers who used crack while pregnant, all of which were seen as threats to the values and stability of the country (Reinarman & Levine, 1989). Take, for instance, crack babies who were portrayed by sensationalist media coverage as the innocent, 'tiniest victims' of the epidemic (Goldman, 1988). The now disproven myth – but very real concern at the time – that prenatal crack exposure would result in physical abnormalities and intellectual disabilities fuelled the fear that these children would be a chronic burden on public services funded by taxpayers (National Public Radio, 2013). This fear was certainly present in the city at the heart of the *United States vs Safehouse* lawsuit. Philadelphia was a centre of the country's crack epidemic, and a 1989 study found that one in six babies born at the city's hospitals were born to a mother who tested positive for cocaine (FitzGerald, 2013). Using this fear to comment on the racialisation of the epidemic, journalist Donovan X. Ramsey (2023, p. 11) summarises the situation well: 'The myth of the crack baby was accepted as gospel, it seems, because it mapped so well onto existing ideas of Black biological inferiority and cultural pathology, and it stoked anxieties regarding violent crime and the cost of America's social safety net.'

To be sure, this is not the first time that the federal government has engaged in a politics of (false) equivalency in the war on drugs. The *Anti-Drug Abuse Act* of 1986, the same legislation that enacted the 'crack house statute', established mandatory minimum sentences for cocaine-related offences. However, the severity of the sentence depended on the form and quantity of cocaine involved. Tougher sentences were given for offences for crack compared to powder cocaine at a ratio of 100-to-1. For example, a crime involving 5 grams of crack would receive the same mandatory minimum sentence as a crime involving 500 grams of powder cocaine. These drastically different amounts were deemed equivalent in the eyes of the law despite the fact that they are two forms of the same drug, the only difference being that crack is powder cocaine cooked with baking powder. The foundation for this equivalency claim was the fact that the majority of people arrested for crack offences were Black. The racial undertone of this legislation – and the war on drugs more broadly – resulted in a sentencing disparity that has had devastating effects on Black communities across the country over the last forty years (Vagins & McCurdy, 2006; Alexander, 2012).

Given this history, the government's comparison of SCS and 'crack houses' makes political sense. As Ramsey (2023, p. 11) observes, crack has long served as 'ammunition' for the war on drugs. Thus, the invocation of crack in the context of the *United States v Safehouse* demonstrates its political utility to a pro-prohibition, anti-harm reduction agenda. The government's argument against Safehouse's proposed SCS is not simply rooted in the belief that the site is 'against the law' but also, as McSwain's colleagues at the Department of Justice describe it, 'an emerging threat to the rule of law: the normalization of criminal behavior' (Huber & Backman, 2019, p. 47).

Conclusion

Why should we care about this politics of (false) equivalency? What is at stake with the operationalisation of comparison in *United States v Safehouse*? First, and most immediately, overdose deaths are at an all-time high in the United States. From 2013 to 2019, overdose deaths related to synthetic opioids (other than methadone), which are driving the overdose trend, increased by 1,040 per cent (Lambdin et al., 2023). And over 107,000 people in the country died from overdose in 2023 alone (Centers for Disease Control and Prevention, 2024). Any delay in the establishment of SCS – a proven overdose prevention strategy – across the country will only contribute to the already too high number of preventable deaths.

Second, the ripple effect of the outcome and conversations surrounding *United States v Safehouse* are negatively influencing local and national politics around supervised consumption. In Philadelphia, the city at the centre of the lawsuit, the city council voted to prohibit the operation of an SCS in most of the county in September 2023 (Orso, 2023). A few months earlier, the Pennsylvania Senate (the US state where Philadelphia is located) approved a bill to ban SCS in the state (Associated Press, 2023a). Since the Pennsylvania House of Representatives did not vote on the issue, a state-wide ban was not enshrined in law. However, a new bipartisan bill supporting a state-wide ban was introduced in the Pennsylvania Senate during the 2025–2026 session (Pennsylvania General Assembly, 2025). Nationally, the continued weaponisation of the CSA contributed to the introduction of US House Bill 6741 (also known as the 'Crack Is Whack Act') in 2022, which would prohibit the use of federal funds to operate or control an 'injection centre' in violation of section 856. The bill also threatened to cut funding to any state or city that allows such a site to open.

Harm reductionists in different parts of the country have worked hard to lay the groundwork to establish their own government-authorised SCS. There have been some notable successes; two more states (Minnesota and Vermont) have authorised SCS (Gray, 2023; Medrano, 2024).[8] Officials in other states, including Colorado, Nevada and New Mexico, are also discussing allowing SCS to operate locally (Associated Press, 2023b). Yet the future of these and other sites is already being threatened by the federal government's successful appeal of the original *United States v Safehouse* ruling. In fact, the US Attorney for the Southern District of New York warned OnPoint NYC, the group that runs the two SCS located in New York City, that the Department of Justice might seek to close the sites for being in violation of not just federal but state and local law (Otterman, 2023), despite their documented success at reversing overdose and providing health and social services (Harocopos et al., 2022). What other courts will do following this decision will potentially save – or risk – thousands of lives in the years to come.

References

Alexander, M. (2012). *The new Jim Crow: Mass incarceration in the age of colorblindness*. The New Press.

Associated Press. (2023a). Pennsylvania Senate votes to ban safe injection sites. *Associated Press*. https://apnews.com/article/opioid-heroin-safe-injection-sites-pennsylvania-drugs-3c94134829464b858e02e3799ac3ae2b.

Associated Press. (2023b). Colorado, New Mexico and Nevada consider 'safe injection sites' to prevent overdoses. *KRWG Public Media*. www.krwg.org/regional/2023-03-03/colorado-new-mexico-and-nevada-consider-safe-injection-sites-to-prevent-overdoses.

[8] One notable exception is California, which has reversed its generally supportive position on harm reduction in recent years. In August 2022, California governor Gavin Newsom vetoed a bill that would have allowed SCS as part of pilot programme in the cities of San Francisco, Los Angeles, and Oakland and Los Angeles County (Cowan, 2022). Additionally, an 'unofficial' SCS that was part of an emergency initiative to address drug use and overdose in San Francisco was closed in December 2022 after less than one year in operation (Johnson, 2022).

Beletsky, L., Davis, C. S., Anderson, E. & Burris, S. (2008). The law (and politics) of safe injection facilities in the United States. *American Journal of Public Health*, 98(2), 231–237.

Boyd, N. (2013). Lessons from INSITE, Vancouver's supervised injection facility: 2003–2012. *Drugs: Education, Prevention and Policy*, 20(3), 234–240.

Brooks, A., & Kotkin, N. (2017, May 17). *Mayor's task force to combat the opioid epidemic in Philadelphia: Final report and recommendations.* City of Philadelphia.

Burris, S., Strathdee, S. A. & Vernick, J. S. (2003). Lethal injections: The law, science, and politics of syringe access for injection drug users. *University of San Francisco Law Review*, 37(4), 813–885.

Candea, M. (2016). On two modalities of comparison in social anthropology. *L'Homme*, 2(218), 1–22.

Carr, E. S. (2019). The work of 'crisis' in the opioid 'crisis'. *Journal of Extreme Anthropology*, 3(2), 161–166.

Centers for Disease Control and Prevention. (2024). U.S. overdose deaths decrease in 2023, first time since 2018. *Centers for Disease Control and Prevention.* www.cdc.gov/nchs/pressroom/nchs_press_releases/2024/20240515.htm.

Chaflin, A., del Pozo, B. & Mitre-Becerril, D. (2023). Overdose prevention centers, crime, and disorder in New York City. *JAMA Network Open*, 6(11), 1–12.

Choy, T. (2011). *Ecologies of comparison: An ethnography of endangerment in Hong Kong.* Duke University Press.

Cohen, S. (2011). *Folk devils and moral panics.* Routledge.

Congressional Record. (1986). *Volume 132, Part 18: Debate on the Controlled Substances Act.* US Government Printing Office.

Controlled Substances Act, 21 U.S.C. s. 856 (1986).

Cowan, J. (2022). Governor Newsom vetoes bill for drug-injection sites in California. *The New York Times.* www.nytimes.com/2022/08/22/us/gavin-newsom-vetoes-drug-injection-sites.html.

Davidson, P. J., Lambdin, B. H., Browne, E. N., Wenger, L. D. & Kral, A. H. (2021). Impact of an unsanctioned safe consumption site on criminal activity, 2010–2019. *Drug and Alcohol Dependence*, 220, 108521.

Deville, J., Guggenheim, M. & Hrdličková, Z. (Eds.). (2016). *Practising comparison: Logics, relations, collaborations.* Mattering Press.

Dickson-Gómez, J., Weeks, M. R., Martinez, M. & Radda, K. (2004). Reciprocity and exploitation: Social dynamics in private drug use sites. *Journal of Drug Issues*, 34(4), 913–932.

Dolan, K., Kimber, J., Fry, C., Fitzgerald, J., McDonald, D. & Trautman, F. (2000). Drug consumption facilities in Europe and the establishment of supervised injecting centres in Australia. *Drug and Alcohol Review*, 19(3), 337–346.

FitzGerald, S. (2013, 21 July). 'Crack baby' study ends with unexpected but clear result. *Philadelphia Inquirer.*

Fraser, S., & Ekendahl, M. (2018). 'Getting better': The politics of comparison in addictiontreatment and research. *Contemporary Drug Problems*, 45(2), 87–106.

Goldman, J. J. (1988). Cocaine's tiniest victims: A struggle from the start. *Los Angeles Times*. www.latimes.com/archives/la-xpm-1988-05-30-mn-2391-story.html.

Gray, C. (2023). Minnesota's legislature passes law opening door to creation of safe injection spaces. *KSTP*. https://kstp.com/kstp-news/top-news/minnesota-legislature-passes-law-opening-door-to-creation-of-safe-injection-spaces.

Handler, R. (2009). The uses of incommensurability in anthropology. *New Literary History*, 40(3), 627–647.

Harocopos, A., Gibson, B. E., Saha, N., McRae, M. T., See, K., Rivera, S. & Chokshi, D. A. (2022). First 2 months of operation at first publicly recognized overdose prevention centers in US. *JAMA Network Open*, 5(7), 1–4.

Huber, J. W., & Backman, D. (2019). Uncivil disobedience: A selfish threat to the rule of law. *Department of Justice Journal of Federal Law and Practice*, 67(4), 47–54.

Johnson, S. (2022). 'Lives are on the line' as S.F. closes only supervised consumption site. *San Francisco Examiner*. www.sfexaminer.com/news/sf-closes-tenderloin-center-only-safe-consumption-site/article_0b534e56-74df-11ed-8340-5fdd4c59df97.html.

Kennedy, M. C., Karamouzian, M. & Kerr, T. (2017). Public health and public order outcomes associated with supervised drug consumption facilities: A systematic review. *Current HIV/AIDS Reports*, 14(2), 161–183.

Kerr, T., Tyndall, M., Li, K., Montaner, J. & Wood, E. (2005). Safer injection facility use and syringe sharing in injection drug users. *The Lancet*, 366(9482), 316–318.

Kinnard, E. N., Howe, C. J., Kerr, T., Hass, V. S. & Marshall, B. D. L. (2014). Self-reported changes in drug use behaviors and syringe disposal methods following the opening of a supervised injecting facility in Copenhagen, Denmark. *Harm Reduction Journal*, 11(29), 1–8.

Kral, A. H., & Davidson, P. J. (2017). Addressing the nation's opioid epidemic: Lessons from an unsanctioned supervised injection site in the U.S. *American Journal of Preventive Medicine*, 53(6), 919–922.

Kral, A. H., Lambdin, B. H., Wenger, L. D., Browne, E. N., Suen, L. W. & Davidson, P. J. (2021). Improved syringe disposal practices associated with unsanctioned safe consumption site use: A cohort study of people who inject drugs in the United States. *Drug and Alcohol Dependence*, 229, 1–9.

Kral, A. H., Lambdin, B. H., Wenger, L. D. & Davidson, P. J. (2020). Evaluation of an unsanctioned safe consumption site in the United States. *The New England Journal of Medicine*, 383(6), 589–590.

Lambdin, B. H., Wenger, L., Bluthenthal, R., Bartholomew, T. S., Tookes, H. E., LaKosky, P., O'Neill, S. & Kral, A. H. (2023). How do contextual factors influence naloxone distribution from syringe service programs in the USA: A cross-sectional study. *Harm Reduction Journal*, 20(1), 1–7.

Levengood, T. W., Yoon, G. H., Davoust, M. J., Ogden, S. N., Marshall, B. D. L., Cahill, S. R. & Bazzi, A. R. (2021). Supervised injection facilities as harm reduction: A systematic review. *American Journal of Preventive Medicine*, 61(5), 738–749.

Marshall, B. D. L., Milloy, M.-J., Wood, E., Montaner, J. S. G. & Kerr, T. (2011). Reduction in overdose mortality after the opening of North America's first medically supervised safer injecting facility: A retrospective population-based study. *The Lancet*, 377(9775), 1429–1437.

McClellan, K. (2022). The politics of equivalence: (Post)colonial care and transnational animal welfare in Jordan. *Social Anthropology*, 30(3), 126–142.

Medrano, K. (2024). VT legalizes safe consumption sites, reversing course on veto override. *Filter*. https://filtermag.org/vermont-safe-consumption-site-veto-override.

National Public Radio. (2013). Decades later, drugs didn't hold 'crack babies' back. *National Public Radio*. www.npr.org/templates/story/story.php?storyId=207292639.

Ng, J., Sutherland, C. & Kolber, M. R. (2017). Does evidence support supervised injection sites? *Canadian Family Physician*, 63(11), 866–867.

Orso, A. (2023, 23 September). Council says no to injection sites in city, overriding a veto by Kenney. *Philadelphia Inquirer*.

Otterman, S. (2023). Federal officials may shut down overdose prevention centers in Manhattan. *New York Times*. www.nytimes.com/2023/08/08/nyregion/drug-overdoses-supervised-consumption-nyc.html.

Pennsylvania General Assembly. (2025). Senate Bill 347: 2025–2026 Regular Session. www.palegis.us/legislation/bills/2025/sb347.

Potier, C., Laprévote, V., Dubois-Arber, F. & Cottencin, O. (2014). Supervised injection services: What has been demonstrated? *Drug and Alcohol Dependence*, 145(1), 48–68.

Radhakrishnan, R. (2009). Why compare? *New Literary History*, 40(3), 453–471.

Ramsey, D. X. (2023). *When crack was king: A people's history of a misunderstood era*. One World.

Reinarman, C., & Levine, H. G. (1989). Crack in context: Politics and media in the making of a drug scare. *Contemporary Drug Problems*, 16(1989), 535–577.

Rhodes, T., Kimber, J., Small, W., Fitzgerald, J., Kerr, T., Hickman, M. & Holloway, G. (2006). Public injecting and the need for 'safe environment interventions' in the reduction of drug-related harm. *Addiction*, 101(10), 1384–1393.

Rosen, J. A. (2020, 4 February). Safe injection sites. *The Philadelphia Inquirer*.

Safehouse. (2023). Who we are. *Safehouse*. www.safehousephilly.org/who-we-are.

Saphos, C. S., Zeldin, M., Harbin, H., Schneider, G. & Hollenhorst, T. M. (1987). *The handbook on the Anti-Drug Abuse Act of 1986*. US Government Printing Office.

Seear, K., Moore, D., Fraser, S., Fomiatti, R. & Aitken, C. (2020). Consumption in contrast: The politics of comparison in healthcare practitioners' accounts of men who inject performance and image-enhancing drugs. *International Journal of Drug Policy*, 85, 102883.

Smith, J. (2022). War in the neighborhood: Anti-drug organizing, 'crack house', and municipal austerity in Philadelphia. *American Quarterly*, 74(1), 119–143.

Stengers, I. (2011). Comparison as a matter of concern. *Common Knowledge*, 17(1), 48–63.

Stoltz, J.-A., Wood, E., Small, W., Li, K., Tyndall, M., Montaner, J. & Kerr, T. (2007). Changes in injecting practices associated with the use of a medically supervised safer injection facility. *Journal of Public Health*, 29(1), 35–39.

United States Attorney's Office Eastern District of Pennsylvania. (2020). U.S. Department of Justice to appeal district court ruling regarding drug injection sites. *United States Department of Justice*. www.justice.gov/usao-edpa/pr/us-department-justice-appeal-district-court-ruling-regarding-drug-injection-sites.

United States v Safehouse. (2019a). *Complaint*. Case No. 2:19-cv-00519-GAM (E.D. Pa., 5 February 2019).

United States v Safehouse. (2019b). *Defendant Safehouse's answer, affirmative defenses, counterclaims to plaintiff's complaint, and third-party complaint*. Civil Action No. 2:19-cv-00519 (E.D. Pa., 3 April 2019).

United States v Safehouse. (2019c). *Memorandum*. Civil Action No. 19-0519 (E.D. Pa., 2 October 2019).

United States v Safehouse. (2020). *Memorandum*. Civil Action No. 19-0519 (E.D. Pa., 25 February 2020).

United States v Safehouse. (2021). *Opinion*. No. 20-1422 (3rd Cir., 2021).

Vagins, D. J., & McCurdy, J. (2006). *Cracks in the system: Twenty years of the unjust federal crack cocaine law*. American Civil Liberties Union.

Weeks, M. R., Clair, S., Singer, M., Radda, K., Schensul, J. J., Wilson, D. S., Martinez, M., Scott, G. & Knight, G. (2001). High-risk drug use sites, meaning and practice: Implications for AIDS prevention. *Journal of Drug Issues*, 31(1), 781–808.

Whelan, A., & Feliciano Reyes, J. (2019, 14 May). Philadelphia's overdose deaths dip overall in 2018 but are 'still at crisis levels'. *The Philadelphia Inquirer*.

Wood, E., Kerr, T., Small, W., Li, K., Marsh, D. C., Montaner, J. S. G. & Tyndall, M. W. (2004). Changes in public order after the opening of a medically supervised safer injecting facility for illicit injection drug users. *CMAJ*, 171(7), 731–734.

Wood, E., Tyndall, M. W., Lai, C., Montaner, J. S. G. & Kerr, T. (2006). Impact of a medically supervised safer injecting facility on drug dealing and other drug-related crime. *Substance Abuse Treatment, Prevention, and Policy*, 1(13), 1–4.

Wood, E., Tyndall, M. W., Zhang, R., Montaner, J. S. G. & Kerr, T. (2007). Rate of detoxification service use and its impact among a cohort of supervised injecting facility users. *Addiction*, 102(6), 916–919.

6

Policing Maintenance

Judicial Restrictions on Medication for Opioid Use Disorder (MOUD) as a Violation of the Americans with Disability Act (ADA)

NANCY D. CAMPBELL

Introduction

Methadone maintenance therapy arose as a treatment for opiate use in the mid 1960s. At the time, neither drug use nor treatment for it were considered disabilities. When Vincent Dole, the Rockefeller Institute metabolic researcher who was one of the progenitors of methadone maintenance therapy (MMT), asked, 'What kind of disablement does a drug produce?' (Courtwright et al., 1989, p. 334), this was a prescient question.[1] Dole's team stabilised patient-subjects on methadone, hoping to displace reliance on shorter-acting opiates, and explored dosages that would enable 'cooperative relationships with patients' (Courtwright, et al., 1989, p. 336). Opposing detoxification and abstinence as the sole basis for treatment, Dole saw opioid use disorder as a metabolic condition that required ongoing pharmacological stability. Contrasting the stabilising effects of one opiate (methadone) to another (heroin), Dole emphasised that drugs should be judged in terms of their social effects – did they improve or undermine capacity for stable relationships with family members, treatment providers or employers? Did they produce 'disablement' or did they instead 'enable' capacities for productive

[1] The Rockefeller team included Enoch Gordis, former head of NIAAA (the National Institute on Alcohol Abuse and Alcoholism); Joyce Lowinson, editor of *Substance Abuse: The Comprehensive Textbook*; Robert Millman, director of substance abuse treatment at Weill Cornell Medical Center; Elizabeth Khuri of Weill Cornell Medical School; Ann Ho of The Rockefeller University; Norman Gordon of Yeshiva University; Phil Appel and Herman Joseph of OASAS (Office of Addiction Services and Supports); and Marie Nyswander. Clinical research assistant Mary Jeanne Kreek became an important addiction researcher in her own right.

citizenship? Such questions dominated the social contexts into which methadone maintenance was inserted. Making stable, productive citizens was adopted as the goal of methadone maintenance.

The past six decades have witnessed methadone's recognition as a medication. Medication-assisted treatment (MAT) or medication for opioid use disorder (MOUD) have become standard, evidence-based treatments, utilising only three medications: methadone, buprenorphine and naltrexone. The subjective and societal effects of each differ from the other. Methadone is an agonist, meaning that it occupies the same opioid receptors as morphine, heroin and fentanyl. Buprenorphine is a partial agonist/antagonist, meaning that it exerts both agonistic and antagonistic effects at these receptors. Naltrexone acts as an antagonist at the receptor site, kicking all other agonists off. Specific treatment settings – methadone clinics or rehab centres – deploy different practices. Methadone is only dispensed in the United States in purpose-built settings. Buprenorphine was made a medication that could be prescribed by doctors from office-based practices (Campbell & Lovell, 2012). The very premise of buprenorphine was to allow physicians to prescribe in their offices on the logic that this would reduce not only the stigma of opioid use but also stigma specific to MAT with methadone, buprenorphine or other drugs (Woods & Joseph, 2015; Hansen et al., 2023). Naltrexone, the pure antagonist, has been under-utilised – and as a pharmacological antagonist, it is no surprise that it is most often encountered as a disciplinary tool in criminal justice settings in the United States. Access to the pharmacological agonist medications approved for OUD treatment – methadone and buprenorphine – has recently been pressed for in criminal justice contexts such as jails, prisons and drug courts (Sue, 2019; Kaye, 2020). A movement to ensure fair, non-discriminatory access to MOUD has arisen; this chapter considers the strategic alliances and tensions being constructed between drug user advocacy and disability rights. In the United States, buprenorphine acted as a disruptive innovation relative to the free-standing methadone clinic system that was institutionalised in the 1970s – whose sole purpose was to dispense methadone. Buprenorphine's disruptive effects have had both temporal and spatial dimensions – each of which have in turn affected the social availability and acceptance of these three main treatments – in part because buprenorphine has 'leaked' everywhere without spatial boundaries.

Drug use disorders – and their treatments – have typically been detached from concerns with disability rights in the United States. The recent convergence is occurring because the Civil Rights Division of the US Department of Justice (DOJ) has recast OUD as a disability under the Americans with Disabilities Act (ADA) (Americans with Disabilities Act, 42 U.S.C. s. 12101 et seq.). The DOJ is attempting to defend, enforce and promulgate that interpretation through a series of lawsuits representing individuals on MOUD against alleged discriminatory practices of employers and healthcare facilities. Defining individuals who are using MOUD as prescribed as disabled before the law is far from commonsense practice in a nation where religious and cultural conservatives continue to impose their sense of moral worth or deservingness upon an array of disabilities, and to dispute the notion that drug users might claim legal protections as members of a disabled class. Nor have harm reductionists, drug user health advocates or drug policy reformers embraced disability as a legal basis for pressing rights claims.

Forced to bring suit against counties, municipalities and states in order to counter unlawful discrimination and retaliation in violation of the ADA, the DOJ has assembled new collateral realities (Law, 2011) in which interruption or withholding of lawfully prescribed MOUD is actionable when individuals are under court supervision, homeless, incarcerated or gainfully employed.[2] Although the United States is notorious for mass incarceration (Alexander, 2010), studies based on the National Survey on Drug Use and Health show that most people under correctional control are not housed in jails or prisons but under some form of community supervision (parole and probation); of the latter, 30 per cent have a diagnosed substance use disorder and 20 per cent a diagnosed mental health disorder, with mortality and morbidity rates exceeding those of the general population (Widra & Jones, 2023). This chapter traces the DOJ's novel therapeutic jurisprudence, assembled from the concrete materialities of drug-using persons' lives but requiring them to accede to a legal and political 'disablement' in order to claim protection from discrimination.

The first ADA case was settled in January 2023 by the DOJ and the US District Court for the Middle District of Tennessee (US Department of Justice, 2023). The Complainant was an anonymous employee of the Cumberland County Sheriff's Office (the Defendant) in Crossville, Tennessee, who had been forced to resign from his job as a correctional

[2] Legal Action Center's complete listing of cases, investigations, settlements and consent decrees involving denial of access to MOUD, or discrimination because of it, appears at www.lac.org/assets/files/Cases-involving-denial-of-access-to-MOUD.pdf.

officer even after positive performance reviews and promotion to a supervisory role while on MOUD. The DOJ argued that the Complainant should be considered a person with a disability, defined in court documents as an

> impairment that substantially limits one or more of his major life activities, including the operation of major bodily functions, and he has a record of such impairments [. . .] OUD substantially limits the operation of Complainant's major bodily functions, such as neurological and brain functions, and substantially limits him in the major life activities of caring for oneself, learning, concentrating, thinking, and/or communicating, absent medication.

The Cumberland County Sheriff's Department's 'drug prohibition policy' avoided questions of body and brain, stating that employees could not possess 'controlled substances [. . .] or any other mind altering or intoxicating substance present in their systems while at work or on duty' (US District Court, Middle District of Tennessee, Northeastern Division, 2023, p. 3), unless they disclosed this to their supervisor. The complainant followed this rule, disclosing that he was on prescribed Bunavil, an easily dissolvable buprenorphine and naloxone film that he had started a few months prior to being hired. After an uneventful year following the disclosure, the complainant was drug-tested and, when he came up positive for Bunavail, he was put on unpaid leave. Despite the disclosure policy, his employer sent him a memo stating, 'It has become necessary to place you on unpaid administrative leave until you are taken off your prescription [. . .] and pass a departmental drug test' (US District Court, Middle District of Tennessee, Northeastern Division, 2023, p. 4). Seeking to keep his job and stay in treatment, he verified compliance with his treatment provider but was put on unpaid leave and told to go off the Bunavil and to complete an outpatient drug treatment programme as a condition of continued employment.

Clearly motivated to remain employed, the complainant satisfactorily completed a drug-free outpatient programme; a memo to the Sheriff's Office stated that he 'proved to be a very compliant participant, turned all assignments in promptly & kept all of his scheduled appointments' (US District Court, Middle District of Tennessee, Northeastern Division, 2023, p. 5). Through 2017 and 2018, he struggled to remain off MOUD to such an extent that his physician advised returning to Suboxone (buprenorphine plus naloxone) rather than return to opioid use. Again he disclosed his Suboxone prescription to a new captain and, not surprisingly, tested positive for buprenorphine. At this point, the captain threatened to fire him and 'tell future employers that he was terminated for a positive drug screen' unless he resigned (US District Court, Middle District of Tennessee, Northeastern Division, 2023, p. 6). Having run out of options, the complainant resigned and sought redress through the Nashville Area Office of the US Equal Employment Opportunity Commission (created to enforce the 1964 Civil Rights Act). He stubbornly sought to inhabit the 'liberal goal of independence through paid employment' (Fraser & valentine, 2008, p. 111). This is not simply a story of the ignorance of the Cumberland County Sheriff's Office, or one in which treatment gets confused for disease. An anti-maintenance stance was so thoroughly naturalised that supervisors did not seem to be equipped to differentiate between the effects of legally prescribed MAT/MOUD and those of extra-legal opioid use. One might ask where the stubborn rejection of the complainant's right to remain on a legally prescribed substance resides?

Due to the recent reframing of opioid use as a disability, treatment medications, including buprenorphine, methadone and naltrexone, were concurrently reframed as 'reasonable accommodations' to disability, the legal standard set by the ADA (US Department of Justice, Office of Public Affairs, 2023). The Cumberland County Sheriff's Department violated the ADA by failing to make 'reasonable accommodations' for an employee to have MOUD present in their system while at work. The 'drug prohibition policy' of the Sheriff's Office treated the complainant, who was maintained on legally prescribed medication, as if he possessed illegal drugs by having metabolites of MOUD in his system. He tested negative for twelve or more 'drugs of abuse' (US District Court, Middle District of Tennessee, Northeastern Division, 2023, p. 4) – only buprenorphine was present during the years of 'random' drug-testing undergone by the complainant. The 'discriminatory conduct' at the hands of the Cumberland County Sheriff's Office (the defendant) was found to have caused years of suffering and emotional distress. As the first ADA settlement resolving claims of employment discrimination based on OUD, this case defined OUD and MOUD as a disability – defined as a physical or mental impairment that 'substantially limit[s] one or more major life activities' (US District Court, Middle District of Tennessee, Northeastern Division, 2023, p. 4), the ADA wording used on the fourth page of the complainant's submission. Disabilities include conditions for which medication is prescribed – but not those in which drugs are used non-medically. The latter fall beyond legal protections against discrimination under the ADA, which distinguish between drugs used within the law, and drugs used outside the law.

Unlike decades in which methadone regulations were restrictively designed to limit patients accessing MMT, policymakers are now encouraged to expand legal access to treatment with Food and Drug Administration (FDA)-approved treatment and maintenance medications and to ensure continuity of care for those enrolled in MAT/MOUD. The ADA proved a useful tool for this expansion project – so useful that the DOJ issued a guidance document, *The Americans with Disabilities Act and the Opioid Crisis: Combating Discrimination against People in Treatment or Recovery*, for the first time in April 2022 (US Department of Justice, 2022). The Civil Rights Department continued to explore enforcement options, signalling that the long-standing pro-prohibition and anti-maintenance drug policy of the United States may be shifting. Along with the Legal Action Center and other entities, the DOJ stepped in to firm up workplace responses to people on MOUD not only in public but private institutions. Similar cases have been settled against medical practices, employment agencies for homeless workers, hospitals and skilled nursing facilities. The rest of this chapter considers a DOJ case brought against a series of counties operating specialised drug courts in the Commonwealth of Pennsylvania.

Summary of the Case: *United States v Unified Judicial System of Pennsylvania*

On February 24, 2022, the Department of Justice (DOJ) filed suit against the Unified Judicial System (UJS) of Pennsylvania, which represents several jurisdictions in the Commonwealth of Pennsylvania. Like the Tennessee case introduced previously, this was neither the first nor the last time that the DOJ would find it necessary to sue state and local governments that encourage, allow or even force interruption of MAT or MOUD. The DOJ views interruption of the three legally prescribed, FDA-approved treatment medications – buprenorphine, methadone and naltrexone – as a form of discrimination under the ADA. If an arm of state and local governments tried to interrupt medication for diabetes, cardiovascular conditions or seizure disorders, this would be considered discriminatory and inhumane. It is the implicit social undesirability of those who suffer from this disability that extends a penumbra of ambiguity over MOUD. Some argue that OUD should be explicitly re-stigmatised by law and society if it is to be contained (Humphreys &

Caulkins, 2023). Researchers and advocates allied with the harm reduction movement have sought to humanise people who use drugs, to use destigmatising language that is more neutral in terms of normative assumptions and value judgments, and to make the case for access to MOUD as a basic civil right if not one of a broader set of human rights.

While it may seem that the DOJ is venturing into medical territory, the Civil Rights Department does exert its authority against that of organised healthcare. For the past four years, the DOJ has seen discrimination on the basis of addiction treatment as a civil rights violation. Surprisingly, these rights are not always violated in places that might be expected given US drug law – such as law enforcement, criminal justice or corrections facilities – but also in skilled nursing facilities or hospitals, including Massachusetts General Hospital in Boston (Black et al., 2023). Generously put, personnel working in such facilities seem not to realise that they are behaving in a discriminatory fashion when they turn down patients or employees who are treated with Suboxone (buprenorphine plus naloxone), methadone or naltrexone. They appear to be functioning without an anti-discrimination frame – as if discrimination against persons with disabilities who have sought treatment for OUD was normalised. According to the Legal Action Center (LAC), which has developed a MAT/MOUD advocacy toolkit and a portal for reporting discrimination on that basis, courts, jails and prisons, probation, parole, child welfare officials, employers, recovery homes, nursing homes and other health care entities often force people to stop taking MOUD against their doctor's recommendations or deny people services because they take MOUD (Cohen et al., 2023). Forcing people off MOUD is illegal, according to LAC's 2021 toolkit (Figure 1). The advocacy toolkit includes sample letters for defence attorneys and treatment providers; educational resources for clients; a list of ongoing civil and criminal litigation; and out-of-court settlements and agreements. Not only do the sample agreements include employers making restitution to affected individuals but they implement employee training programmes to guard against future discrimination. The LAC also worked with physicians from Yale School of Medicine, University of Washington and Boston Medical Center to publish a call for an end to physicians' role in 'medical complicity' with this form of discrimination by skilled nursing facilities and emergency medicine departments (Cohen et al., 2023).

Emergency rooms and departments are also sites where discrimination against individuals on MOUD occurs so frequently that the LAC posted a downloadable flyer detailing the rights of persons who use drugs to be

ORDER OF COURT

AND NOW, this 3rd day of August, 2018, this Court and its probation department dealing with opiate abuse by probationers, and this Court finding that the vast majority (well in excess of 80%) of individuals prescribed with Suboxone, Methadone, Subutex and other opiate based treatment programs, abuse those drugs with regularity; and further that it makes these probationers ineffective and nearly impossible to manage; and finally, it does not appear to help the patients in any way to become productive members of society. It should be noted that among the thousands of individuals who have been on probation while prescribed these drugs, there have been less than 15 people who have successfully completed treatment and been completely weaned off of these drugs.

IT IS HEREBY ORDERED AND DECREED that effective immediately but beginning with this Court's sentencing on August 15, 2018, no individual who is sentenced to ARD, Probation, Parole, Intermediate Punishment or Drug Court shall be permitted to take Suboxone, Subutex, Methadone or any other opiate based treatment medication regardless of whether not these drugs are prescribed, they will be completely clean of the substance with in 30 days of the date of their sentence or face probation revocation.

IT IS FURTHER ORDERED AND DECREED that the only exception shall be pregnant probationers (who are pregnant upon commencement of probation) during pregnancy and with the permission of their obstetrician/gynecologist. These probationers shall be off opiates and free of the substance within 30 days of the end of their pregnancy.

Figure 1 Signs of discrimination in admission to skilled nursing facilities. Legal Action Center Advocacy Toolkit.

free from discrimination based on the stigmatisation of their condition ('addiction') as well discrimination based on their medication. Widespread normalisation of such stigma continues for other forms of disability; only recently has freedom from stigmatisation been reframed as disability rights; and many staff of such facilities continue to casually make stigmatising comments (as demonstrated in Figure 2).

To overcome normalised discrimination, the Justice Department has sued counties (which deliver addiction treatment and prevention services in the United States with state and federal certification and oversight); municipalities; states (which have legal oversight over treatment and prevention programmes); and hospitals and other healthcare facilities. The Justice Department filed suit against the UJS of Pennsylvania on grounds that Pennsylvania's 'problem-solving courts' prohibited or limited lawfully prescribed MOUD, thus discriminating against and violating the civil rights of individuals under court supervision in the Northumberland and Jefferson County Courts of Common Pleas.[3] Three named complainants were ordered to stop using legally prescribed

[3] The DOJ named six Pennsylvania counties considered to have 'problematic' policies and practices: Allegheny, Blair, Butler, Clinton, Delaware and York.

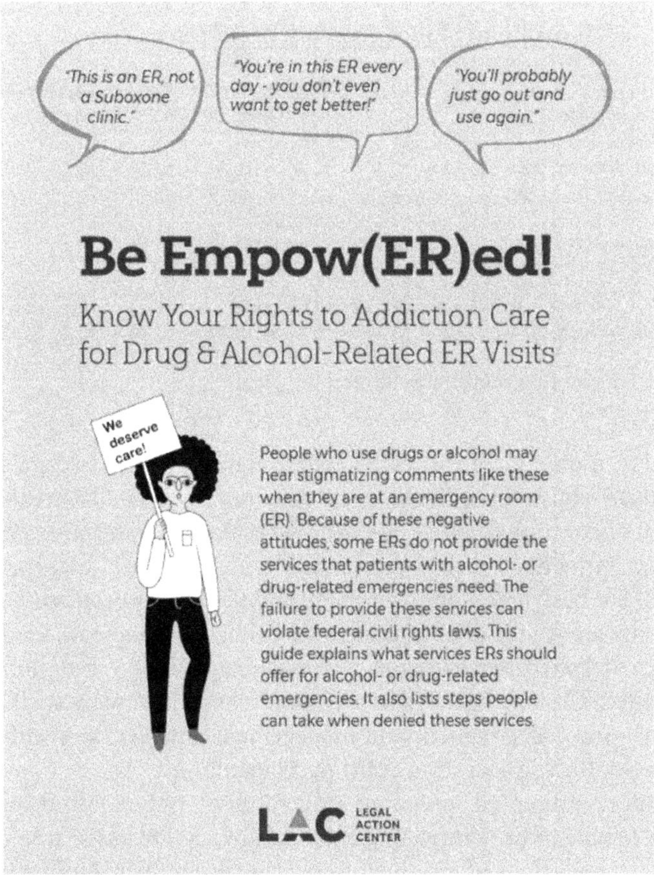

Figure 2 Know your rights to addiction care for drug and alcohol-related ER visits. Legal Action Center Advocacy Toolkit.

medication by authorities whose edicts they could not disobey. One of the most egregious of these is discussed in the next paragraph.

On 3 August 2018, Judge Foradora, who presided over a Jefferson County drug court, issued an Order of Court based on his finding that the 'vast majority [. . .] of individuals prescribed with Suboxone, Methadone, Subutex and other opiate based treatment program, abuse those drugs with regularity; and further that it makes these probationers ineffective and nearly impossible to manage; and finally, it does not appear to help the patients in any way to become productive members of society'.

Admission to Skilled Nursing Facilities

(including nursing homes and long-term care facilities)

People needing care at a skilled nursing facility (SNF) are often denied admission because they take methadone or buprenorphine to treat opioid use disorder (OUD). The U.S. Department of Justice has stated that these practices are illegal discrimination.

Signs of discrimination include:

- SNF has a policy not to admit people taking methadone or buprenorphine
- SNF says someone must taper off of MOUD to be admitted
- SNF says it cannot provide the "type of services" someone with OUD needs
- SNF denies someone admission after commenting about their substance use

For help, call the Legal Action Center: (212) 243-1313

Visit LAC's MAT ADVOCACY TOOLKIT for materials that can help you advocate!

Figure 3 Judge Foradora's administrative decree.

There is a lot to unpack in this court order (Figure 3). In Foradora's order, the phrase 'abuse those drugs with regularity' implies that treatment is a form of continued 'abuse' for the 'vast majority', and leaves no indication that individuals use these named and unnamed drugs as prescribed. All are designated unmanageable and thereby unproductive. This order designates the goal of treatment as 'being completely weaned off these drugs' despite their use as part of ongoing relapse prevention and maintenance. Clearly, this order was most concerned with social control, behavioural comportment and management – rather than with the health and well-being – of drug court participants.

Judge Foradora exempted 'pregnant probationers' but required all non-pregnant people to be 'completely clean' of any 'opiate based treatment medication regardless of whether or not these drugs are prescribed' within thirty days. Judge Foradora's goal was abstinence or complete 'weaning', not only from illegal opioids but also from MOUD. He cast continued maintenance as evidence of failure and a sign of weakness and ineffectiveness. If 'patients' – who, it must be recalled, were participants in a drug court – were not off their addiction treatment drugs within thirty days, they faced revocation of probation and return to jail. This order was not rescinded for close to five months.

Impact on individuals affected by Judge Foradora's order was profound. Complainant A (later identified as Sonya Mosey by the LAC and the American Civil Liberties Union of Pennsylvania) and Complainant B (unidentified) were told by probation officers that they had to endure the misery and risk of going off MOUD regardless of strenuous objections from their prescribing physicians. Despite doing well on buprenorphine, which 'has helped her stay stable, enabling her to buy a house, start a small business, and be a better parent to her young child', Complainant C (unidentified) of Northumberland County was ordered to taper off buprenorphine completely (US District Court, Eastern District of Pennsylvania 2023b, pp. 5–6). This requirement held even after Complainant C's doctor informed the court that tapering off 'could put her at increased risk of relapse, overdose, and death' (US District Court, Eastern District of Pennsylvania 2023b, p. 6). The list of somatic suffering endured by these attempts to enforce abstinence included 'significant emotional distress and severe side effects as a result, including loss of appetite and energy, body aches, soreness, backpain, diarrhoea, depression, and anxiety' (US District Court, Eastern District of Pennsylvania 2023b, p. 6). The DOJ asked UJS to guarantee that no court in the statewide system adopted discriminatory policies and practices such as Judge Foradora's Order of Court (Figure 3). No judge should be allowed to discriminate in policy or practice because someone was on prescribed MOUD.

The ADA offered a concrete path to recast methadone, buprenorphine and naltrexone as 'disability-related medications' (US Department of Justice, Office of Public Affairs, 2022). While people on MOUD 'too often face discrimination rooted in stereotypes and myths rather than in science', noted Assistant Attorney General Kristen Clarke:

> ensuring that court-involved individuals with Opioid Use Disorder have access to the medications they need is critical to support recovery efforts and to break the cycles of opioid addiction that have harmed families and communities across our country. Ensuring that courts are employing science-driven and data-informed approaches to this crisis is an important priority for the Civil Rights Division.
>
> (*US Department of Justice, Office of Public Affairs,* 2022)

Science and data are invoked to fend off prejudice and discrimination in service of civil rights. Yet there is little recognition that the new term 'disability-related medications' harnesses specific pharmacological treatments to a broader category of access supports for the disabled that joins common physical aspects of the post-ADA built environment such as grab bars, ramps, elevators, and so forth – thus forcing drug users on MOUD to take up positions as disabled subjects with which they may not identify (Bunn, 2019; Seear, 2020). The unusual relationship between maintenance medications and their users is such that they *must* use them as prescribed in order to claim and defend legal protections in order to maintain their status on MOUD. The question is who gets to determine appropriate use of 'disability-related medications', as well as the rights of individuals with OUD. Strategically, legal subjects must identify as both 'disabled' and 'addicted' (Bunn, 2019). Only this will maintain their access to legally prescribed medications – even then, they may subscribe to this subject position and lose access due to misconceptions about OUD and MOUD on the part of advocates and judges. As Kate Seear argues in *Law, Drugs and the Making of Addiction: Just Habits* (2020), lawyers play a role in 'strategically constituting the addicted subject' but also distance themselves from 'their own interpellative practices, including processes of anticipation, pondering, hesitation, hailing and calling through advocacy' (Seear, 2020, p. 76). The strength of the interpellation at the 'disabled/addicted' intersection is such that it may 'spill' onto advocates and even judges associated with drug courts – who in turn seek to manage their identities through appeals to abstinence so as not to be soiled.

The UJS of Pennsylvania sought to have the DOJ's case against it dismissed. Judge Mitchell S. Goldberg, Eastern District of Pennsylvania, granted UJS's motion to dismiss, finding the DOJ too short on 'facts' to warrant him to order the state judiciary to comply with federal law. The UJS successfully argued that it should not be 'held responsible for a handful of isolated incidents that occurred at the local level of individual courts of common pleas' (county-level courts). These 'isolated incidents' were blamed on the idiosyncrasies of judges, as opposed to a blanket policy to which the DOJ's claim could stick. But Judge Goldberg allowed the DOJ to amend its initial complaint, if it could do so in good faith. In September 2023, the DOJ added six more unidentified complainants in an amended complaint finding that eleven UJS courts in Pennsylvania had administrative policies either restricting use of MOUD or limiting it to naltrexone. Courts such as the Luzerne County Court of Common Pleas and the Berks County Drug Treatment Court had even adopted prohibitions on buprenorphine or methadone *after* the DOJ had formally notified the UJS that these policies were discriminatory under the ADA (Am. Compl., ECF No. 28, pp. 123–4, 132). Others changed their policies 'begrudgingly while its Drug Court personnel continued as a matter of policy and practice to pressure participants to wean off OUD medication'.

Blair County Drug Court representatives 'told participants in the Drug Court that they were allowing OUD medication "against our will"', indicating that the federal DOJ had pressured them into it. Not only had some drug court representatives pressured complainants into weaning off maintenance medications, they ordered some to do so in ways that forced them into withdrawal with a variety of social and health consequences. Complainant D (unidentified) spent the Thanksgiving holiday in 'forced inpatient treatment, away from his family, vomiting, twitching, and feeling like he wanted to die. Id. ¶ 40. The UJS could have prevented the harm done to Complainant D. Id. ¶¶ 11–12, 138–39. Instead, it did nothing. Id. ¶ 143'. Despite being at high risk of relapse, Complainant D did not resume use of MOUD 'because he fears that he may be forced off it again in the future' (p. 11). Complainant E (unidentified), a regular user of legal and illegal opioids after a string of occupational injuries, was forcibly withdrawn from buprenorphine against medical advice due to the Blair County policy, and described withdrawal as a 'savage' weeks-long ordeal that was 'the most terrible thing imaginable' (p. 12). Following this incident, Complainant E tried heroin *for the first time*, became addicted, went to jail, was separated from his family, and spent more than four years under drug court supervision – a saga that was attributed to his 'being continuously denied access to his lawfully prescribed medication treatment'.

These unidentified complainant's stories indicate a pattern in which 'disability-related medications' are prescribed by physicians yet controlled by court supervision programmes that decide which forms of MOUD may or may not be used. In suing state court systems, the federal DOJ plays an adversarial role in enforcing the fundamental right of equal access to and benefit from courts and court supervision programmes for people with disabilities. Charging the Supreme Court of Pennsylvania with failing to fulfil its obligations under the ADA to ensure that all the Commonwealth's courts are fairly administering justice to individuals with OUD (US District Court, Eastern District of Pennsylvania, 2023a, p. 14), the DOJ is claiming that Pennsylvania's courts are harming residents (US District Court, Eastern District of Pennsylvania, 2023a, p. 5). The Commonwealth of Pennsylvania requires drug court participants to become 'drug-free' by forcing them off even legally prescribed treatment medications. The struggle over who gets to decide what forms of MOUD are allowed or disallowed has become an arena of concrete struggle between state and federal governments in the United States.

Conceptual and Critical Approach: Drug-Free Zones

Drug-free zones are a form of policing practice based on limited tolerance for the presence of drugs and those who use them in public space – and upon the mistaken assumption that drug use can be eliminated from such 'zones' as schools, parks and public employment. Writing about the relationship between liberal democracies and subjects on methadone, Suzanne Fraser and kylie valentine interrogate the 'intra-activity of space and time', building upon the materialism of Karen Barad's (2007) concept of agential realism to understand what they call the 'chronotype of the queue[s]' at methadone dosing points (Fraser & valentine, 2008, pp. 91–112). While lining up for daily dosing at the methadone clinic marked patients by requiring complex daily transportation routines, singling them out, and otherwise demarcating them, the distributed model of responsibility for maintenance of buprenorphine in physicians' offices sheered away these necessities (but created new problems; see Hansen et al., 2023). Changing guidelines for accessing methadone also occurred in response to the COVID-19 pandemic, which disturbed long-standing chronotypes as well as physical locations. Naltrexone/Vivitrol, too, is prescribed and administered within different parameters, as it requires at least two weeks of complete abstinence from all opioids before initiation. Induction onto buprenorphine also requires medical supervision due to the unique pharmacological profile of a mixed agonist/antagonist. Each aspect of MOUD now has different 'chronotypes' and 'treatment identities' (Fraser & valentine 2008, p. 113) that may be glimpsed when MOUD status is invoked outside treatment settings and contexts of employment, social service provision and healthcare. These new, supposedly 'destigmatised', identities are bound more to the spatial logics of policing, accomplished through boundary-setting and exclusion of all forms of drug selling and use from purified 'drug-free zones', than to strictly medical logics. These drug-using identities embody a performative biopolitical process through which 'destigmatisation' has been remade with the very tools that once contributed to stigmatisation of anyone using opioids for any purpose. The drug-free space must now expand to include people on MOUD, as well as people on opioids for pain, and it is difficult for anyone to distinguish them beyond the ways in which they confound attempts at moral purity. Wars on drugs can no longer be 'total' but must instead admit a complex array of exceptions.

Drug-free zone laws were first enacted as part of the federal Comprehensive Drug Abuse, Prevention and Control Act of 1970 (Comprehensive Drug Abuse, Prevention and Control Act, 1970), amended in 1984 and 1988. The Anti-Drug Abuse Act (1988) was motivated by media attention to crack cocaine, which led Congress to pass 102 Stat. 4296 P.L. 100–690-NOV. 18, 1988 21 USC 1502. Opposition to drug legalisation was painted explicitly as being an 'unconscionable surrender' in the all-encompassing or 'total' war on drugs: 'The

Congress finds that legalisation of illegal drugs, on the Federal or State level, is an unconscionable surrender in a war in which, for the future of our country and the lives of our children, there can be no substitute for total victory' (Public Law 100–690, 102 Stat. 4296, 1988, Title V – User Accountability, Section 5011). In this discourse there is no possible relationship between disability, civil rights or movements for or against drug policy reform.

This all-or-nothing jurisdictional intent to cordon off drug-free schools, public housing and workplaces contained Subtitle F, a 'Drug-Free America' policy that set the deadline of 1995 for the nation to become 'drug-free'. Due in part to the US Congress finding that (102 Stat. 4310, 14) 'the use of illicit drugs affects moods and emotions, chemically alters the brain, and causes loss of control, paranoia, reduction of inhibition, and unprovoked anger' (102 Stat. 4310), the policy mentioned heroin and cocaine. The threat of the latter was cited in finding (102 Stat. 4310, 16) '8 of 10 men arrested for serious crimes in New York City test positive for cocaine use', and this finding was called out as motivating the act's denial of federal benefits to drug traffickers and 'drug possessors' (102 Stat. 4310–4311). In Subtitle F, the 'sense' of the Congress 'That Proposals to Legalize Illicit Drugs Should Be Rejected' (102 Stat. 4359) was explicit:

> It is the sense of Congress that (1) proposals to combat sale and use of illicit drugs by legalisation should be rejected; and (2) consideration should be given only to proposals to attack directly the supply of, and demand for, illicit drugs, such as proposals to strengthen and expand penalties for sale and use, proposals to encourage greater multinational cooperation in eradication and interdiction, and proposals to promote educational awareness programs for young people.

This latter purpose centred on places where young people congregate, creating special penalties for those distributing or intending to distribute drugs within a thousand feet of a schoolyard (Public Law 100–690, 102 Stat. 4373, 1988, s. 6457).

Signs declaring drug-free zones have proliferated around schools, parks, swimming pools and playgrounds in the United States since the 1980s. The rhetoric of the 'drug-free' nation partakes of ritual cleansing, expulsion of 'dirty' from 'clean', and propulsion of drug users to social perimeters that refuse them the rights of productive citizens. These enactments 'reveal[] the co-constitutive dependency of the one on the other', serving the 'symbolic goal of securing a drug-free nation, a mythical status to which the United

States ever aspires and never embodies' (Campbell, 2006, p. 57). The morally cleansed drug-free zone is not only about space but has been extended to the temporal rhythms of home and work. Simon Flacks (2021) discusses political discourses of 'spatial purity', in which the *sight* of drugs is considered to endanger innocent children who inhabit 'privileged sites of child development', wherein harms are considered to derive from the 'mere presence of [drugs] in a place in which the very essence of childhood was performed through play' (Flacks, 2021, pp. 100–1). Segmentation of public space, its division into designated zones for purposes of law enforcement and the courts began to be enacted in several states in the 1970s. These were rolled into federal legislation with the Reagan–Bush era policy reforms that laid the groundwork for mass incarceration (Alexander, 2010; Hinton, 2016).

Drug-free zone warriors appeared to think that they were creating impermeable walls to cordon off those who used drugs from those who did not. These boundaries are permeable and the constitutive impurity of maintenance confounds purity-based laws in a regulatory state bent upon making itself 'drug-free'. The co-constitutive making of 'disability-related medications' disturbs both the epistemic cultures of disability law (which allow medications but disallow 'drugs') and those of drug law and regulatory policy (defined without regard for disability). Drug users and harm reduction advocates 'do disability' differently from DOJ imperatives. If hospitals, schools, and workplaces, including those of local law enforcement and state government cannot be 'purified' due to the presence of people on MOUD, this will push a reckoning with the difference between 'doing drugs' to get well/stay employed, and 'doing drugs' to get high/avoid withdrawal. The common ground between MOUD and OUD may become the site upon which the dignity, recognition and protections against discrimination that have been sought and won by the disability rights movement are extended to drug users.

Harm reduction and drug user activism are both culturally wide-ranging practices conjoined through pragmatism and recognition of dignity. These epistemic cultures range in terms of their resistance to, and at times even defiance of, the law. Harm reduction organisations 'do safety' differently, resulting in 'illegal subjectivities' produced by decades of underground activism that have only recently sought to become legally sanctioned in the form of safer injection sites for the purpose of overdose prevention or drug users' recent attempts to create 'safer supply' policies and practices that combat heightened toxicity in the illegal drug supply (Ivsins et al., 2020). Such efforts recognise that 'drug-free zones' are based upon untenable notions that will do harm – just as restrictions on which forms of MOUD may be used to do harm to individuals forced thereby to become 'drug-free' for ideological rather than medical reasons.

Drug-free zones are not evidence-based practice – they are a harmful policing practice based on limited tolerance for the presence of drugs and those who use them. The notion that drug courts should be drug-free zones is a harmful one that denies dignity at the limits of tolerance for medical maintenance and MAT. According to Kerwin Kaye, author of a book on New York City drug courts, 'drugs courts in their current formulation represent a devil's bargain' (Kaye, 2020, p. 40). They condition rights and privileges of social inclusion upon participants appearing to buy into becoming 'Normal Ordinary Responsible Persons, or NORPs' (Kaye, 2020, p. 34). Such courts engage in punitive as well as well-meaning tactics designed to extract 'compliance' with the terms of the power and authority enacted through them: '[D]rug courts necessarily position themselves as the safeguards of an upright citizenry against beastly outsiders, even as they simultaneously offer the possibility of redemption for those who successfully "civilize" themselves' (Kaye, 2020, p. 41).

For the evidence-based practice of MAT/MOUD, there is the troubling finding that because of the affordability of drug-free treatment modalities in jails and prisons, the pharmacologically based regimens are rarely available, often interrupted and always stigmatised. Physician-ethnographer Kimberley Sue found that women rarely sought 'humane and evidence-based' MAT before leaving prison, instead buying into drug-free programmes that 'reflect the American belief that total abstinence from substances was the only right course of action' (Sue, 2019, p. 82). Instead, 'what women wanted most of all, desperately, was some kind of absolution. They wanted forgiveness for their sins, to be washed clean and able to start anew [. . .].' (Sue, 2019, 82). To become drug-free, they were willing to go along with dangerous practices of abstinence and withdrawal that increased risk for relapse, opioid overdose and continued court supervision. Whether imposed by judges or by internalised stigma, intolerance for MOUD causes a great deal of harm, the remedy for which must currently be sought in disability rights.

Discussion: Beyond Freedom and Dignity

As evidence-based medications, the benefits of methadone and buprenorphine have been thoroughly scrutinised by the National Academies of Science, most recently in a report entitled *Methadone Treatment for*

Opioid Use Disorder: Improving Access Through Regulatory and Legal Change (2022), which built on *Medications for Opioid Use Disorder Save Lives* (NASEM, 2019). The 2022 report contained testimony from a Pennsylvania state trial court judge, the Honourable Michael Barrasse, president judge in the Lackawanna County, Pennsylvania, Court of Common Pleas, who said,

> From the perspective of a judge who adjudicates cases of people with OUD charged with criminal offenses on the ground, the number one obstacle to MOUD in the criminal justice system is stigma. The criminal justice system is slow to change [. . .] It is adversarial and was never meant to be a change agent in dealing with behavioral health.
>
> (NASEM, 2022, p. 66)

Pointing to *USA v UJS of Pennsylvania*, Judge Barrasse illustrated how naturalised the insistence on being 'completely clean' has been throughout the Pennsylvania judicial system. He called out the benighted state of MAT in the Commonwealth, referencing Judge Foradora's court order and indicating that his colleague on the bench felt that these treatments did not 'appear to help the patient in any way to become productive members of society' (NASEM, 2022, pp. 67–8). These beliefs are hardly swayed by science or evidence. Most Pennsylvania jails do not include methadone or buprenorphine on their medication formularies and rarely have MOUD on offer. To remedy this, Barrasse applauded the civil rights litigation to hold Pennsylvania accountable for continuing established patterns of discrimination towards people using MOUD. He hoped to 'transform the system from punitive to restorative' by 'champion[ing] proven strategies within the judicial system that empower drug-using people to change their lives' (NASEM, 2022, pp. 67–8).

The National Association of Drug Court Professionals (NADCP), a non-profit drug court organisation that Barrasse once chaired, changed its name in the summer of 2023 to 'All Rise', and described its mission as a 'training, membership, and advocacy organization for justice system innovation addressing substance use and mental health for individuals at every intercept point' (All Rise, 2023, p. 1). All Rise offers resources to educate drug court professionals on the merits of MAT, including a peer-reviewed journal underwritten by the White House Office of National Drug Control Policy. Authors note that MAT remains under-utilised throughout the justice system (Westreich, 2019, p. 5), as do advocacy organisations including the National Sheriff's Association. The DOJ strategy has filtered down to Attorneys General (federal prosecutors), who are not just targeting drug courts but also jails and prisons and signalling that 'blanket prohibitions against MAT for inmates and detainees are no longer constitutionally or statutorily acceptable [...] If your jails and prisons do not permit MAT, especially for opioid addiction, maybe now is a good time to bring this authority to their attention' (Meyer, 2019, p. 139). Reporting on *Pesce v Coppinger* (2018), a case in the Federal District Court of the District of Massachusetts (Civil Action 18–11972-DJC D. Mass. Nov. 26, 2018) indicates that theory and practice are not yet meeting in this arena. As ethnographers, drug policy reformers and human rights organisations consistently document, treatment is so regularly withheld in the US criminal justice system that it will need to be redressed from bottom up and top down. If we take seriously that legality is 'a way in which the world is assembled, an attribute that is attached to events, people, documents, and other objects when they become part of the decision-making process' (Levi & Valverde, 2008, p. 806), the test cases in which the DOJ is engaged are an exercise in re-worlding.

References

Alexander, M. (2010). *The new Jim Crow: Mass incarceration in the age of colorblindness*. The New Press.

All Rise. (2023). About us. *All Rise*. https://allrise.org/.

Anti-Drug Abuse Act of 1988, Pub. L. No. 100–690, 102 Stat. 4296 (1988).

Barad, K. (2007). *Meeting the universe halfway: Quantum physics and the entanglement of matter and meaning*. Duke University Press.

Black, A., Gardner, T. M., Joab, R., Johnston, D., Reid, D. A., Seitz, J. & Warren, A. (2023). Substance use-based discrimination in health care: A conversation with LAC staff on drug user health rights. *No health = no justice podcast*. Legal Action Center. www.lac.org/news/substance-use-based-discrimination-in-health-care-a-conversation-with-lac-staff-on-drug-user-health-rights.

Bunn, R. (2019). Conceptualizing addiction as disability in discrimination law: A situated comparison. *Contemporary Drug Problems*, 46(1), 58–77.

Campbell, N. D. (2006). Everyday insecurities: The micro-behavioural politics of intrusive surveillance. In T. Monahan (Ed.), *Surveillance and security: Technological politics and power in everyday life* (pp. 57–75). Routledge.

Campbell, N. D., & Lovell, A. M. (2012). The history of the development of buprenorphine as an addiction therapeutic. *Annals of the New York Academy of Sciences*, 1248(1), 124–139.

Civil Action No. 18–11972-DJC (D. Mass. 26 November 2018).

Cohen, S. M., Joab, R., Bolles, K. M., Friedman, S. & Kimmel, S. D. (2023). Ending medical complicity with skilled-nursing facility discrimination against people with opioid use disorder. *Annals of Internal Medicine*, 176(3), 410–412.

Comprehensive Drug Abuse Prevention and Control Act of 1970, 21 U.S.C. ss. 801 et seq. (1970), as amended by the Anti-Drug Abuse Act of 1984, Pub. L. No. 98–473, 98 Stat. 1837, and the Anti-Drug Abuse Act of 1988, Pub. L. No. 100–690, 102 Stat. 4181.

Courtwright, D., Joseph, H. & Des Jarlais, D. (1989). *Addicts who survived: An oral history of narcotic use in America, 1923–1965.* University of Tennessee Press.

Fanning, C. (2018). Get to know Judge Michael Barrasse. *Happenings Magazine.* www.happeningsmagazinepa.com/2018/05/31/get-to-know-judge-michael-j-barrasse/.

Flacks, S. (2021). *Law, drugs and the politics of childhood: From protection to punishment.* Routledge.

Fraser, S., & valentine, K. (2008). *Substance and substitution: Methadone subjects in liberal societies.* Palgrave Macmillan.

Fraser, S., Pienaar, K., Dilkes-Frayne, E., Moore, D., Kokanovic, R., Treloar, C. & Dunlop, A. (2017). Addiction stigma and the biopolitics of liberal modernity: A qualitative analysis. *International Journal of Drug Policy*, 44, 192–201.

Hansen, H., Netherland, J. & Herzberg, D. (2023). *Whiteout: How racial capitalism changed the colour of opioids in America.* University of California Press.

Hinton, E. (2016). *From the war on poverty to the war on crime: The making of mass incarceration in America.* Harvard University Press.

Humphreys, K., & Caulkins, J. (2023). Destigmatizing drug use has been a profound mistake. *The Atlantic.* www.theatlantic.com/ideas/archive/2023/12/destigmatizing-drug-use-mistake-opioid-crisis/676292/.

Ivsins, A., Boyd, J., Beletsky, L. & McNeil, R. (2020). Tackling the overdose crisis: The role of safe supply. *International Journal of Drug Policy*, 80, 1–5.

Kaye, K. (2020). *Enforcing freedom: Drug courts, therapeutic communities, and the intimacies of the state.* Columbia University Press.

Law, J. (2011). Collateral realities. In F. Rubio & P. Baert (Eds.), *The politics of knowledge* (pp. 156–178). Routledge.

Legal Action Center. (2021). *MAT/MOUD advocacy toolkit.* www.lac.org/assets/files/SNF-MOUD-Info-Sheet-June-2021-ak-formatted.pdf.

Levi, R., & Valverde, M. (2008). Studying law by association: Bruno Latour goes to the Conseil d'État. *Law & Social Inquiry*, 33(3), 805–825.

Meyer, W. G. (2019). Two cases that will make a difference. *Journal for Advancing Justice*, 2, 131–139.

National Academies of Sciences, Engineering, and Medicine. (2019). *Medications for opioid use disorder save lives.* The National Academies Press. https://nap.nationalacademies.org/catalog/25310/medications-for-opioid-use-disorder-save-lives.

National Academies of Sciences, Engineering, and Medicine. (2022). *Methadone treatment for opioid use disorder: Improving access through regulatory and legal change.* The National Academies Press.

Pesce v Coppinger, No. 18–11972-DJC, 2018 US Dist. LEXIS 199265 (D. Mass. 26 November 2018).

Public Law 100–690, 102 Stat. 4296 (1988). Title V – User Accountability, Section 5011.

Seear, K. (2020). *Law, drugs and the making of addiction: Just habits.* Routledge.

Sue, K. (2019). *Getting wrecked: Women, incarceration, and the American opioid crisis.* University of California Press.

US Congress. (1990). Americans with Disabilities Act of 1990, s. 933, 101st Cong, 2nd Sess.

US Department of Justice. (2022). *The Americans with Disabilities Act and the opioid crisis: Combating discrimination against people in treatment or recovery.* US Department of Justice.

US Department of Justice, Office of Public Affairs. (2022). *Justice Department finds that Pennsylvania courts discriminated against people with opioid use disorder.* US Department of Justice. www.justice.gov/opa/pr/justice-department-finds-pennsylvania-courts-discriminated-against-people-opioid-use.

US Department of Justice, Office of Public Affairs. (2023, 18 January). *Cumberland County, Tennessee agrees to end discrimination based on opioid use disorder.* US Department of Justice. www.justice.gov/opa/pr/cumberland-county-tennessee-agrees-end-discrimination-based-opioid-use-disorder.

US District Court, Eastern District of Pennsylvania. (2023a). *United States of America's opposition to defendants' motion to dismiss*, No. 22-cv-00709.

US District Court, Eastern District of Pennsylvania. (2023b). *United States of America, plaintiff, v Unified Judicial System of the Commonwealth of Pennsylvania, defendant*, Civil Action No. 22–709.

US District Court for the Middle District of Tennessee, Northeastern Division. (2023). *United States of America v Cumberland County, Tennessee*, Case No. 3:23-mc-09999, Document 28 [Complaint]. US Department of Justice. www.justice.gov/crt/case-document/file/1563011/download.

Westreich, L. M. (2019). Use of medication-assisted treatment in the justice system: A medical perspective. In D. B. Marlowe (Ed.), *Best practices in the justice system for addressing the opioid epidemic* (pp. 5–19). National Association of Drug Court Professionals.

Widra, E., & Jones, A. (2023). Mortality, health, and poverty: The unmet needs of people on probation and parole. *Prison Policy Initiative.* www.prisonpolicy.org/blog/2023/04/03/nsduh_probation_parole/.

Woods, J. S., & Joseph, H. (2015). Stigma from the viewpoint of the patient. *Journal of Addictive Diseases*, 34(2–3), 238–247.

7

'This Is Only the Beginning'

Drug-Induced Homicide, a Test Case and the Construction of Death-Worlds in the US Overdose Crisis

ALLISON V. SCHLOSSER

State of Ohio v Jamie N. Maynard

On 27 April 2015, Jamie Maynard and Courtney Penix met in a strip mall parking lot in Columbus, Ohio, a city in the Midwestern United States (US). Earlier that day, Courtney had sent Jamie a series of text messages asking if she could get her $150 worth of heroin. Jamie said that she could, plus two 'rigs' (equipment to inject the drug), for $175 total. They arranged to meet that evening to make the trade before Jamie headed to work at a local casino. Jamie and Courtney, both White women in their mid twenties, met earlier that spring through a friend-of-a-friend. They initially connected to exchange drugs: heroin, to which both had developed habits, and the pharmaceuticals Suboxone, used to ease painful opioid withdrawal symptoms, and Xanax, used to ease anxiety and sometimes used in combination with opioids to amplify the effects of the drugs. They quickly developed a casual friendship, communicating regularly by text messages and phone calls. They vented about their jobs, shared stories about their struggles to maintain their drug habits, and offered drugs to one another to keep each other 'well' (i.e., to stave off withdrawal) (Williams, 2020).

When Jamie met Courtney in the parking lot that April evening, she gave her the heroin and rigs after a few minutes of conversation. Noticing that Courtney was slurring her words, Jamie asked if she had recently used Xanax. Jamie was concerned that Courtney would be vulnerable to drug overdose if she were to take heroin in addition to the sedative. When Courtney said that she had not used Xanax since the previous night, explaining that her speech was slurred due to impending opioid withdrawal symptoms, Jamie gave her the heroin and rigs and left for work. Courtney went to a nearby gas station bathroom to use the heroin but never emerged. An hour later, she was found dead of a drug overdose (Williams, 2020).

That spring and summer, detectives used text messages and video surveillance footage from area businesses to determine that the heroin Courtney had purchased and used prior to her death was purchased from Jamie (Decker, 2015). By August 2015, local Franklin County Prosecutor Ron O'Brien and Sheriff Zach Scott announced that Jamie would be arrested for Courtney's death. Sheriff Scott warned: 'Once you cause a death of someone by providing them with a substance, we're going to come after you' (Decker, 2015, para. 6). Jamie was charged with involuntary manslaughter, corrupting another with drugs and trafficking in heroin.

Drug-induced homicide (DIH) prosecutions such as this one charge people who sell or deliver drugs to another person who subsequently dies of an overdose with manslaughter or homicide (Beletsky, 2019). Facing over twenty years in prison, Jamie plead guilty to involuntary manslaughter (a first-degree felony) and trafficking in heroin (a fifth-degree felony). In January 2017, Courtney was sentenced to four years and eleven months in prison. Prosecutor O'Brien framed the case as an exemplar of the county's future approach to its escalating drug problem: 'Based on the soaring heroin overdose death rate in Franklin County, and as with this case, we will continue to aggressively investigate drug overdose deaths immediately after a body has been discovered in an attempt to identify the source of the drugs' (Franklin County Prosecuting Attorney, 2017, para. 1).

Local news media extensively covered the case, often celebrating the approach as a new tool in the ever-escalating 'overdose crisis'. Of the case, the local Columbus Fox News affiliate proclaimed, 'Investigators say it can actually be pretty challenging to connect the addict who dies to the dealer who gave them the drugs, but tonight for the first time detectives say they have done it – and this is only the beginning' (Williams, 2020, p. 22). Following a critical drug studies approach, I analyse this case to track how DIH prosecutions constitute crime out of unintentional overdose death, make truths about people who use drugs, examine the consequences of these truths, and explore other possible truths under different legal approaches.

Introduction

The US continues to struggle with a now decades-long rise in drug overdose death, often referred to as the 'overdose crisis', with nearly 110,000 people dying of drug overdose in 2022 alone (Kariisa et al., 2023). While efforts to frame drug overdose as a public health problem have gained momentum, the criminal legal system remains deeply involved in responding to overdose death punitively (Carroll et al., 2021). Since the mid 2010s, DIH prosecutions have become a prominent legal response to drug overdose death in the US (Beletsky, 2019). Some criminal legal and public health safety representatives justify this approach by framing people who are charged with DIH as large-scale 'kingpin' drug distributors whose removal from communities will disrupt drug markets, despite all available data suggesting that they are often friends or family of the deceased who engage in small-scale drug trades or sharing (The Action Lab, 2024).

Ohio, a US state hit especially hard by the overdose crisis, is one of the US states that has most aggressively prosecuted DIH cases (DPA, 2017). Drug-induced homicide cases are often covered in local news, circulating moralised discourses that define some drug market actors as 'victims' and others as 'villains' (Carroll et al., 2021; El-Sabawi et al., 2023). These representations provide opportunities for compassion or derision; social belonging or exclusion. The case of *State of Ohio v Jamie N. Maynard* (*Ohio v Maynard*, 2016) played a key role in advancing DIH prosecutions in the state; local criminal legal actors and public safety advocates considered it a 'test case' of the viability of this prosecutorial strategy as tool in the evolving US war on drugs.

Drawing on theories of *ethico-ontological politics* (Seear, 2020) and *necropolitics* (Mbembé, 2003), using this DIH case as an example, this chapter explores the co-construction of life and death in legal practices that constitute 'addicts' and drug 'dealers' in relation to disparate models of addiction, related notions of agency and responsibility, and gendered and racialised framings of the US 'overdose crisis'. It draws on analyses of legal documents, statements about the case made by criminal legal actors, and local media coverage of the case illuminate the politics of life and death in reflected in DIH prosecutions and the broader US war on drugs.

Background

The Origins of Drug-Induced Homicide

While the war on drugs has deep roots in US law's punitive response to drug use, DIH as a prosecutorial strategy emerged to prominence during the 1980s rise in crime and drug use when crack cocaine use was represented in racialised and gendered media coverage, stoking public hysteria (Gorga, 2020; Hansen et al., 2023). It is in this context that the story of Len Bias gained media attention, intensifying public concern about drug use. Bias was a rising basketball star drafted as the second overall pick in the National Basketball Association (NBA) draft by the Boston Celtics in June 1986. Yet he died of heart arrhythmia induced by cocaine use just two days later, leading to public outrage and advocacy for more punitive drug policy. After Bias's alleged drug supplier was acquitted of drug-related charges, public attention focused on calls to prosecute drug suppliers for murder. In 1988, the Anti-Drug Abuse Act was signed into law, establishing a federal mandatory minimum sentence of twenty years and up to life in prison for supplying drugs that result in death (Gorga, 2020). While DIH prosecutions emerged in this context, they were rarely pursued before the mid-2010s rise of the US 'overdose crisis'.

The 'Overdose Crisis' in the United States

In the US, the rise in opioid use and overdose death has upended core beliefs about drug use and addiction (Hansen et al., 2023). The rapid rise in opioid use since the 2000s involved intersecting prescription opioid and illicit opioid use trends. From 2000 to 2012, prescription opioids were the cause of most unintentional drug overdoses; by 2012, prescription opioid-related overdose deaths levelled off and heroin-related overdose deaths rose significantly (National Institute on Drug Abuse (NIDA), 2017). As prescription opioids such as OxyContin were reformulated to prevent their illicit use, people who had become dependent on them often switched to heroin as a cheaper and highly available alternative (Hansen et al., 2023). In this shift, new race and gender patterns in drug use emerged. By the mid 2010s, more women than men entering treatment reported heroin as their 'drug of choice' and more White Americans than Black Americans reported heroin use (Massatti et al., 2014).

These sociodemographic changes disrupted racialised gender norms and incited moral panic; that is, public anxiety fuelled by attention to illicit drug use among relatively socioeconomically privileged people. News media portrayed sympathetic images of suburban White people who use drugs – often women like Courtney and Jamie – in stark contrast to the previously more common representations of criminalised urban Black and brown people who use drugs (Netherland & Hansen, 2016). Presumptively innocent, middle-class White women who use opioids became symbols of 'wasted whiteness', their value in society seemingly squandered, obscuring the harms of opioids among communities of colour (Hansen, 2017). These representations challenged the engrained belief that 'addiction' is a problem of criminality and influenced calls for understanding it as a biological brain disease. Yet 'addiction' is a culturally constructed concept, and the brain disease model of 'addiction' is contested and controversial (Reinarman, 2005). While some advocates argued that a shift from a criminological to a brain disease model would be destigmatising – part of a 'gentler approach' to drug problems focused on treatment and not punishment (Hansen, 2017) – evidence for the brain disease model is limited and its effect on public perceptions and policies toward drug use has been modest (Hall et al., 2015).

Calls for a 'gentler approach' to drug problems did not translate into a clear shift from criminological to biological responses to drug problems, and overdose deaths continued to rise. In 2010, 21,089 individuals died of opioid-related overdose; by 2021, that number rose to 80,411 (NIDA, 2023). As deaths rose, criminal legal actors increasingly touted DIH in response to the overwhelming loss of life, framing it as a way to get 'dealers' off the streets, disrupting drug markets and saving lives. In 2012, 109 DIH cases were prosecuted; by 2018, that number rose to 696 (Beletsky et al., 2022). Media coverage of DIH prosecutions also rose significantly. From 2011 to 2016, the number of DIH cases covered in the news rose 300 per cent (Beletsky & Siegal, 2018). By 2019, twenty-five states had approved specific legislation allowing for prosecutors and judges to implement DIH charges (Beletsky et al., 2022). Notably, when a state does not have a specific DIH statute, such as Ohio, prosecutors often use existing criminal law to treat a unintentional overdose as a homicide or manslaughter (Beletsky & Siegal, 2018). In 2018, the National District Attorneys Association encouraged DIH prosecutions, urging law enforcement and prosecutors to 'treat every overdose death as a homicide and assign homicide detectives to respond to these scenes' (National District Attorneys Association (NDAA), 2018, p. 9).

Drug-Induced Homicide in Ohio

Since 2007, unintentional drug overdoses, largely opioid-related, have been the top cause of injury-related death in the state of Ohio (ODH, 2015). In Franklin County, where *State of Ohio v Jamie N. Maynard* was prosecuted, there was an 83.9 per cent increase in drug overdose deaths from 2017 to 2020 (Ortiz, 2020). Like other states hit hard by the rise in overdose death, Ohio prosecutors have embraced DIH prosecutions. As of 2019, Ohio pursued more DIH charges than all but one other US state, with Franklin County identified as one of the most active counties pursuing DIH prosecutions (Beety et al., 2019). Local media frequently featured these cases. In 2019, Ohio ranked as the number one state in news mentions of DIH prosecutions (Beletsky, 2019). Franklin County Prosecutor Ron O'Brien appeared in local news extolling the number of DIH prosecutions he pursued and the lengthy prison sentences that resulted (Beety et al., 2019).

Amid this prosecutorial zeal, legal scholars asked the Ohio Criminal Sentencing Commission to reassess DIH prosecutions in the state, emphasising that these prosecutions do not deter substance use, make communities less safe by discouraging people from seeking help in the event of an overdose, and result in lengthy periods of incarceration that divert funding from evidence-based responses to overdose (Beety et al., 2019). Soon after, the Ohio Prosecuting Attorneys Association submitted a letter to the commission critiquing the legal scholars' use of data, their description of 'evidence-based' programmes available in the state, and their interpretation of the primary intent of felony charges (i.e., according to association, to protect the public from future crime and to punish the offender) (Tobin, 2019). While the Ohio Criminal Sentencing Commission considered these letters, it rejects the legal scholars' request to formally reassess DIH prosecutions in the state (Ohio Prosecuting Attorneys Association, 2020).

Justifying Drug-Induced Homicide

Drug-induced homicide prosecutions gained prominence as a legal response to drug overdose in the 'emergency imaginary' (Calhoun, 2013) of the US 'overdose crisis'. Emergency imaginaries focus attention on immediate needs, diverting attention from fundamental societal structures and beliefs that underlie a problem. Drawing on this perspective, E. Summerson Carr (2018) urges us to question what lines of analysis and modes of representation are constrained and enlivened by the word 'crisis'. Crisis, Carr (2018) stresses, 'tells us that even if there are no good answers at the ready, something must be done here and now' (p. 163). As overdose deaths rose, prosecutors felt pressure from 'communities in crisis to "just do something" about overdose deaths' (Beletsky & Siegal, 2018, para. 4) and landed on DIH as the legal mechanism with which to respond.

While prosecutors and other criminal legal actors often claim that DIH prosecutions reduce overdose deaths, there is little evidence of this effect (Carroll et al., 2023). Instead, DIH prosecutions undermine 911 Good Samaritan laws that provide legal immunity, although often limited, to bystanders seeking medical assistance in the event of an overdose (Carroll et al., 2023). The most frequently cited reason bystanders state for not calling 911 emergency responders in the event of an overdose is fear of law enforcement involvement (DPA, 2017). However, some prosecutors believe that DIH prosecutions are a necessary social and moral response to overdose death. El-Sabawi, Carroll and Godvin (2023) found that prosecutors from the US Attorney's Office in the state of Connecticut reported the belief that, 'prosecuting overdose deaths to the fullest extent possible constitutes a morally necessary acknowledgment of the value of the life that was lost to overdose' (p. 1385).

Such arguments make a clear distinction between the value of the lives of people who use drugs and people who distribute them, with the former understood as 'victims' and the latter as 'villains', consistent with moralised popular narratives (El-Sabawi et al., 2023). Yet these categories of 'victim' and 'villain' create a false binary that is inconsistent with the lived experiences of people who use and distribute drugs. Ethnographic research shows that there is no clear separation between people who use drugs and those who distribute them; for example, people who use drugs often also distribute when 'hustling' to survive and to help others avoid painful drug withdrawal (DPA, 2017; Preble & Casey, 1976). Moreover, scholars argue that the victim/villain framing infantilises people who use drugs and those who distribute them by obscuring their complex motivations and situated rationalities (El-Sabawi et al., 2023).

Additionally, DIH prosecutions are often considered a 'teaching type of case' because 'prosecutors must explain why one person should be convicted for the willing act of another' (Morrissey et al., 2024, p. 9), troubling notions of agency and responsibility. Drug-induced homicide prosecutions strip the person who died of overdose of agency and responsibility, framing them as sick and their deaths as mournable. In contrast, DIH prosecutions grant agency, and thus responsibility, to the person charged with distribution, rendering them criminal and punishable (Gorga, 2020). By framing agency and responsibility in these ways, prosecutors use the criminal legal system, which largely operates on binary logics, to actively engage in the ontological work of making the meaning of 'addict' and 'dealer' in simplified terms consistent with broader social beliefs related to 'addiction' (Morrissey et al., 2024).

Theoretical Approach

Ethico-ontological Politics of Drug-Induced Homicide

Critical drug studies scholars have stressed the importance of law in the making of worlds and have called for analyses of the *ethico-ontological politics* of legal proceedings, recognising that legal actors make 'addicted realities, subjects and objects' (Seear, 2020, p. 143). This lens is consistent with the social harm approach taken up by critical criminologists, which holds that '*crime has no ontological reality* – there is nothing intrinsic to an event that constitutes it as a "crime". Rather, crimes are necessarily constituted through a range of social and political processes, such as detection and decision-making by police, trial proceedings, conviction, and so on' (Dertadian & Askew, 2024, p. 3).

From this perspective, DIH prosecutions like *State of Ohio v Jamie N. Maynard* can be seen as making an unintentional overdose death into a crime through the decision-making of legal actors. Critical scholarship has also illuminated how legal practices make truths about the often taken-for-granted categories of 'addicts' and drug 'dealers' (Campbell & Herzberg, 2017; Seear, 2020). This occurs, for example, when lawyers enact people who use drugs as 'addicts' who are 'sick', and thus non-agentive and irrational, based on strategic legal imperatives (Seear, 2020, p. 150). Thus, 'addiction' is a concept that is 'made in practice and capable of being made anew' (Seear, 2020, p. 163).

Furthermore, critical drugs studies scholars stress the need for gender analyses in studies of drug use, drug trade and drug policy (Campbell & Herzberg, 2017). Nancy Campbell (2000), for example, shows how gendered discourses on drugs form 'governing mentalities' that uphold gendered and racialised expectations of biosocial reproduction. Women who use drugs are often punished for not conforming to these racialised gender roles. Scholars have also documented the gendered binaries that undergird discourses on drug use – disease versus crime and victim versus agent (Campbell & Herzberg, 2017). Drug-induced homicide prosecutions reflect these racialised gender dynamics that shape the use of biological and criminological models of addiction in making 'addicts' and 'dealers' through their legal proceedings and media coverage of them.

Necropolitics: Social Life and Death

In addition to the ethico-ontological politics of legal proceedings, this chapter draws on *necropolitical* theory (Mbembé, 2003). Political theorist Mbembé (2003) developed this approach to examine expressions of power dictating who may live and who may die under conditions of extreme violence such as war, colonial rule and extermination camps. Mbembé (2003) writes that power 'continuously refers and appeals to exception, emergency, and a fictionalized notion of the enemy. It also labors to produce that same exception, emergency, and fictionalized enemy' (p. 16). Further, Mbembé (2003) describes the creation of 'deathworlds': 'new and unique forms of social existence in which vast populations are subjected to conditions of life conferring upon them the status of living dead' (p. 40). In the state of apparent emergency that had emerged from the US 'overdose crisis', necropolitics provides a productive lens through which to explore questions central to understanding the ontological work of DIH prosecutions in this context: How do legal proceedings frame *certain* people who use drugs as 'addicts' whose deaths are to be mourned and morally redeemed via DIH prosecutions while *other* people who use drugs are framed as criminal 'dealers' to be punished? Who is granted social life and death in these processes?

This chapter explores how the ethico-ontological politics of legal proceedings and necropolitics intersect through the case of *State of Ohio v Jamie N Maynard*. In this case, Courtney, a young White woman from a middle-class background who died of drug overdose, was made into a mournable, 'sick' addict in DIH legal proceedings and in media coverage, reflecting fears of 'wasted whiteness' (Hansen, 2017). Her social life was redeemed in death via Jamie's DIH prosecution. In contrast, Jamie, also a middle-class White woman, was made into a criminal 'dealer', defying gendered and racialised expectations and stoking fear that anyone could become a deviant criminal in the 'overdose crisis'. In the process, Jamie's social life was stripped and made only redeemable through abstinence-based recovery and 'good' motherhood.

Analysis: Making Crime, 'Addicts' and 'Dealers'

Legal Proceedings

Both Courtney Penix and Jamie Maynard struggled with drug use. Jamie had an on-and-off history of using drugs recreationally before she began to habitually use opioid pain medication when working as a casino blackjack dealer. When the pills became too expensive to manage her growing need, she switched to the less expensive but readily available heroin. Courtney, who worked as a nanny in suburban Columbus, had struggled with drug use since high school and had been to rehabilitation programmes twice by the time she met Jamie. After autopsy, Courtney's death was recorded as an unintentional overdose resulting from Xanax and heroin use (Williams, 2020).

By August 2015, Franklin County Prosecutor Ron O'Brien and Sheriff Zach Scott announced the formation of a task force charged with responding to the rise in drug overdose: Heroin Overdose Prevention and Education (HOPE). The task force was charged with investigating overdose deaths as homicides and worked to link Courtney's death to Jamie. That month, Prosecutor O'Brien and Sheriff Scott announced Jamie's arrest for Courtney's death and charged with involuntary manslaughter, corrupting another with drugs and trafficking in heroin. Scott warned: 'Once you cause a death of someone by providing them with a substance, we're going to come after you' (Decker, 2015, para. 6). The case was the county's first to involve an involuntary manslaughter charge associated with drug delivery resulting in death, and one that O'Brien considered an ideal test of the viability of this prosecutorial approach.

Jamie pled guilty to involuntary manslaughter and trafficking in heroin. Since being charged, she had learned that she was pregnant and feared the up to twenty years she could face if convicted. In early 2017, her attorney submitted a sentencing memorandum urging the judge to accept the plea deal. The memorandum contextualised the relationship between Jamie and Courtney and the events of the night of Courtney's death: 'Jamie had known Ms. Penix for a period of time and had become friendly with her. Jamie indicated to detectives that she was trying to help Ms. Penix because she was going through withdrawals and did not want her to be sick' (*State of Ohio v Jamie N. Maynard*, 2017a, p. 3). The memorandum adds that Courtney made the decision to seek out Jamie for heroin and that Courtney's use of Xanax influenced the overdose in combination with the heroin she purchased from Jamie. Further, it notes that 'Jamie was not present when Ms. Penix injected herself with the provided heroin' (*State of Ohio v Jamie N. Maynard*, 2017a, p. 3).

The memorandum also describes Jamie's past struggle with 'addiction' and desire to get 'sober and clean' for the sake of her children:

> Like many other young people, Jamie has suffered from addiction. She has used heroin in the past. Recently, she has entered a suboxone treatment program for the health of the unborn baby and her own health and well-being. This process has set off alarms and has been eye opening for Jamie. She has committed herself to becoming sober and clean. She realizes she must be clean in order to care and provide for her children.
>
> (*State of Ohio v Jamie N. Maynard*, 2017a, p. 2)

While acknowledging the contexts of Courtney's death, the argument for the plea agreement is rooted in Jamie's willingness to take responsibility for Courtney's death, acceptance of her incarceration, and her desire to get 'clean' so that she can be a 'good mother'.

Courtney was sentenced to four years and eleven months in prison. In the judgment entry outlining Jamie's sentence, the state opposed judicial early release and stated the requirement for Jamie to serve consecutive sentences to 'protect the public from future crimes or to punish the offender' (Judgment Entry, 2017, p. 5). Moreover, the court imposed a mandatory five-year period of post-release control and disapproved of Jamie's placement in special programmes that would provide her with education, vocational training and substance use disorder treatment in prison and facilitate her transition back into the community after release.

These legal processes, decisions and documents configured Courtney's death, originally defined as an unintentional overdose, as a homicide. Both women had histories of drug use that could be understood as biological sickness limiting their decision-making capacity. They could also be understood as rational actors engaged in mutual caregiving (e.g., Jamie delivering a drug to Courtney that would prevent painful withdrawal). Yet understandings of both women were reduced through the problematic and simplistic binary of biological disease versus criminal deviance. Jamie was ultimately held to the criminological model: a drug 'dealer' (the criminal villain) – and Courtney the sick, but sympathetic 'addict' (her victim).

Media Coverage

Local news frequently covered the case.[1] Coverage often humanised Courtney, presenting a complex picture of her life. Articles prominently featured Courtney's family's pain in the wake of her death. In one story, the journalist described 'two Courtneys': one Courtney was a former member of the 4-H (a youth development group) and loved her horse named Taco; the other Courtney struggled with drug use since age nineteen, causing pain for her sister and parents (Decker, 2015). According to the story, Courtney was a 'victim of the flood of heroin that has found its way into all corners of Ohio' (Decker, 2015, para. 7).

[1] *The New Yorker* American magazine published an article about the case in 2020 (Williams, 2020). This article depicts the life histories of Jamie and Courtney and critiques DIH as a legal response to overdose death. I focus on local media coverage in this chapter to capture the local media discourses where the case was prosecuted.

In local media, Courtney was mainly framed as a victim, although news reports also noted the pain that her actions caused to her family. In contrast, media often framed Jamie as the drug 'dealer' or 'supplier' whose punishment could both stem the influx of opioids into the area and ease Courtney's family's pain. Media often emphasised Courtney's family's grief and their hope to prevent future overdose deaths via DIH prosecutions. One story featured Courtney's mother's perspective: 'It doesn't forgive the people that are using the drugs but it's so easy to get drugs [. . .] They are so accessible out there and they need to put something in place to stop these people from selling them' (Wicker, 2015, para. 9). Another story focused on Courtney's father's response to DIH charges. It noted that 'he's never heard of drug dealers being held accountable like this in overdose deaths, and hopes efforts will lead detectives straight to the drug suppliers [. . .] he wants Maynard to serve the maximum sentence' (Faugl, 2015, para. 5). Another story underscored Courtney's father's sense that DIH prosecutions indicated law enforcement's recognition of and attempt to respond to his pain: 'They know what we are going through but they don't know what we are going through. So we can't commend them enough' (Wicker, 2015, para. 13). While Courtney's parents were more prominently featured, one article, which included more of Jamie's life history than others, quoted Jamie's defence attorney, who stressed that Jamie 'worked full time. I don't think the depiction of her as a big-time dealer is accurate' (Decker, 2015, para. 29).

Criminal legal representatives were often featured in local news about the case. County Sheriff Scott was frequently quoted touting DIH as a new and promising tool to reduce overdose death. He appeared on one local television story stressing that 'we are going to actually go after the supplier too. The amount of drugs they've been bringing in. We're still going to do everything we've been doing but we're just going to add another tool to our tool belt on this one [DIH prosecutions]' (Wicker, 2015, para. 11). He later added, 'It's an effort that gives hope to parents just like [Courtney's]' (Wicker, 2015, para. 12).

This coverage reinforced the making of Courtney's overdose death – initially described as an unintentional – into a crime, Courtney as a victim, making Jamie a villain in legal proceedings. Images that accompanied stories further made Jamie into a villain by depicting her mugshot (e.g., Futty, 2017) and Courtney into a victim by depicting her seemingly happy, smiling brightly (e.g., Faugl, 2015). Yet public debates about the case in comments sections of social media posts reveal tensions in responses to the 'overdose crisis'. Responding to a Facebook post entitled '27-year-old Jamie Maynard allegedly sold heroin to a woman who overdosed in a Meijer bathroom' on the local NBC affiliate's page (National Broadcasting Company (NBC) 4, 2016), one commenter referred to Jamie's appearance as a young, attractive White woman, defying expectations of drug 'dealers': 'Not just another pretty face. This is what a 2016 drug dealer looks like. The way you look on the outside can never totally cover up a rotten inside. I hope she never sees the outside of a prison wall.' Another commenter asked, 'Where's the responsibility of the addict fit in? Quit doing dope and it'll put drug dealers out of business ... '. Yet another questioned, 'Why don't they prosecute doctor's [*sic*] or pharmacist? Think real hard ... Hmmmm ... Double standard thinking ... '. These responses reflect how DIH prosecutions trouble beliefs about 'addicts' and 'dealers' based on the racialised and gendered 'overdose crisis', both reinforcing and challenging the criminological models of addiction, its source in individual choice, and attributions of responsibility for the problem.

Consequences of Drug-Induced Homicide: Social Life in Death, Social Death in Life

Jamie was released from prison early in April 2019, but her life was permanently changed by the felony involuntary manslaughter conviction. Gorga (2020) urges us to 'Consider what a felony drug charge does to an individual's opportunities in life: amongst other things, it significantly hinders their ability to vote, find employment, find housing, enlist in the armed forces, obtain a passport, or obtain federal student aid [...] [the war on drugs has] effectively rendered entire swaths of our nation second-class citizens' (Gorga, 2020, pp. 171–2). Jamie's life opportunities were indeed limited by the DIH conviction. Ohio revoked Jamie's gaming license, so she could not return to her work at the casino. Instead, she began temporary work as a janitor in a factory, juggling early-morning shifts at the low-wage job while caring for her children and attending regular Alcoholics Anonymous (AA) meetings in her effort toward abstinence-based recovery[2] (Williams, 2020).

Returning to Mbembé's (2003) necropolitical theory, DIH can be viewed as a legal mechanism to create 'death-worlds' that confer social

[2] In the US, AA meeting attendance is often a condition of post-release control; however, whether this was a requirement for Jamie is unclear.

death upon those convicted of DIH by restricting their social and economic life opportunities just as they aim to redeem the social belonging of the deceased 'addict'. As Mbembé (2003) writes, 'death in the present is the mediator of redemption' (p. 39). In the context of long-standing beliefs about 'addiction' in the US rooted in the clean/dirty moral binary, the only reliable way to escape social death for people who use drugs is redemption through abstinence-based recovery. Jamie is faced with *social death in life* as she was treated as a criminal drug dealer in the legal proceedings and in media coverage that largely stripped her of the contexts and complexity of her life. Jamie sought redemption by shifting from criminal drug dealer to sick addict pursuing recovery, against the significant barriers of a felony conviction and the marked publicity of the case. Meanwhile, the framing of Courtney's life and death in legal proceedings and media coverage granted her *social life in death* as the victim of Jamie's crime. Unlike Jamie, Courtney was portrayed through her unique life history, social relationships and complex contexts that shaped her drug use. The framing of her death facilitated her redemption, yet only in her death and at the expense of Jamie's social life.

Critical drug studies scholars such as Fraser and colleagues (2018) have drawn on Judith Butler's (2016) lens of 'grievable lives' to explore the politics of drug-related death, calling us to ask, 'What kind of death warrants grief and memorialisation? What makes a proper life; a life worth preserving or mourning?' (p. 28) and 'What kind of loss is this, and to what ends is the loss of death by overdose turned?' (p. 33). Analysing newspaper coverage of opioid overdose deaths in Australian, Fraser and colleagues (2018) find that

> These deaths are significant not because of the injustice of life denied the deceased, but because of the suffering they cause those left behind, and because they can be mobilised for political change. Here we can ask incidentally to what purposes a death must be turned to become reportable as news (and, in any meaningful sense, publicly grievable).
>
> (pp. 33–4)

The media response to Courtney's death, focused heavily on her grieving family, echoes this finding. In the politics of the 'overdose crisis', Courtney's death was mobilised to support DIH as a new tool to ease familial grief and to fight overdose death. In the process, compassion for Courtney's family was weaponised to support yet another punitive response to the drug problem.

The necropolitics of the case also underscore the racialised, gendered 'overdose crisis'. Notably, Jamie's DIH sentence was significantly shorter than average sentences for DIH convictions for Black, Indigenous, and People of Color (BIPOC). While it is not possible to determine the race of people investigated for DIH based on available research, it is likely that BIPOC will be disproportionately subject to such charges given the history of racism in the US criminal legal system (DPA, 2017). Research does, however, show that BIPOC are more likely to receive longer sentences than White individuals (six years for White Americans; ten years for African Americans; thirteen-and-a-half years for Asian, American Indian and Alaskan Native, and other People of Color) (The Action Lab, 2024). This suggests that DIH prosecutions are likely to deepen racial disparities fuelled by the criminal legal system.

While the *State of Ohio v Jamie N. Maynard* does not reflect the disproportionate impact of DIH prosecutions on BIPOC, it underscores the racialised and gendered moral panic that has emerged from the US 'overdose crisis' that has been described by critical drug studies scholars (Hansen, Netherland & Herzberg, 2023). Jamie's depiction as an attractive White woman who became a criminal drug 'dealer' reflects fear of contagion of crime and addiction from stigmatised Black and brown communities to privileged White ones in the drug panic. Now, even young White women are drug dealers, their whiteness wasted (Hansen, 2017). Moreover, Jamie's framing as a drug 'dealer' in legal proceedings and media accounts troubled racialised cultural beliefs about the 'good mother' as anchor of social order and facilitator of biosocial reproduction, likely influencing her punishment and opportunity for redemption through devoting herself to the abstinence-based recovery and the care of her children.

Conclusion: Making Different Truths in the Wake of Overdose Death

Drug-induced homicide prosecutions reveal how life and death constitute one another in the 'overdose crisis' through ethico-ontological and necropolitical processes. In DIH legal proceedings and the media coverage of them, overdose death is constituted as a crime. In the process, certain people who use drugs are granted redemption – social life – when framed as non-agentic 'addicts' with a sickness, but only after their overdose and death. In contrast, other people who use drugs are made into drug 'dealers' with agency but are subject to punishment as criminals. The stakes for people who use drugs and those who care for them are high.

Drug-induced homicide prosecutions often occur when prosecutors aim to show they are taking action to stem drug overdose death and the circumstance of the death enable them to blame another person for it, making DIH a convenient response. Yet DIH is an ineffective response with harmful ontological effects that intersect with and deepen existing, multilevel stigma that marginalises people who use drugs. Drug-induced homicide prosecutions do nothing to change the broader social and political structures that lead to drug death (e.g., drug criminalisation), but they lead to deeper socioeconomic marginalisation of the prosecuted, may cause more pain for loved ones of both the prosecuted and decent, and deepen social stigma against people who use drugs. As Seear (2020) stresses, there is great potential for legal practices to 'enact, reinforce, and entrench stigma' (p. 159). Legal practices may result in public understandings of people who use drugs in harmful and unrealistic ways, for example, by promoting the belief that all people who share or exchange drugs are villainous 'dealers' and all people who use drugs are 'sick', widening the net for criminal legal system and biomedical control. Perhaps most concerning, legal practices can 'entrench understandings of drug use that ultimately restrict the capacity of publics and governments to think differently about drugs, and the capacity for social change' (Seear, 2020, p. 154).

Can we create policies and practices that make different truths about overdose death and people who use drugs? The social harm approach, with its focus on social harm rather than legally defined notions of harm, has potential to move away from carceral logics and pathologising narratives to promote human flourishing (Dertadian & Askew, 2024). This approach 'asks us to abandon the concept of crime, and by extension the legal institutions that derive from and uphold it, to broaden out our understanding of what is harmful and what kind of harm matters in conversations about drugs' (Dertadian & Askew, 2024, p. 2). From this perspective, 'crime' cannot address large-scale, systemic forms of harm that produce drug overdose death (Dertadian & Askew, 2024). Moreover, this approach recognises that laws are entangled with the social and political processes that produce them. Finally, in broadening our understanding of harm, this approach has potential to make the necropolitics of DIH prosecutions more visible by facilitating broader attention to and critique of which deaths are rendered grievable, and which persons are seen as socially disposable, in the 'overdose crisis'. These perspectives are essential to centre when considering DIH prosecutions that purport to stem the rise in drug overdose death, a claim often fervently made by criminal legal actors, but which do nothing to address the social structures that have fuelled their increase.

What might such an approach look like in practice? Legal scholars recognise that:

> Prosecutors – who exercise tremendous discretion in charging and disposition decisions and also have a powerful voice in their community's public safety conversations – can play a critical role in ensuring that communities adopt harm reduction strategies that have proven more effective than overly punitive approaches such as drug-induced homicide charges.
>
> (Fair & Just Prosecution, 2022, p. 9)

Moreover, research shows that lawyers 'recognize the constitutive power of their practices' (Seear, 2020, p. 172). Given lawyers' power and their recognition of it, Seear (2020) suggests that lawyers adopt an *onto-advocacy* approach that encourages them to 'rethink lawyering in light of the power they hold to constitute objects, subjects and outcomes' (p. 172). An *onto-advocacy* approach requires lawyers to consider the consequences of their legal strategies by recognising how they constitute realities and how these realities present profoundly political and ethical problems. It asks them to consider the consequences of these emergent political and ethical realities, urges them to harness the law's constituted power deliberately to reduce the harms of drug policy, and calls for them to work in meaningful collaboration with drug user organisations and peers who are most impacted by legal interventions.

Legal actors can join existing actions by drug user organisations and others impacted by overdose death, such as efforts among people who use drugs to 'reframe the blame' for drug overdose death by creating 'Do Not Prosecute' (DNP) orders that protect the person that provided them with drugs should they subsequently die of an overdose (Szalavitz, 2018). Prosecutors can also work more ethically with family members of people lost to drug overdose. Such collaboration should aim to reduce the social harms of drug use and drug death by cultivating grief support and harm reduction approaches that address the broader societal structures that harm people who use drugs. Again, these onto-advocacy efforts can join the work of existing groups such as Broken No More (Snodgrass, 2023).

Such an approach combining onto-advocacy and the social harm perspective emphasises the need to question what kind of harm matters and focuses our attention on human flourishing. These shifts have potential to counter the emergency mentality of the 'overdose crisis' that fuels misguided legal interventions like DIH that result in even more suffering for people who use drugs, their loved ones and the communities in which they live.

References

The Action Lab. (2024). *Drug-induced homicide*. The Action Lab. www.healthinjustice.org/drug-induced-homicide.

Beety, V., Beletsky, L., Berman, D., Goulka, J. & Kreit, A. (2019). Open letter to the Ohio Criminal Sentencing Commission. *The Supreme Court of Ohio*. www.supremecourt.ohio.gov/docs/Boards/Sentencing/materials/2019/Dec/openLetter.pdf.

Beletsky, L. (2019). America's favourite antidote: Drug-induced homicide in the age of the overdose crisis. *Utah Law Review*, 2019(4), 833–890.

Beletsky, L., Rock, E. & Kang, S. (2022). Drug-induced panic: Overdose moralities and related harms require a public health response, not more criminalization and incarceration. *Inquest*. https://inquest.org/drug-induced-panic/.

Beletsky, L., & Siegal, Z. A. (2018). Charging 'dealers' with homicide: Explained. *The Appeal*. https://theappeal.org/the-lab/explainers/charging-dealers-with-homicide-explained/.

Butler, J. (2016). *Frames of war: When is life grievable?* Verso Books.

Calhoun, C. (2013). The idea of emergency: Humanitarian action and global (dis) order. In D. Fassin & M. Pandolfi (Eds.), *Contemporary states of emergency: The politics of military and humanitarian interventions* (pp. 29–58). Zone Books.

Campbell, N. D. (2000). *Using women: Gender, drug policy, and social justice*. Routledge.

Campbell, N. D., & Herzberg, D. (2017). Gender and critical drug studies: An introduction and an invitation. *Contemporary Drug Problems*, 44(4), 251–264.

Carr, E. S. (2018). The work of 'crisis' in the 'opioid crisis.' *Journal of Extreme Anthropology*, 3(2), 161–166.

Carroll, J. J., Bevis, L., El-Sabawi, T., Figgatt, M., Dasgupta, N., Beletsky, L., Leiberman, A., Dennis, A. & Davis, C. S. (2023). A discussion of critical errors in a longitudinal study on the deterrent effect of drug-induced homicide laws on opioid-related mortality across 92 counties and the District of Columbia in the United States. *World Medical & Health Policy*, 15(4), 587–612.

Carroll, J. J., Ostrach, B., Wilson, L., Dunlap, J. L., Getty, R. & Bennett, J. (2021). Drug-induced homicide laws may worsen opioid-related harms: An example from rural North Carolina. *International Journal of Drug Policy*, 97(1), 103406.

Decker, T. (2015). Heroin addiction ended in a lonely death. *The Columbus Dispatch*. www.dispatch.com/story/news/crime/2015/09/20/heroin-addiction-ended-in-lonely/23520896007/.

Dertadian, G. C., & Askew, R. (2024). Towards a social harm approach in drug policy. *International Journal of Drug Policy*, 127, 104425.

Drug Policy Alliance (DPA). (2017). *An overdose death is not murder: Why drug-induced homicide laws are counterproductive and inhumane.* Drug Policy Alliance. https://drugpolicy.org/wp-content/uploads/2023/05/Overdose_Death_Is_Not_Murder_Report.pdf.

El-Sabawi, T., Carroll, J. J. & Godvin, M. (2023). Drug-induced homicide laws and false beliefs about drug distributors: Three myths that are leaving prosecutors misinformed. *American Criminal Law Review*, 60(4), 1381–1402.

Fair and Just Prosecution (2022). *Drug-induced homicide prosecutions.* Fair and Just Prosecution. https://fairandjustprosecution.org/wp-content/uploads/2022/07/FJP-Drug-Induced-Homicide-Brief.pdf.

Faugl, E. (2015). Detectives using woman's overdose death to go after suspected dealer. *FOX 28 Columbus.* https://myfox28columbus.com/news/local/detectives-using-woman39s-overdose-death-to-go-after-suspected-dealer-10-09-2015.

Franklin County Prosecuting Attorney. (2017). Madison County woman sentenced to 4 years and 11 months for involuntary manslaughter in connection with heroin drug overdose death for selling drugs that caused the overdose. *Franklin County Prosecuting Attorney.* https://prosecutor.franklincountyohio.gov/press-releases/madison-county-woman-sentenced-to-4-years-and-11-m.

Fraser, S., Farrugia, A. & Dwyer, R. (2018). Grievable lives? Death by opioid overdose in Australian newspaper coverage. *International Journal of Drug Policy*, 59, 28–35.

Futty, J. (2017). Woman sentenced for supplying fatal dose of heroin. *The Columbus Dispatch.* www.dispatch.com/story/news/courts/2017/01/19/woman-sentenced-for-supplying-fatal/22637807007/.

Gorga, J. (2020). Retribution, not solution: Drug-induced homicide in North Carolina. *Campbell Law Review*, 42(1), 161–190.

Hall, W., Carter, A. & Forlini, C. (2015). The brain disease model of addiction: Is it supported by the evidence and has it delivered on its promises? *The Lancet Psychiatry*, 2(1), 105–110.

Hansen, H. (2017). Assisted technologies of social reproduction: Pharmaceutical prosthesis for gender, race, and class in the white opioid 'crisis'. *Contemporary Drug Problems*, 44(4), 321–338.

Hansen, H., Netherland, J. & Herzberg, D. (2023). *Whiteout: How racial capitalism changed the color of opioids in America.* University of California Press.

Kariisa, M., O'Donnell, J., Kumar, S., Mattson, C. L. & Goldberger, B. A. (2023). Illicitly manufactured fentanyl–involved overdose deaths with detected Xylazine: United States, January 2019–June 2022. *Morbidity and Mortality Weekly Report*, 72(26), 721–727.

Massatti, R., Beeghly, C., Hall, O., Kariisa, M. & Potts, L. (2014). *Increasing heroin overdoses in Ohio: Understanding the issue.* Ohio Department of Mental Health and Addiction Services.

Mbembé, A. (2003). Necropolitics. *Public Culture*, 15(1), 11–40.

Morrissey, B., El-Sabawi, T. & Carroll, J. J. (2024). Prosecuting overdose: An exploratory study of prosecutorial motivations for drug-induced homicide prosecutions in North Carolina. *International Journal of Drug Policy*, 125, 104344.

National Broadcasting Company (NBC). (2016). 27-year-old Jamie Maynard allegedly sold heroin to a woman who overdosed in a Meijer bathroom. [Status update]. *Facebook*. www.facebook.com/NBC4Columbus/posts/27-year-old-jamie-maynard-allegedly-sold-heroin-to-a-woman-who-overdosed-in-a-me/10153758870647751/.

National District Attorneys Association (NDAA). (2018). *The opioid epidemic: A state and local prosecutor response*. National District Attorneys Association. https://ndaa.org/wp-content/uploads/NDAA-Opioid-White-Paper.pdf.

National Institute on Drug Abuse (NIDA). (2017). *Overdose death rates*. National District Attorneys Association. www.drugabuse.gov/related-topics/trends-statistics/overdose-death-rates.

National Institute on Drug Abuse (NIDA). (2023). *Drug overdose death rates*. National District Attorneys Association. https://nida.nih.gov/research-topics/trends-statistics/overdose-death-rates.

Netherland, J., & Hansen, H. (2016). The war on drugs that wasn't: Wasted whiteness, 'dirty doctors', and race in media coverage of prescription opioid misuse. *Culture, Medicine, & Psychiatry*, 40, 664–686.

Ohio Department of Health (ODH). (2015). *2015 Ohio drug overdose data: General findings*. www.odh.ohio.gov/-/media/ODH/ASSETS/Files/health/injury-prevention/2015-Overdose-Data/2015-Ohio-Drug-Overdose-Data-Report-FINAL.pdf?la=en.

Ohio Prosecuting Attorney's Association. (2020). *The Ohio Prosecutor – January 2020 newsletter*. www.ohiopa.org/top0120.pdf.

Ortiz, A. M. (2020). *Franklin County overdose fatalities data brief: 2020*. www.nbc4i.com/wp-content/uploads/sites/18/2021/07/Franklin-County-Overdose-Fatalities-Data-Brief.pdf.

Preble, E., & Casey, J. J. (1976). Taking care of business: The heroin user's life on the street. In R. H. Coombs, L. J. Fry & P. G. Lewis (Ed.), *Socialization in drug abuse* (pp. 309–331). Springer.

Reinarman, C. (2005). Addiction as accomplishment: The discursive construction of disease. *Addiction Research & Theory*, 13(4), 307–320.

Seear, K. (2020). *Law, drugs and the making of addiction*. Routledge.

Siegel, Z. A., & Beletsky, L. (2018). Charging 'dealers' with homicide: Explained. *The Appeal*. https://theappeal.org/the-lab/explainers/charging-dealers-with-homicide-explained/.

Snodgrass, S. (2023). Drug-induced homicide: Broken No More position statement. *Broken No More*. https://broken-no-more.org/drug-induced-homicide/.

State of Ohio v Maynard, No. 15CR 1492 (Ohio Ct. Com. Pl. 2016).

State of Ohio v Maynard, No. 15CR 1492 (Ohio Ct. Com. Pl. 16 January 2017a) (Sentencing Memorandum).

State of Ohio v Maynard, No. 15CR 1492 (Ohio Ct. Com. Pl. 19 January 2017b) (Judgment Entry).

Szalavitz, M. (2018). These drug users don't want their dealer prosecuted if they OD. *VICE*. www.vice.com/en/article/kzyk7n/these-drug-users-dont-want-their-dealer-prosecuted-if-they-od.

Tobin, L. (2019). *Ohio Prosecuting Attorneys Association letter to Ohio Criminal sentencing commission*. The Supreme Court of Ohio. www.supremecourt.ohio.gov/docs/Boards/Sentencing/materials/2019/Dec/OPAALetter.pdf.

Wicker, V. (2015). Suspect charged with manslaughter after woman dies from heroin overdose. *10 WBNS*. www.10tv.com/article/news/crime/crime-tracker/suspect-charged-manslaughter-after-woman-dies-heroin-overdose/530-76c99a06-c5ee-405b-a5d1-56026dfdd507.

Williams, P. (2020). The wrong way to fight the opioid crisis: People struggling with addiction who share a lethal dose of drugs are being prosecuted as killers. *The New Yorker*. www.newyorker.com/magazine/2020/02/10/the-wrong-way-to-fight-the-opioid-crisis.

8

'Speaking Legally' to Rule Out Emergency Claims in Swedish Cannabis Cases

MATS EKENDAHL

Two Legal Cases

This chapter concerns emergency claims in cannabis offence cases. The provision in the Swedish criminal code that regulates invocations of emergency (SFS 1962:700, Chapter 24, Section 4, my translation) reads like this:

> An act committed by a person in a state of emergency in cases other than those previously mentioned in this Chapter only constitutes an offence if, in view of the nature of the danger, the damage caused to another, and the other circumstances, it is unjustifiable. Emergency exists when a danger threatens life, health, property or some other important interest that is protected by the legal order.

A juridical commentary to this provision further states: '[t]hat which is protected is to be worth more than that which is harmed and the danger is not to be avoidable through any other means' (Anonymous, 2025, see: https://lagen.nu/1962:700#K24).

Case 1

New Juridical Archive (NJA) (2012): In 2012, Two Danish men (A and B) were accused of smuggling 68 kilograms of cannabis from Denmark to Sweden. A was twenty-one years of age and did not provide information about the context of the crime (although later on in the court proceedings, his defence attorney suggested he had acted under duress). In addition to the charge, A was also accused of smuggling 1.26 grams of cocaine and 4.98 grams of cannabis into Sweden one month previously. B was twenty years of age and claimed to have committed the crime under duress from a person to whom he was indebted. The District Court judged both guilty of severe drug smuggling, and they were sentenced to six (A) and four (B) years imprisonment. The District Court accepted that B acted under duress, but that this was not a 'state of emergency', which would have excused the crime (according to SFS 1962:700, Chapter 24, Section 4). As a result of his young age, he received a suspended sentence of two years.

In the Appeal Court, the prosecutor asked for tougher penalties, whereas A requested a lighter sentence. B asked for an acquittal on the grounds of emergency, or at least a lighter penalty. The Appeal Court concluded, like the District Court, that none of the accused had acted in a state of emergency, and that B's reference to threats could only marginally reduce the time in prison. A's sentence was consolidated (six years), while B's was increased (to five years and six months). Both were convicted of severe drug smuggling.

In the Supreme Court, A and B requested lighter penalties, and the prosecutor objected. After assessment of all relevant factors in the case, the Supreme Court endorsed the Appeal Court's decision regarding the defendants' (primarily B's) references to threats, and agreed that they did not qualify as states of emergency. After new facts about the case emerged, the criminal classification was changed from severe drug smuggling to severe drug offence. The Supreme Court concluded that the sentence should not exceed five years. The sentences were reduced to four years and six months (A) and four years for the slightly younger defendant (B).

Case 2

NJA (2017): In 2017, a Swedish man (C) was accused of cultivating and possessing 83.9 grams of plant material containing cannabis and 125 grams of homemade mixture containing some cannabis (regular drug offence), plus for using these preparations (minor drug offence). C denied the offence by invoking a state of emergency, and argued that these offences should at least be classed as minor. His plead to be excused was based on medical reasons. He was paralysed and in constant pain following an injury. Medication had not eased his pain. As a last resort he tried illegal cannabis, which provided relief. The District Court did not question C's reasons for cultivating and using cannabis and he was excused. The court consisted of one chairperson and three elected laypeople. The chairperson dissented from the majority decision to acquit, maintaining that 'C cannot be considered to have been in a state of emergency'.

In the Appeal Court, the prosecutor rejected the District Court's acquittal and charged C with minor (use) and regular drug offence (cultivation). C claimed innocence, or to be prosecuted for minor drug offence only. The court concluded that C's situation was not acute, and so he could not invoke a state of emergency. It also maintained that the drug offence must be considered regular rather than minor, since the volume of cannabis was 'not insignificant' and sophistically 'produced in a tent', even though 'partly low on THC-levels'. The court ruled in favour of the prosecutor and sentenced C to probation and daily fines (90 days × €13). One elected layperson disagreed and supported the District Court's ruling.

C appealed to the Supreme Court, asking to be found innocent or to at least be charged with a minor drug offence on the first count of cultivating and possessing cannabis, and to be acquitted on the second count of cannabis use. The Attorney General disagreed and maintained that the charge still amounted to regular drug offence, but that the charge for using should be considered superseded if C was sentenced on the first count. He was convicted for minor drug offence and sentenced with daily fines (40 days × €13).

Background

A common-sense notion posits that the law works to protect the rights of all citizens. Another widespread idea is that legal processes are concerned with the establishment of truths about events, acts and people, so that fair verdicts can be reached. Being based on norms, values and interests that have been passed down over time and have created a common awareness of justice in society, 'law on the books' is expected to wash away jurists' subjective preferences and concerns from rulings. Law, thus, is supposedly a crucial, predictable and lasting aspect of democratic societies. As Bruno Latour (2010, p. 276) writes in his ethnography of a French court: 'One should be able to say of law that it is there at birth. It precedes us and survives us. We live in its house. Yet it says nothing, informs us of nothing; we have to do all the work.'

In this section, Latour emphasises that law is never self-explicatory, natural, agentic or informative in its own right. Instead, we need to study the *practice* of law to uncover its functions and effects. Such endeavours can shed light on 'the process by which humble practices of interaction metamorphose into objective truth', and can prevent this from remaining 'a trade secret known only by initiates' (Latour, 2010, p. 196). Following previous attempts to open the black box of law (Latour, 2010; McGee, 2015a, Seear, 2020; Valverde & Weaver, 2015), this chapter aims to unpack Swedish case law related to cannabis offences in Sweden.

Cannabis is globally the most widely used illegal drug, and its harmfulness is highly contested (Månsson, 2017; Wheeldon & Heidt, 2023). In Sweden, drug policy and law does not differentiate between so-called soft and hard drugs, which warrants experiences of stigmatisation and marginalisation among cannabis users (Tham, 2021). Still, it is well known that legal proceedings include assessments of evidence, actors and deeds that can be either lenient or harsh, and that these produce specific 'truths' relied on within rulings. I have chosen here to pinpoint two cannabis offence cases that should bring to the fore either leniency or harshness, namely those where the defendants argued that their offence should be excused because they acted under a 'state of emergency'.

I will interpret assessments and verdicts with the help of Latour's argument that truths in the law are not discovered but *made up* through the assemblages of people, beliefs, legislations, precedent cases, symbols, and so on that conjure up law 'in action'; thus the act of 'speaking legally' (Latour, 2010, p. ix). Drawing also on Ben Anderson and colleagues' work on 'slow emergencies', I will discuss the cases as illustrations of two opposing ways in which a state of emergency can be invoked: on behalf of the prosecution as a 'state of exception' (Adey et al., 2015, p. 4), and on behalf of the defence as a 'spark of hope' (Anderson, 2017, pp. 474–5).

Theoretical Approach

In a discussion of Latour's work, Levi and Valverde (2008) encourages us to look beyond the dichotomy between 'law on the books' and 'law in action' and instead treat law as: 'a network of people and of things in which legality is [. . .] a way in which the world is assembled, an attribute that is attached to events, people, documents, and other objects when they become part of the decision-making process' (Levi & Valverde, 2008, p. 806). Latour thus analyses the law similarly as he would society in general, not as a separate ontological domain or a 'structure', but a process composed of 'action, actors, communication, imitation and translation, networks, knowledge flows' (Levi & Valverde, 2008, p. 807). Starting out from actor network theory (ANT), Latour's interest is in the practice of law, that is on the 'immense difference, very easy to grasp, between speaking *about* law and speaking *legally*' (Latour, 2010, p. ix; original emphasis). This means to target the situated and material practice of law that ties together phenomena (Latour, 2010, p. x) and to identify instances when law not only enunciates truth through 'rational application of rules and principles to fact situations' (Matthews & Veitch, 2016, p. 351) but produces it through legal reasoning. The content of the law is of minor interest, and more so is the process of making the law and the effects that legal truth claims have for people (Matthews & Veitch, 2016).

Inspired by calls to 'slow down' and 'peer in' (McGee, 2015b, p. 62), this study concerns the 'passage of law' (Latour, 2010, p. 88) as it enfolds in two legal cases. I analyse textual reports of court proceedings (Seear, 2020) and ask what 'speaking legally' encompasses in the embodied practice of Swedish drug offences case law. To do this, the point of departure will be McGee's discussion on legal devices, which he defines as 'assemblages of mostly non-legal beings deployed for a legal purpose, namely to give consistency and objectivity, as well as direction, to a specific legal trajectory' (McGee, 2015b, p. 64). The device, which can be anything (e.g., an actor, object or circumstance) introduced into legal proceedings with a specific intention, 'formats and translates' entities and agents into legally valid phenomena that legitimise rulings.

As noted by McGee (2015b, p. 67), when reality is simplified in legal proceedings and placed in either the 'fact' box or the 'law' box '[c]ertain enunciative positions are emphasised and elaborated or exaggerated, others ignored, played down or silenced altogether'. This stabilisation of 'collectives of humans and non-humans' McGee (2015a, p. 3), from messy and complex to firm and demarcated, is necessary for verdicts. In referencing cases that are handled by administrative courts, Latour emphasises the dissimilarity between what real people experience and how this is represented in the court: 'There is quite a distance between groaning, growling or protest and the writing of a claim' (Latour, 2010, p. 72). By reading the two cannabis cases with legal devices in mind, both apparently non-legal (e.g., character traits, situational analyses, assumptions about drugs) and apparently legal (e.g., precedent cases, technical evidence, law on the books), my analysis uncovers how emergency claims are dealt with in Swedish cannabis case law.

In Anderson and colleagues' critical scrutiny of emergency as a social phenomenon, it is not considered an objectively identifiable event with fixed characteristics, but rather a 'descriptor, technique and legal-political device' (Anderson, 2017, p. 463) to apprehend and govern space, time and people. They argue (Grove et al., 2022, p. 6): 'Alongside crisis, disaster, and catastrophe, emergency is one of the few genres we have for making sense of situations which, in some way, threaten to open up different, usually unwanted futures, and therefore demand action to bring them to an end.' A government's declaration of emergency depicts the difference between an exceptional situation and a state of normality that can and should be returned to through extreme measures (Anderson, 2017, p. 464). This warrants potential debate concerning what counts as emergency and normality, what is problematic in a given society, whose interests are worth protecting, and when and what measures should be taken in order to return to normality. With examples drawn from the structural and racialised violence highlighted by the US 'BlackLivesMatter' movement (Anderson, 2017), the devastating effects of European colonialism on indigenous peoples (Anderson et al., 2020) and the preservation of racially uneven life chances through COVID-19 public health interventions (Grove et al., 2022), the authors show that governmental responses to emergency claims depend on who makes them (Anderson, et al., 2020, p. 633).

Invocations of emergency can be sparks of hope for people trying to get their 'slow', everyday suffering recognised, but are more often rejected as invalid descriptors of the acute states of exception that deserve special attention from governments. This difference between slow and acute emergencies (Anderson et al., 2020) pinpoints the significance of time in emergencies and the exceptional responses they warrant. Anderson (2015, p. 20) explains the 'interval' as 'the space-time of an event's becoming; or the separating of and separation between normal reality and some kind of changed reality'. The practice of state governance through emergencies – which is ill-suited to deal with 'slow emergencies' – rests on the idea that the 'interval' can be responded to in a timely way so that the problematic situation can be stifled or improved 'before harm, damage or loss becomes irreversible' (Anderson, 2015, p. 20).

Method and Data

The research involved a survey of cannabis cases in order to better understand how Swedish prohibitionist drug policy affects drug sentencing, including penalties for the possession of minor quantities of cannabis, and how courts considered mitigating circumstances. Starting out from the documented mismatch between what marginalised people perceive as desperate situations and what the state authorises as 'real' emergencies, I searched an archive of Swedish legal documents open for public view (see: https://lagen.nu) for cases that included both 'cannabis' and 'emergency' (*nöd* in Swedish). This resulted in six hits. I chose two of them for further analysis since they contained lengthy reasoning on emergencies. The study was approved by the Swedish Ethical Review Authority (Dnr 2022–05462–02). The analysis was conducted through a content-based coding of the two cases in Nvivo, yielding codes such as: 'how is cannabis described'; 'how is emergency defined'; 'who are the defendants'; 'assessments and facts', and so forth. I then read the relevant codes from the perspective of what 'speaking legally' can entail (regarding truth claims, legal devices and the space-time of events, i.e., the interval). The analysis was guided by the following questions: How are the realities of the defendants transformed so that they point towards certain verdicts? What entities are approached as legal devices that should direct legal trajectories? How is the interval described to rule out emergency claims?

The material consists of written judgments only. The analysis does not specifically consider differences in assessments between the three court instances (there were more similarities than differences between the courts' rulings) but rather takes a comprehensive look at the legal proceedings. The results are presented under two main themes that illustrate how emergency claims were dealt with and rejected in cannabis offence cases. Quotes have been translated by me with the ambition to stay close to the original wording.

Distinguishing Some Legal Devices to Produce 'Truth'

All events that find their way into courts are being subject to profound transformations when real people's acts are dissected, structured and juxtaposed with the law and made ripe for legal assessment and verdict (McGee, 2015b, p. 62).

The realities of the two drugs smugglers, A and B (NJA, 2012), are condensed into a series of indices that determine their roles in the crime. There are several passages in the case that inform about when and where the two defendants met up (indicating that the crime was preconceived rather than spontaneous due to threats), who were in possession of a cell phone (indicating collaboration), and with whom they interacted before and during the crime (indicating the existence of threats). While the settling of who did what to whom – that is, identifying and presenting evidence – is standard in legal proceedings, the ambition to disentangle the relevant from the irrelevant also transforms the lives of the two young drug smugglers into 'facts' about events. The web of people, settings and deeds entailed in the crime is condensed into circumstances that point towards the two men having acted together in a deliberate manner. This is exemplified by the District Court, where certain aspects of the situation, through assessments, are made into legal devices that influence the ruling. For example, it is concluded that B's lack of knowledge regarding who was to pick up the suitcase with cannabis 'does not appear credible at all', amounting to 'an improbable situation', since it is 'more or less obvious that the person in charge would provide clear information' (NJA, 2012, District Court's assessment). This settles a 'truth' about the two defendants' joint and equal responsibility for the crime.

Needless to say, drug smuggling is a serious crime in most jurisdictions, but it should be noted that there is room in the legal proceedings to highlight certain issues and ignore others. This means, for instance, that it would have been possible for the court to acknowledge that specifying a threatening person (which B did) could have been perceived as rather remarkable considering the risk of retribution it placed him in. The information presented to the court, namely that only one of the two defendants (B, not A) chose to name the threatening person, could also have been taken as evidence that the person did coerce the two men into drug smuggling, but that only one of the defendants dared to mention the threat. This incidence, however, is not transformed into a legal device that informs assessments. It is 'silenced altogether' (McGee, 2015b, p. 67) in favour of other issues, such as the defendants' ages during the crime, their collaboration and what sentences cannabis smuggling affords.

There are many 'non-legal beings' employed as legal devices to warrant a conviction, and they substantiate that the ruling is meticulous, impartial and hesitant (Latour, 2010). The actors and events are laid out in a pattern that can only indicate conviction. In addition to legal devices such as technical evidence and drug analyses, the courts include in their assessments non-legal beings in the form of the defendants' character traits and other circumstances that settle a specific (somewhat reduced) sentence. Their motivation to get involved in the drugs trade is bolstered by citing histories of unemployment and cannabis use. Moreover, their lack of cunningness as criminals is deduced from the fact that they are considered 'minor and easily replaceable actor(s) in a greater scheme' who were not supposed to 'obtain any share of the drug smuggling profit' (NJA, 2012, District Court's assessment). The importance of their acts is also lessened by pointing to a lack of 'sophistication' (NJA, 2012, Supreme Court, point 34) in being bottom-level 'couriers' (NJA, 2012, Supreme Court, point 12).

As regards the threat referenced by the defendants, the courts are less lenient and do not include it as a legal device. In a concluding remark, the Supreme Court argues that they 'might have been in a stressful situation', but that this does not warrant non-culpability according to the law, and that it is to be expected in criminal environments.

> It rather concerns a predicament of a kind probably not uncommon during participation in the handling and smuggling of large amounts of narcotic drugs, and which normally should not – and not in this case either – influence the assessment of the deed.
>
> (NJA, 2012, Supreme Court, point 32)

This shows how the courts assess and add some non-legal beings but not others. The making of drug realities, that is, the transformation of some eventualities into legal devices that affect rulings, is evident in the case about medical cannabis use as well (NJA, 2017).

Previous research discusses cannabis as a polysemic sign that can be anything from a dangerous illegal drug of abuse to a harmless plant with great medical potential (see, e.g., Månsson, 2017; Wheeldon & Heidt, 2023). The court proceedings in C's case show how this complexity is handled and ultimately resisted. There are, for instance, references to levels of tetrahydrocannabinol (THC; the primary psychoactive agent in cannabis) detected through drugs analyses, which are assumed to determine the potency and dangerousness of the seized cannabis. It is stated that the cannabis C cultivated 'was low on THC and should be considered of limited interest to those who want to get intoxicated' (NJA, 2017, Supreme Court, point 21). While this reasoning acknowledges the existence of cannabis with differing potency, it also stabilises that substances' intoxicating properties and abuse potential are key to determining the severity of the crime (see also NJA, 2012, Supreme Court, point 23). The multitude of meanings that can be assigned to cannabis is downplayed through the legislator's focus on potency, harm and seizures of a substance that according to Swedish law is always illegal.

In addition to discussing THC levels that can affect penalties, C's case shows how the defendant tries to make his medical reasons for cannabis use into a legal device that will either excuse his behaviour or reduce the punishment (NJA, 2017). This, however, is challenged by the prosecutors and the courts. The transformation of cannabis from a personal painkiller in C's world into a generic 'drug of abuse' fit for ruling can be tracked by explicating some references to the substance in the case. In the District Court, where C was acquitted, there is mention of 'cannabis' (defendant) and 'narcotics' (prosecutor). The Appeal Court, in turn, cites 'plant materials containing cannabis' (summary of defendant's argument) but also the more generic 'narcotics' (summary of the court's assessment).

In the Supreme Court, finally, such differences in labelling are displaced in favour of wordings such as 'C has produced narcotics intended for abuse' (NJA, 2017, Supreme Court, point 5), and 'abuse designates consumption that is not supported by a duly administered prescription' (point 6). Through establishing medical purposes as unworthy of legal consideration, the Supreme Court subsumes cannabis cultivation, possession and use under one demarcated legal device, 'criminal intent', that must influence the verdict. In a concluding remark, the court argues that 'it does not matter if C himself would classify the planned consumption as abuse', from which follows that C 'had a criminal intent regarding his production of narcotics intended for abuse' (point 18). This shows how the legal proceedings produce 'truths' about cannabis, its use and users that are rejected by the defendant, but also by elected laypeople in the District Court and the Appeal Court. The law thus stabilises cannabis as a 'drug of abuse'.

Circumscribing the Interval to Rule Out 'Slow Emergencies'

The District Court's acquittal of C in the medical cannabis case (NJA, 2017), which was later refuted by the higher courts, stated in line with the defence that the defendant's production of cannabis was his only means to 'lead a decent life'. It claimed that C tried everything the healthcare system could offer, and that he was in a state of emergency which made his acts legal. There is no mention of emergencies as having to be 'acute', and not of the short interval for taking legitimate action that higher courts refer to. This notion is, however, picked up by the chairperson of the District Court, who dissented from the ruling. She proclaimed that:

> Emergency is at hand according to 24 chap. 4 § BrB when a danger threatens life, health, property or any other important interest protected by the legal order. I have no reason to doubt what C has disclosed about his situation and his suffering. The emergency provision shall however be deployed restrictively and it is necessary for the situation to appear acute for C to be considered being in a state of emergency. C had the opportunity and did also consult healthcare for help with his pain. The fact that the medicines healthcare had to offer gave C negative side effects or are very

> expensive is obviously difficult for him, but it does not warrant that C should be perceived as having been in a state of emergency.
>
> (NJA, 2017, District Court, addendum)

This quote shows how the judge differs between what Latour (2010) describes as 'law in action' (law as practice or pragmatism) and 'law on the books' (law as theory or doctrine). At this stage of the legal proceedings, C's precarious situation, suffering and use of medicines with damaging side effects and high costs are considered realistic ('no reason to doubt') but irrelevant indicators of emergency, since the emergency provision 'shall be deployed restrictively' and 'it is necessary for the situation to appear acute'. This reasoning uses truth claims to regulate what counts as emergency, ruling out C's long-time pain and suffering, that is, the kind of slow emergency that is common among marginalised users of illegal drugs.

Moreover, the statement is later cited in the Appeal Court ('as *made clear* by the dissenting meaning in the District Court', NJA, 2017; emphasis added), which introduces a precedent case about another type of crime to vindicate that C was not in a state of emergency. This case concerns environmental activists who tried to prevent potential health risks by obstructing future storage of nuclear waste and who invoked a state of emergency as excuse. They were found guilty since nuclear waste storage, according to the court's ruling, relies on the government's 'principal acceptance of included accident risks' (NJA, 1982, p. 621), and that these risks are not acute threats to the defendants' lives. By drawing on a precedent case, and thereby juxtaposing two different crimes (cannabis cultivation and obstruction of industrial work), the Appeal Court provides legal 'evidence' that emergencies cannot be slow and pending. They must be acute and afford a short interval in which action is taken to avoid threatening dangers.

The same verdict is later reached by the Supreme Court, although its reasoning is more complex and references yet another precedent case, plus some clarification of the legislator's interests. The court concludes that a state of emergency can in fact be present when the threat is 'impending' or 'relatively impending' (NJA, 2017, point 10) by citing a precedent case in which a farmer killed a wolf that was about to attack live stock. Since the wolf's behaviour, however, was considered 'an *uncertain* future threat' (point 10; emphasis added), the farmer had not acted in a state of emergency and was convicted for a severe hunting offence.

In addition to this more flexible view on the temporality of emergencies – stretching the space-time of the event's becoming (Anderson, 2015, p. 20) by stating that the risk was 'relatively impending' – the Supreme Court concludes that 'being free from pain is such an interest that can suggest deployment of the emergency provision' (point 11). Knowing the court's final verdict (C was convicted), this reasoning illustrates how the law attempts to appear impartial, or as Latour (2010, p. 273) says: 'legal fiction calms and reassures'. It increases the legitimacy of the passage of law by demonstrating meticulousness and hesitancy, while at the same time claiming to be unable to excuse C's acts (Latour, 2010). In the next quote, the Supreme Court emphasises its willingness to increase the length of the interval when action should be taken, but anyhow dismisses C's claims as irrelevant due to the nature of his acts:

> The circumstance that C's condition is enduring and that the appointed act, to cultivate cannabis, could only in the long run contribute to diminish the infringement of interest, does not prevent it from being done in a state of emergency. It is another thing that the character of the emergency situation – considering that a penalised act can seldom be a justifiable means to handle a more enduring problem – can influence the assessment of whether the act is allowed according to some section of the law. The act is not allowed according to the emergency provision.
>
> (NJA, 2017, Supreme Court, point 12)

The court's ruling is based on the following logic: a crime can be excused if it is committed in an emergency, enduring pain can be an emergency, but a penalised act can seldom be excused if it is committed as a response to an enduring problem. It arrives at the notion that medical cannabis cultivation and use are inexcusable by linking C's case with a 'corpus of precedents' that determines the ruling in the individual case (Latour 2010, p. 257), but also by contrasting the interest in being free from pain with society's interest in controlling narcotics. The legislator has also, in this way, provided a way in which the interest of being free from pain can be accommodated and instituted an order for controlled distribution of narcotics for medical use. An act which includes a narcotics offence and is conducted to relieve pain is thereby only defensible in strictly exceptional cases, for example, in an acute situation when instant supply of regular healthcare is lacking (NJA, 2017, Supreme Court, point 15).

While acknowledging C's 'appropriate interest in avoiding pain' (point 16), the Supreme Court concludes that it is 'impossible to take into consideration that his act according to a more general assessment can be regarded as in some way excusable' (point 19). The court gives and takes. This example of 'speaking legally' illustrates how both hard facts and underlying principles are made up during legal proceedings. As McGee explains:

> The principle inscribed in the judgment will emerge only gradually from the shudders and hesitations of legal reason; the legal facts become so only through an exhausting process of qualification and a cascade of transformations set in motion by the resonance among allegations, proofs, rhetorical acumen, ingenious readings of texts, a curious detachment (libido judicandi) and a litany of semiotic objects that the case engenders and puts into circulation.
>
> (McGee, 2015a, p. 3)

The reference to 'narcotics offence' is important because it connects C's reasonable acts on the individual level with the maintenance of strict drug control on the societal level. Or as Latour puts it when discussing how a sheet of paper can be linked to a legal machinery that authenticates ownership: 'The link is tiny yet total; the grip is infinitely small yet capable of linking up with all the rest' (Latour, 2010, p. 265). Here, evidence of a narcotics offence warrants a legal machinery that deploys the emergency provision restrictively, disregards people's motives for breaking the law and reflects the stance of political authorities that valorise harsh rather than lenient interpretations of drug prohibition.

I conclude this analysis with a glance at the drug smuggling case (NJA, 2012), from the perspective of the time-space of the event's becoming. The three courts do not dwell on if the two defendants were or were not under threat and acted in states of emergency. Their claims appear to have been easily dismissed, and the legal assessments concern what sentences are correct considering their crimes and ages. The District Court emphasises that 'the emergency provision is meant to be deployed in strictly exceptional cases', that the danger 'must be relatively acute' and that the legal assessment shall consider 'if options to act differently were available'. This sets the stage for a sternly circumscribed interval and ignorance of the defendants' interest in avoiding imminent violence. Acknowledging but also downplaying this threat, the District Court concludes that the defendant could have handled it differently:

> B has been threatened on the 2nd of September, i.e., the day before he smuggled the narcotics to Sweden. B had thus plenty of time to contact the police in diverse conceivable ways. Even if the threatening person held

> a gun, this person did not point it towards B and no explicit threats were made to seriously injure or kill B or his family. These circumstances entail that B cannot be considered having been in a state of emergency and he had no reason to perceive it like that either. Freedom of responsibility shall thereby not ensue.
>
> (NJA, 2012, District Court's assessment)

This conclusion was never questioned by the higher courts. While drawing on the emergency provision's demand for acuteness (no direct gunpoint) and the potential of other acts than the chosen to avoid danger (contact police), the court circumscribes the interval (Anderson, 2015, p. 20) and dismisses the defendant's experience of being threatened to life. It is assumed that since several hours passed between the threat and the crime, B should have named the threatening person to the authorities. It is also assumed that being commanded to smuggle a large amount of cannabis by a person involved in the illegal drugs trade who held a gun in their hand does not qualify as an emergency. This exemplifies, again, how B's beliefs regarding what harm the threatening person was capable of doing are displaced in favour of available evidence of what happened. The court disregards the 'slow emergency' of being a 'minor and easily replaceable actor in a greater scheme' (NJA, 2012, p. 535). In this way, 'speaking legally' entails assessing the relevance of the emergency provision with reference to *direct* gunpoint, thus neglecting powerlessness, drug debts, subtle threats and violence towards police informers.

Discussion

The defendants' emergency claims in these cannabis cases were ignored by the courts through reproducing truths about drugs of abuse and of people who smuggle or use them, and through circumscribing the space-time of events that can excuse exceptional measures, or through what McGee (2015, p. 1) terms: 'constructive practices that shape legal truths'. The data show how the courts *made up* drug realities that rest on assertions about why people smuggle drugs, the skill levels of criminals, the trustworthiness of different actors, the quantifiable dangers of drugs, and the qualitative difference between illegal drugs and medicines. Since courts are supposed to enact governmental drug policy, the prohibitionist line of reasoning evident in these cases is expected. Still, my analysis shows that 'speaking legally' can and does entail something more than 'law on the books', which also displays the capacity of law to strive for change. A lesson learned is that courts, through their ability to pick and choose what legal devices to consider, have an unexploited potential to spur bottom-up drug policy reform. From my perspective, the cases studied here showcase that it would have been possible for the courts to reach wholly different verdicts, which would have had a major impact on the 'corpus of precedents' that absorbs and guides similar cases in the future (Latour 2010, p. 257).

It should be noted that the temporal intervals discussed in the two cases were dissimilar but that 'speaking legally' refined both into demarcated situations in which certain rational actions were proscribed. The precarious lives of the drug smugglers were boiled down to a few hours when they had the chance to inform authorities about the threats (NJA, 2012). Their claims were therefore rejected. The medical cannabis case involved months of suffering and the ambition to ease pain in the long run (NJA, 2017). The defendant's emergency was rejected because he never lacked physical access to regular healthcare. This was how 'slow emergencies' were effectively ruled out.

Looking back at the previously mentioned addendum to the emergency provision in Swedish law, it can be concluded that saving the defendants' interests was not deemed by the courts as outweighing the harm their exceptional measures caused. It can be concluded that avoiding repercussions from organised crime and avoiding persistent pain were worth less than reinforcing the legislator's tough stance towards drugs. While one ruling challenged this notion (the District Court in C's case), this was accomplished by laypeople and not a judge, which illustrates a potential conflict between the common awareness of justice and what 'speaking legally' involves in practice. Even if C's case attracted some media coverage, the public interest in the verdicts did not in any detectable way bend the Supreme Court towards acquittal. This, together with the same court's acknowledgement (point 19) that C's acts 'according to a more general assessment can be regarded as in some way excusable', shows how the law declares that its assessments, interpretations and weighing of interests are not flexible. It reaches a verdict, *as if* it was predetermined.

The emergency claims in the cannabis smuggling case received less attention, in the media as well as in the court proceedings. It is as if the defendants' pleads could be rejected as futile attempts to reduce their punishments. Still, it might be interesting to think through why the two types of emergency claims were responded to differently by the courts. Was it about the defendants' credibility, the perceived magnitude of their crimes or other factors that might influence how jurors define justice. While the two cases were clearly dissimilar, it appears impossible to rule out some circumstances from consideration. In the legal proceedings, A and B were depicted as deviant villains already by the time of the crime (contacts with drug sellers, use of cannabis, drug debts, unemployment, etc.), while C was presented as victim of a difficult situation (pain, helplessness, cannabis naïveté, parenting difficulties, etc.). All defendants were finally convicted, but my analysis highlights that some people's 'slow emergencies' are considered more pressing, and also more eligible than others to be transformed into legal devices that affect rulings.

Recognising Lauren Berlant's work on 'slow death' (2011), Anderson with colleagues conceptualise the everyday and lasting suffering people are exposed to through unemployment, poverty, stigma and violence as 'slow emergencies' that lack a distinct separation from normality (Anderson et al., 2020, p. 622), 'because the emergency is the everyday and the everyday is an emergency' (Anderson, 2017, p. 475). They show that the endemic problems of the poor are less prone to trigger political action in liberal democracies than the spatially and temporally demarcated problems of those who are affluent and included in society.

This is crucial to consider in times when harsher penalties and more policing have become hegemonic in criminal law related to illegal drugs. Not least in Sweden, today, the government takes measures to fight gang-related violence with deterrence and control, rather than with prevention and care (SOU, 2023). The 'slow emergencies' of young men who are forced or lured into organised crime are displaced, making room for the political idea that minors are responsible agents who should be locked up (cf., Khoshnood, 2019; Hermansson, 2022). While there appears to be no quick fix to the policy dilemma of children who commit turf war murders, scholarly work on 'slow emergencies' reminds us to acknowledge whose emergencies count in society and what qualifies as a state of exception. We also need to question the idea, popularised in the media (Ekendahl et al., 2023) that drugs in their own right contribute to violence, marginalisation and ruined lives, that they are and will always be problematic and therefore prohibited.

In this chapter I have tried to show that cannabis offence cases include the appointment of non-legal beings such as the defendants' living conditions, motivations and skills into court rulings. This illustrates that 'law on the books' is completely different than 'speaking legally' (Latour, 2010, p. ix) when assessing emergency claims. If politicians are reluctant to think nuancedly and anew when it comes to what drugs 'are' and how they should be controlled, maybe it is time for our courts to deploy the leeway in assessments this study pinpoints and use it to give the benefit of the doubt?

References

Adey, P., Anderson, B. & Graham, S. (2015). Introduction: Governing emergencies – Beyond exceptionality. *Theory, Culture & Society*, 32(2), 3–17.

Anderson, B. (2016). Governing emergencies: The politics of delay and the logic of response. *Transactions of the Institute of British Geographers*, 41(1), 14–26.

Anderson, B. (2017). Emergency futures: Exception, urgency, interval, hope. *The Sociological Review*, 65(3), 463–77.

Anderson, B., Grove, K., Rickards, L. & Kearnes, M. (2020). Slow emergencies: Temporality and the racialized biopolitics of emergency governance. *Progress in Human Geography*, 44(4), 621–39.

Anonymous (2025). Commentary to the Swedish Criminal Code, Chapter 24, Section 4. https://lagen.nu/1962:700#K24.

Berlant, L. (2011). *Cruel optimism*. Duke University Press.

Ekendahl, M., Månsson, J. & Karlsson, P. (2023). Media constructions of an illegal drug: The link between cannabis and organized crime in Swedish newspapers. *Drugs: Education, Prevention and Policy*, 31(3), 300–309.

Grove, K., Rickards, L., Anderson, B. & Kearnes, M. (2022). The uneven distribution of futurity: Slow emergencies and the event of COVID-19. *Geographical Research*, 60(1), 6–17.

Hermansson, K. (2022). The symbolic potential of security: On collective emotions in Swedish criminal policy discourse. *Emotions and Society*, 4(3), 395–410.

Khoshnood, A. (2019). Holding Sweden hostage: Firearm-related violence. *Forensic Sciences Research*, 4(1), 88–93.

Latour, B. (2010). *The making of law: An ethnography of the Conseil d'État*. Polity Press.

Levi, R., & Valverde, M. (2008). Studying law by association: Bruno Latour goes to the Conseil d'État. *Law & Social Inquiry*, 33(3), 805–25.

Månsson, J. (2017). *Cannabis discourses in contemporary Sweden: Continuity and change* (Doctoral dissertation). Stockholm University.

Matthews, D., & Veitch, S. (2016). The limits of critique and the forces of law. *Law Critique*, 27, 349–61.

McGee, K. (2015a). Introduction. In K. McGee (Ed.), *Latour and the passage of law* (pp. 1–16). Edinburgh University Press.

McGee, K. (2015b). On devices and logics of legal sense: Toward socio-technical legal analysis. In K. McGee (Ed.), *Latour and the passage of law* (pp. 61–92). Edinburgh University Press.

New Juridical Archive (1982). *I syfte att skapa politisk opinion mot tilltänkt förvaring i urberget av radioaktivt avfall*, p. 621. https://lagen.nu/dom/nja/1982s621.

New Juridical Archive (2012). *Brottsrubricering och straffvärdebedömning avseende en narkotikatransport från Danmark till Sverige (drygt 67 kg cannabis)*, p. 535. https://lagen.nu/dom/nja/2012s535.

New Juridical Archive (2017). *Att cannabis har odlats i smärtlindringssyfte har inte medfört ansvarsfrihet med stöd av bestämmelsen om nöd i 24 kap. 4 § BrB. Även fråga om rubricering och påföljd, p. 872.* https://lagen.nu/dom/nja/2017s872.

Seear, K. (2020). *Law, drugs and the making of addiction: Just habits.* Routledge.

SFS 1962:700. *Brottsbalk.* www.riksdagen.se/sv/dokument-och-lagar/dokument/svensk-forfattningssamling/brottsbalk-1962700_sfs-1962-700/.

SOU (2023). *Utökade möjligheter att använda preventiva tvångsmedel 2: Slutbetänkande av Utredningen om preventiva tvångsmedel.* Statens Offentliga Utredningar, SOU 2023:60. www.regeringen.se/49bb1f/contentassets/dc2b23f7e20044b8b75ad90b0272332a/sou-202360_webb.pdf.

Tham, H. (Ed.). (2021). *Retreat or entrenchment? Drug policies in the Nordic countries at a crossroads.* Stockholm University Press.

Valverde, M., & Weaver, A. (2015). 'The crown wears many hats': Canadian aboriginal law and the black-boxing of empire. In K. McGee (Ed.), *Latour and the passage of law* (pp. 93–121). Edinburgh University Press.

Wheeldon, J., & Heidt, J. (2023). Cannabis, research ethics, and a duty of care. *Research Ethics*, 19(3), 250–87.

9

Rethinking the Sexual Subject

Assembling Intoxication, Gender and Consent in the Law

RENAE FOMIATTI, KIRAN PIENAAR AND GEMMA NOURSE

Introduction

The rise of the #MeToo movement has prompted a public reckoning with sexual consent, with public discourse now squarely focused on issues of sexual coercion and culpability. However, the principle of consent has a much longer history and wider significance beyond recent events. Bolstered by a social contract model that prioritises individual personhood and the protection of private property, consent has been central to the development of modern law and liberal societies (Munro, 2008). As feminist legal scholar Vanessa Munro argues, in Western legal settings, it 'demarcate[s] the terrain between acceptable and unacceptable intrusions upon property / bodies' (Munro, 2008, pp. 923–4) and accredits the liberal subject with its defining features of individuality, rationality and autonomy. In the specific context of sexual violence, consent is endowed with significant power (Hindes, 2022): it is used to arbitrate legal disputes over sexual assault and violence, and determine whether violation has occurred.

A key factor in some legal deliberations over sexual violence is the role of alcohol or other drug consumption, particularly in cases involving individuals deemed to be drug-affected or intoxicated. Thus, the concept of intoxication and how it is understood and mobilised in the law has significance for assumptions and ideals underpinning sexual consent and, we argue, for sexual politics more broadly. Intoxication, with its attendant meanings of excess and transgression, undermines liberal ideals of rationality, agency and reason (Fraser et al., 2022; Reith, 2022) and as such, can pose a challenge to the presumed rational negotiation of consent. As Fraser and colleagues (2022) observe, prevailing understandings of intoxication rely on and reproduce Cartesian binaries between reason and emotion, rationality and irrationality, legitimacy and illegitimacy, and order and disorder. These meanings take on a particular significance in the context of sexual practices, where the equation of intoxication with impairment, combined with gendered ideals of sexual agency and responsibility, means that intoxicated sex is typically framed as ambiguous, dangerous and, crucially, as undermining rational decision-making and thus the capacity to give consent. Of course, there are numerous public and legal examples of cases where intoxication *does* impact upon or limit the exercise or consent, including examples of people who are sexually assaulted while intoxicated. In the following discussion we do not wish to minimise these experiences, nor the very real harms enacted through sexual violence and experienced by victim-survivors, but rather to draw attention to the assumptions and liberal ideals buttressing dominant conceptions of intoxication. In doing so we build on contemporary research that has critiqued conventional assumptions about intoxication, agency and responsibility for their tendency to overdetermine a relation of risk and coercion (Pienaar et al., 2020; Hunt et al., 2022; Race et al., 2022). Instead, intoxication is understood as a technology through which gender and sexuality is made, and new selves and cultural relations produced and vice versa. It follow then that gender and sexuality are technologies for making and transforming intoxicated selves. On this view, intoxication entails forms of corporeal and affective modulation, but it is not necessarily antithetical to reason or capacity; rather it is understood in broader, less normative terms as creating a new relation with the self and others (Keane, 2020; Fraser et al., 2022). Following this conception, and for the purposes of this chapter, we define intoxication as a socially and culturally contingent phenomenon (Reinarman, 2023) involving a temporary change of state associated with the consumption of a wide range of substances including, but not limited to, nicotine, alcohol, cannabis, opiates and sedatives.

Notwithstanding these critiques of the normative politics of intoxication, the criminal law often instates narrower definitions of intoxication as a state of diminished rational capacity that compromises an individual's capacity to consent. Intoxication has been found to be legally significant in criminal deliberations, shaping the parameters of criminal responsibility in multiple, sometimes contradictory ways (Cowan, 2008; Gotell, 2008; Benedet, 2010; McNamara, 2017). In this chapter, we build on this scholarship to analyse how intoxication in the appellate court case *Still v The Queen* NSWCCA 131 (23 June 2010) works to reinforce gendered standards of consent. By drawing on theorisations of performativity (Race, 2018) and science and technology studies (STS) scholarship on standards and standardisation (Bowker & Star, 1999), we track how the law consistently performs intoxication as a non-ideal condition for the exercise of consent. This is achieved by the law's reliance on a conventional account of intoxication as impairment and disorder, one that is sustained and stabilised through the gendering of consent standards. However, we argue that, far from being a non-ideal condition of consent, that is, a situational factor that undermines the full autonomy required for consent, intoxication *preserves* a liberal notion of consent in the law – as rational, orderly and autonomous. As such, it functions as an *ideal* condition (e.g., a normative standard) for the creation of consent. To conclude, we consider the implications of intoxication and consent for the sexual subject in the law, and for the law itself.

Intoxication, Consent and the Law

A large body of critical legal scholarship analyses how the law constitutes thresholds or 'standards' for capacity in relation to intoxication (Wertheimer, 2001; Ryan, 2004; Finch & Munro, 2007; Cowan, 2008) to make determinations in sexual violence cases. While the law has historically developed standards and statutes for forced or involuntary intoxication and sexual assault (e.g., including phenomena often colloquially referred to as 'date rape') it has developed fewer standards on unwanted sexual intercourse with 'voluntarily' intoxicated peoples (Wallerstein, 2009). As Buchhandler-Raphael (2017) argues, voluntary intoxication presents the law with a 'conundrum' at the heart of which is an understanding that underlying sexual encounters is 'the question of how to distinguish intoxicated yet consensual sex – perfectly lawful, even if regrettable after the fact – from a sex crime' (Buchhandler-Raphael, 2017, p. 1034). Or in other words, how does the law determine the threshold at which a person reaches a state of 'incapacity' to consent due to intoxication? And what gendered and political effects might the making of this threshold have?

Courts often use a 'capacity-based' standard to determine whether the victim's intoxication reached a level that rendered them incapable of consenting to sex (Munro, 2008; Benedet, 2010). Undertaking a comprehensive review of Canadian case law involving intoxicated complainants, Craig (2020, p. 70) argues that Canadian law entails a 'legal standard that is too low and an evidentiary threshold that is too high'. For example, unconsciousness is often used 'as the evidentiary proxy for lack of capacity', which might inadvertently perpetuate the idea that if a person is anything less than unconscious during a sexual encounter, they are capable of consenting to sex (Craig, 2020, p. 81). As a result, no matter how severely intoxicated a person is when sexual contact occurred, courts are unlikely to find that the victim lacked capacity to consent unless they were unconscious during some or all of the sexual activity, thus narrowly circumscribing the legal definition of diminished capacity to a state of unconsciousness.

As might already be evident, gender is central to assessments of intoxication and consent, with the law approaching voluntary intoxication differently for men and women (Ryan, 2004), and by extension trans or gender-diverse people (although considerations of the issues for these populations are notably absent in the extant scholarship). In line with binary gendered assumptions about sexual agency, intoxication is often understood to increase sexual aggression and arousal for men. Conversely, intoxication is seen as lowering women's inhibition, making them more willing to engage in sex and also at greater risk of experiencing gendered sexual violence (Seear & Fraser, 2013; Seear & Mulcahy, 2022). Finch and Munro (2007) argue that intoxication among women is widely stigmatised and plays a role in jurors' attributions of responsibility in sexual assault cases. More recently, Richards (2020) found that expert and forensic evidence used in cases involving sexual assault against women is frequently unable to provide precise conclusions about a complainant's level of intoxication. This can result in inconclusive evidence and opinion being used to undermine the complainant's narrative, which in turn can uphold damaging stereotypes about sexually assaulted women, such as the claim that intoxicated women are sexually promiscuous, amoral or courting sexual violence (Finch & Munro, 2005).

In addition to critiquing the legal standard for incapacitation, other legal research highlights the contradictory application of intoxication and incapacity standards, raising questions about how the law should handle intoxicated sex (McNamara et al., 2017). For example, research on UK case law (Cowan, 2008; Wallerstein, 2009; Clough, 2019) found that intoxication can be used to both strengthen and cast doubt upon whether consent occurred. The defendant can claim the complainant was not intoxicated at all or that she was not intoxicated to the degree that she was incapable of consenting or there could be a disagreement about whether consent occurred at all (Cowan, 2008). Highlighting the performative and unstable qualities of legal processes, Canadian case law on incapacity to consent due to intoxication has been found to be contradictory and incomplete, with the doctrines of incapacity and involuntariness applied in an ad hoc manner (Benedet, 2010).

While universal approaches to intoxicated sex in the law are widely thought to be ineffective because of contextual variables in intoxicated sexual encounters (Ryan, 2004), some scholars have developed recommendations for developing greater legislative clarity on the issue of capacity and intoxicated sex (Cowan, 2008). These include the need for consistent interpretations of consent across criminal law (Wallerstein, 2009), guiding standards and sliding scales for evaluating consent and distinguishing between degrees of intoxication, or even legally prohibiting sex with severely intoxicated individuals (Buchhandler-Raphael, 2017; Cole, 2017; Goodman, 2009). Overall, prevailing intoxication and consent standards are contested and largely seen as insufficient for adjudicating the complexities involved in the sexual assault of intoxicated victims (Buchhandler-Raphael, 2017), with much of this criticism focusing on the law's inability to handle context and complexity – including in relation to matters of gender – in such cases (Benedet, 2010).

Taking a broader perspective on 'context', feminist analysis has pointed to how the legislative focus on incapacity obscures the gendered and socio-structural constraints on sexual agency and autonomy more generally for all citizens (Kukla, 2021). Munro (2008, p. 925), for example, argues that common legislative frameworks do little to recognise the complex ways in which 'entrenched power disparities, material inequalities, relational dynamics, and socio-sexual norms operate to construct and constrain women's ability to say no and to have refusal accredited by society and law'. She adds that prevailing legal frameworks also fail to uphold the contemporary standard of enthusiastic consent where women are able 'to say "yes", at least in the kind of free and unfettered way that the liberal model of autonomy often seems to presume' (Munro, 2008, p. 925). For these reasons, Munro (2008) argues that rather than doing away with consent as the central legal principle for judging cases of sexual violence, we need to move beyond 'consensual minimalism', by which she means very low, minimum standards for consent, to a model of consent that prioritises critical self-engagement and deliberative choice regarding sexual acts. Feminist ethics and philosophy scholar Kukla (2021) elaborates on these concerns in her examination of consent under 'non-ideal' conditions, including intoxication, that do not fit the standard criteria for rational autonomy. She argues that most sex and therefore conditions of consent are non-ideal because individual autonomy is always necessarily partial within patriarchal power relations. As such, Kukla is interested in exploring ways to scaffold agency and consensual sex under conditions of partial autonomy but refrains from applying this examination to the law.

Overall, this scholarship provides important context for the law case that we examine in this chapter, as it highlights the role of the law in shaping how we think about intoxication and consent, the role of gender in performing legal standards and thresholds, the socially mediated character of consent and opportunities for improvements in how the law handles intoxication in cases of sexual violence. In this chapter, we build on this work to examine how the law approaches intoxication as a non-ideal condition underpinned by the fiction of judicial impartiality, and how these, together, reinforce a gendered double standard in relation to sexual consent.

Approach

Our theoretical approach in this chapter combines the concept of performativity with STS scholarship on standards. The concept of performativity has a long history in poststructuralist feminist theory, especially in the influential work of gender theorist Judith Butler (1993). For Butler, sex-gendered subjects are produced through iterative socio-material practices, and these are characterised by dynamics of inclusion and exclusion. As Butler explains, it is only through the identification, production and exclusion of a range of abjected Others who 'circumscribe the domain of the subject' that the legitimate and intelligible subject comes to be formed (Butler, 1993, p. 3). To theorise performativity and its relationship to the law, we turn to some observations by renowned queer scholar Kane Race:

> To ask about the performativity of the law is to ask a series of questions about whether and when the law does what it says, and whether these doings are desirable. Certain statements or enactments of the law might be said to be successful, bringing about the social reality that they name; binding subjects in desired ways. And certain enactments or statements of the law may be seen to misfire, producing circumstances in which the law does not quite do what it says, or worse, can be seen to be participating in processes that undermine some of its express aims.
>
> (Race, 2018, p. 115)

Race's aim here is to highlight the performative or constitutive function of the law and legal deliberations in producing particular truths and realities, with significant regulatory and subjectification effects. In other words, legal practices and processes, like other institutional practices, do not simply respond to a stable, preexisting reality; rather they are active in making realities (in the plural), hence their performative role in shaping social worlds in both expected and unforeseen ways. As Race notes, it is not always possible to predict the consequences of particular statements or practices of the law or to ensure ethical outcomes. Legal and drug scholar Kate Seear also draws attention to the performativity of the law and legal deliberations in her book *Just Habits* (2020) in which she draws on Latour (2009) and the work of legal scholar Kyle McGee (2015) to argue that the essence of the law does not lie in texts but in social and legal practices which perform or constitute law, and in so doing, perform bodies, subjects, objects and relations. According to this view, the law has its own processes of veridiction or truth-making, and it is these processes that a performative analytic approach seeks to make visible by tracing the politics and ethics of law-making practices and the normative assumptions that underpin them. Such an approach exposes how widely accepted 'legal truths' come to be constituted and stabilised through legal practices including sentencing statements, legal deliberations, advocacy strategies and legislative processes.

In this chapter we attend to one actor in the legal process of veridiction (or truth-making) – that of standards. Going beyond the analysis of the sufficiency of legal standards, which is a concern in the literature we discussed earlier, we draw on sociological and STS theorisations of the performativity of standards and standardisation to analyse what these standards do in the law generally, and in constituting liberal consent and the sexual subject, in particular. Here, the work of Bowker and Star in their now classic book *Sorting things out: Classification and its consequences* (1999) is useful for thinking about the work that standards perform. While Bowker and Star are primarily focused on the performative work of classifications and classificatory systems, they also analyse the political and social function of standards in social life. They distinguish classifications from standards by arguing that while classifications are a 'spatio-temporal' segmentation of the world, displaying a consistent principle of ordering, a standard is 'any set of agreed-upon rules for the production of (textual or material) objects' (Bowker & Star, 1999, p. 13). Successful standards impose classifications systems, valorise specific points of view and silence others (Bowker & Star, 1999, p. 5). As such they contain and espouse particular ethical agendas and produce material effects, including elevating certain social groups and marginalising others; or as Bowker and Star put it, 'for any individual, group or situation, classifications and standards give advantage or give suffering' (Bowker & Star, 1999, p. 6).

While sociological work on standards often emphasises the link between standardisation and homogenisation, the dominant focus of much science studies research on standardisations has been on the local and the contingent (Timmermans & Epstein, 2010), including the ways in which standards enact 'coordination' and 'comparability' across time, space and contexts. Timmermans and Epstein argue that a key issue for studying 'standard creation' is to 'map the interactions among the multiple parties involved in the creation process, even paying attention to those that could reasonably be expected to be included but are currently not part of the creation process' (Timmermans & Epstein, 2010, p. 75). In the law, as in other institutional domains, legal standards coordinate people and things into social configurations with particular outcomes, some of which advantage some social groups while disadvantaging others.

In our analysis, we focus on how standards work in the case of *Still*, an Australian appellate court case in the New South Wales Court of Criminal Appeal. An appellate court has jurisdiction or authority to hear and determine appeals from judgments handed down in other courts. In the original case in 2009 at the Newcastle District Court, the appellant, a taxi driver, was charged with detaining the complainant (a passenger) in his taxi, stealing items of her clothing and indecent assault. The jury acquitted him on the charge of aggravated detainment for advantage (Count 1) and convicted him of indecent assault and stealing (Counts 2 and 3). In the appeal, the appellant challenged his conviction of the indecent assault count only upon the grounds of factually inconsistent verdicts between the charges of detainment and assault. The appellate court found that the inconsistency between the verdicts was not established and that there was sufficient evidence to support the conviction for indecent assault. In sum, the appeal was dismissed.

As we argue in the next section, the case draws on intoxication to support a range of arguments, some of which are inconsistent, ethically fraught and require closer scrutiny. Key questions at stake in this case include: How does the law enact intoxication as limiting or altering the capacity to consent, and what are the implications of this enactment for intoxicated sex? What constitutes the standard of incapacity in intoxicated sex? How does voluntary intoxication affect responsibility attribution in sexual assault and rape trials? Despite important differences in the substance and implications of these questions, they are interrelated insofar as they demonstrate an orientation to the law and intoxication which emphasises contingency, complexity and relationality. We argue that the law *consistently* constitutes intoxication as a non-ideal condition for the exercise of consent. This is achieved by the law's reliance on a conventional understanding of intoxication as a state of impairment, which is produced and stabilised through what we identify in the second section as the gendering of consent standards. However, far from being a non-ideal condition of consent, this enactment of intoxication has the inadvertent effect of strengthening and preserving a liberal notion of consent in the law – as rational, orderly and autonomous. As such, we argue that intoxication in fact shores up the liberal model of consent and the sexual subject, and in this respect can be understood to function as an *ideal* condition for the standard creation of autonomous liberal consent. We now turn to the case of *Still* to provide an example of how this works in the law.

Intoxication: An Ideal Condition for Consent Standard Creation

In *Still*, the court restates the evidence presented in the district trial to provide context for the appellant's grounds of appeal. We discuss this here as much of what constitutes contextual or circumstantial evidence for the indecent assault of the complainant (known in the case only as 'KG') focuses on alcohol intoxication.[1] This includes the procurement of large quantities of alcohol by KG and her friends, a subsequent heavy drinking session that spans multiple locations, witnesses' descriptions of the complainant's intoxicated, impaired behaviour and the complainant's own descriptions of alcohol-related memory loss. For example:

> On Saturday 22 March 2008, the complainant, KG, went out with a friend, Kerrie Delaney. Ms Delaney picked up KG in her car and drove to a hotel where they had lunch. The complainant had two glasses of white wine and after a couple of hours, they went to the home of another friend, Nadine Martin, of Adamstown Heights. On the way, they stopped at a bottle shop and purchased two bottles of white wine. After arriving at Ms Martin's place they decided to stay, so they returned to the bottle shop where Ms Delaney purchased a two-litre cask of white wine. They returned to Ms Martin's place about 4.30 pm and continued to drink.
>
> (paragraph 13)

[1] In Australian criminal law, the person who makes a complaint of sexual assault is typically referred to as 'the complainant' (as opposed to the 'victim' or 'alleged victim').

And shortly after:

> By 7.30 pm, *the complainant was observed by Ms Delaney to be quite intoxicated*, and was *upset and crying* and *had knocked over a few glasses and broken them*. At about 8.00 pm, Ms Delaney called a taxi to take the complainant to her home at Merewether. Ms Delaney had asked the complainant why she was upset, but *could not make sense of the complainant, who was slurring her words*.
>
> (paragraph 15; emphasis added)

While these descriptions of alcohol consumption seem like neutral descriptions of fact, it is worth reflecting on how intoxication is identified and performed through the law as a significant actor shaping responsibility and culpability in cases concerning assault and consent. Introduced early in the description of evidence (paragraph 13) and repeatedly referenced thereafter, intoxication is elevated as a dominant contextual factor and assumes legal significance as a risk or aggravating factor for sexual violence. The focus on intoxicated states and behaviours in these extracts (e.g., emotional volatility, physical clumsiness, slurring) is shaped by a gendered double standard in relation to consumption: while the women's drinking is presented in a 'factual' style, it is marked as noteworthy because it does not accord with dominant gender norms governing safe, respectable behaviour for young women. These gendered overtones work to mobilise a feminised enactment of intoxication as impairment, which implicitly depicts drunk women and intoxication as sources of risk and vulnerability. Tacit appeals to this gendered double standard are repeated throughout the case via references to the intoxicated state and conduct of the complainant. In line with the performative approach adopted in this chapter, we argue that this conventional politics of intoxication helps to perform the *normative standards* of consent in legal deliberations as free, unfettered, rational and sober. Significantly, this conventional enactment of intoxication thus helps to coordinate, regulate and calibrate normative standards of sexual practice, agency and consent, and ultimately standards of normative, autonomous subjecthood.

In this case and more broadly in legal deliberations involving sexual assault, intoxication functions in other ways to establish a liberal humanist standard of consent. In *Still*, descriptions of incoherence, often in the form of fragmented memory and time, operate as the normative conventions of intoxication. For example, in the following extract, after consuming the alcohol described earlier, KG reports having no memory of leaving her friend's house. Evidence of fragmented memories include noticing her mobile phone and items of clothing were missing (notably her underpants):

> KG said in evidence that she had no recollection of leaving Ms Martin's place. She recalled waking up in the early hours of the morning of Sunday, 23 March 2008, just after 2.00 am, in bed at her Merewether home. She noticed that one of her mobile phones (a black Nokia N80) was missing, so she tried to ring it from her other phone. It rang for a couple of rings and it then cut out, so she tried ringing again, with the same result. The phone was set to ring for 30 seconds before it went to message bank, but it only rang for about 10 seconds on these occasions. KG could not see her green boob-tube and noticed that she did not have any underpants on. She went back to sleep.
>
> (paragraph 55)

In contrast to this description of dissociation and partial memory loss, evidence originating from the original trial but presented later in the Court of Appeal transcript describes fragmented memories of physical assault:

> KG said in evidence that she had a memory (described as a 'vision') of lying backwards and a man over the top of her saying 'Shh, it'll be OK'. She described the man as 'a biggish sort of man, big build with short brown hair and a button up shirt'.
>
> (paragraph 19)

The court later describes this evidence as 'the thought processes of a heavily intoxicated person who, after some hours of sleep, awoke to find injuries to her body and items of her clothing and her mobile phone gone'. Here, intoxicated states are treated as noteworthy and suspicious in the law because of their association with disinhibition and the threat they are seen to pose to the ideal of the rational, autonomous subject, and to related notions of order and time that shore up the rational model of consent. Importantly, it is not the purpose of this analysis to cast doubt upon the verdict or the complainant's sexual assault but to explore how intoxication functions in relation to consent. In these extracts we can see how liberal consent relies upon linear temporal logics that take for granted singular accounts of events, at the centre of which is the rational, decision-making subject. Intoxicated states are handled in the law as overflowing with social excess and temporal disorder and are treated as an aberration from 'normal' social order and interactions, and an impediment to unambiguous consensual sexual encounters. While in some cases – especially in cases of extreme impairment – intoxication may contribute to memory loss or greatly diminished capacity, intoxication in general is performed as suspicious and an impediment to the proper function of the law itself, by, for example, making the 'facts' of the case less amenable to rational investigation, by casting doubt on a singular, stable version of events that can be uncovered through careful legal deliberations. For example, KG's inability to clearly recall the sequence of the events and her reference to 'visions' are seen in this case to complicate the proper function of the law by making singular, objective 'facts' more ambiguous and less amenable to rational investigation. These performances of intoxication as non-ideal contribute to a normative standard for consent as best expressed and negotiated in the context of sober sex, minimising the often diffuse, shape-shifting power dynamics that underpin all sexual practice, intoxicated or otherwise (Farrugia, 2023). As we noted earlier, it is not our intention to disprove that the complainant was intoxicated or to cast doubt upon her assault. Rather, our point is to show how a normative liberal standard of consent as a rational and autonomous process is established and upheld in the law, in part *through* conventional – and, as we explore in the following section, highly gendered – accounts of intoxication. In this way, insofar as intoxication is eschewed as a non-ideal condition for consent, it becomes a key constitutive norm governing the liberal model and standard of consent.

Gendering Consent Standards

In this section we explore how the values underpinning the liberal consent standard are gendered in relation to intoxication and argue that as a result, references to intoxication in legal deliberations involving sexual violence can work to reformulate a masculine standard of consent along a normative axis of masculine and feminine agency. As we noted earlier, consent thresholds are thoroughly 'saturated with sexuality' insofar as they typically work to reproduce the female body as imbued with an 'inherently dangerous female sexuality' (Munro, 2008, p. 936). As we go on to show, in *Still*, the appellant's defence references intoxication in ways that both draw on and reproduce normative standards and stereotypical understandings of sex, gender and agency. For example, intoxication is articulated in the case via a binary, sexualised notion of risk. In the first extract from the defence barrister, the female complainant is depicted as sexually unrestrained and flirtatious and in the second, taken from the appellant's response under cross-examination, as vulnerable to sexual exploitation because she was intoxicated:

> It was his version that the complainant entered the taxi and soon after told him he was '*a nice bloke*' and put her hand on the inside of his leg. He said that the complainant was '*very flirtatious and full on*' and did not seem too intoxicated. He told her to take her hand off his leg and then she put her arm around his neck. He pulled over to the side of the road because he could not drive, and told the complainant that she had to stop, but she said that she did not want to stop. The Appellant said that he continued driving and the complainant started removing her clothing. She took off her see-through top and her boob-tube and put it on the floor of the taxi, exposing both of her breasts. She put her hand back on his leg and he pulled over after the Brunker Street lights because he knew '*he couldn't shrug her off again*'
>
> (paragraphs 35–6; original emphasis)

The appellant denied that he had diverted the complainant because she was too drunk to say she did not want to be with him. He denied taking advantage of her because of her clear state of intoxication, and denied that this was why he kept her clothes and her mobile phone (paragraph 43).

In the first example, the complainant's level of intoxication is disputed by the appellant to challenge the complainant's status as 'victim' and to refigure her as sexually agentive, 'flirtatious' and as making sexual overtures to the appellant ('put[ting] her hand on his leg', 'her arm around his neck', 'removing her clothing . . . and exposing her breasts' and refusing to stop despite the appellant's request). In line with legal research on the highly gendered figure of the 'reasonable person' in case law that establishes standards and expectations for how women should behave in response to perceived or actual threats and violence – ideally as a 'victim who needs protection' – (Cahn, 1992, p. 20), it is evident that intoxication also works to regulate and calibrate sexual standards along conventional sex-gendered lines. Male sexual agency is valorised as natural and legitimate while female sexual agency is denigrated as illegitimate and inappropriate, allowing the male appellant to present the female complainant's alleged flirtation and initiation of sexual contact as 'full on' (i.e., extreme, unrestrained and persistent in that 'he couldn't shrug her off') and as straightforwardly related to her level of intoxication. This framing is also enacted along specifically gendered lines insofar as it suggests that he is a rational and sober victim of an unwanted sexual advance; and she is potentially a wayward intoxicated woman whom he needs to control.

Several normative gendered assumptions are at work here. First, a causal link is drawn between intoxication and the risk of experiencing gendered, sexual violence. According to this gendered logic, the fact that the female complainant was intoxicated puts her at increased risk of 'being taken advantage of' sexually, which in turn relies on and reinforces a stereotype of men as inherently sexual, aggressive and unable to restrain their sexual impulses. In this case, the appellant presents himself as a 'nice bloke' who did not take advantage of the complainant despite her alleged 'full on' sexual overtures to him. Secondly, as other scholars have noted, the ideal victim is often constituted in sexual assault decisions as embodying a number of normative gendered attributes: she is 'rape-preventing', 'respectable' (i.e., morally and sexually virtuous, and unprovocative), cautious and blameless in that she exercises appropriate caution to minimise the risk of experiencing sexual violence (Larcombe, 2002; Bows, 2018). Of course, appropriate caution entails a never-ending constellation of practices that women are encouraged to undertake to 'protect' themselves against sexual violence, including maintaining sobriety or at least limiting alcohol and other drug consumption. This commonplace approach to sexual violence allows an overdetermined focus on the actions and conduct of victim-survivors (usually women), sidelining the role of perpetrators (usually men) and the cultures of violence and misogyny that enable gendered violence (Fahs, 2016). While female agency and consent are gendered differently in these enactments of intoxication above (i.e., as sexually permissive versus passive), they ultimately work to preserve an active masculine sexuality (Gotell, 2008) and a gendered version of subjecthood more broadly; the male appellant is consistently enacted as the one in control at all times and upon whom questions of choice and agency hinge. In this sense, and in keeping with the ways in which standards work to advantage certain groups and disadvantage others (Bowker & Star, 1999), the gendered double standard in relation to sexuality and intoxication functions to preserve a masculinist standard of sexual consent that significantly disadvantages women by inoculating male conduct from critique.

In contrast to the appellant's defence that reproduces masculinist norms which denigrate women's sexual agency and presents intoxication as increasing women's risk of experiencing gendered violence, the court handles intoxication in the case differently. To demonstrate the inability to give consent, intoxication, as we noted earlier, is constructed as a state of severe impairment: the complainant is described as 'heavily affected by alcohol, incoherent in her speech shortly before entering the taxi and probably bordering upon comatose'. This account of impairment, along with the fact that the appellant was unknown to the complainant, is then mobilised in support of the complainant to demonstrate that she was physically incapable of consenting: 'These were significant aspects bearing upon the giving of consent to sexual activity with the appellant, who was a complete stranger' (paragraph 66). Regarding the count of indecent assault, the court continues that 'it would have been open to the jury to conclude that the complainant was unconscious at times whilst she was in the taxi, and that this was a significant aspect on the issue of consent on the indecent assault charge' (paragraph 91). In this example, incapacity-through-intoxication evidences and provides a standard for non-consent despite the complainant's gaps in memory and temporal fragmentation. As previously noted, our intention is not to question the charge of indecent assault or the complainant's account, but it is notable here that the law requires certainty, and as such it appeals to intoxication as a standard of ambiguous or risky behaviour and sexual practice to make legal decisions, valorise specific points of view and silence particular subjects (Bowker & Star, 1999). In this way, via the dictates of consent and non-consent, and a feminised notion of intoxication as beyond reason, the legal determination of incapacity-through-intoxication also strengthens the alignment of the law with rationality and reason, and thus with masculinity itself.

Conclusion: Rethinking Consent and the Sexual Subject in the Law

Much of the legal deliberation in this case includes assembling the 'facts' of the indecent assault, which involves the court trying to establish the legal implications of the complainant's state of intoxication in this specific encounter. In many respects this attention to local, specific circumstances makes the law flexible and adroit at registering social context. Yet, in encountering social complexity and a range of non-ideal conditions (most notably, the complainant's state of intoxication), the law is tasked with establishing standards or thresholds to determine where violation and criminal action have occurred. Drawing on critical thinking about performativity and standards, in this chapter we have argued that intoxication is a significant legal actor which, while treated as a non-ideal condition for exercising consent, in fact shores up liberal consent via appeals to gendered ideals of individual autonomy and rationality. In this sense, by establishing the 'constitutive outside' (Butler, 1990, 1993) or definitional boundaries for liberal consent, the notion of incapacity-through-intoxication serves as the dialectical standard for the normative ideals of consent. In other words, insofar as intoxication is seen to impair individual agency and rationality, it functions as a non-ideal condition for consent while paradoxically preserving the ideal of consent as requiring a fully cognisant, agentive and rational subject, best exercised in a field of deliberate and ordered social activity.

In addition, we drew on the work of Bowker and Star (1999) on the performativity of standards to explore how normative standards work in relation to intoxicated sex to advantage men and disadvantage women. We argued that standards of voluntary intoxication, consent and non-consent buttress a pernicious gendered double standard: they are inflected with prevailing gender norms that disadvantage women (as the primary targets of gendered violence) and obscure the role of men (as the main perpetrators of such violence). For example, gendered stereotypes depict women as sexually disinhibited when intoxicated and thus as more readily consenting to sex, although perhaps mistakenly or regrettably. Conversely, intoxication is presumed to make women more susceptible and vulnerable to sexual violence. Key here is that the law is ill-equipped to handle women who become intoxicated through their own 'choices' and actions (or more complicated accounts of relational social action), as conventional accounts of intoxication necessarily entail a compromised form of affect and agency. The law is more adept at recognising and handling sexual violence when its patterning and materialisation conforms to normative gender binaries of activity and passivity, vulnerability and strength, capacity and incapacity. We have argued that the gendered double standard underpinning dominant accounts of intoxication and sexual risk functions to preserve a masculinist standard of consent in the law and, by extension, more widely in sexual practice.

To draw these threads together by way of concluding, we offer some reflections on how this relationship between intoxication, gender and consent shapes the figure of the autonomous sexual subject in the law and what intoxication does *for the law*. While we have argued that the notion of consent accredits the liberal subject with its defining features of individuality, rationality and distinctness from other subjects and beings, it also performs a socially detached model of sexual subjecthood and sexual agency that relies on and reproduces a view of feminine agency as necessarily compromised in the various ways we have previously explored. This model of sexual subjecthood, premised upon the rhetoric of liberalism which is foundational to the law, disguises the more complex realities of consent and sexual practice, and the extent to which human agency is always partial and constrained (Munro, 2008), even without the 'mediating factor' of intoxication. This gendered figure of sexual consent and the prevailing notion of consent in the law warrants careful scrutiny to interrogate its foundational notions of 'abstract subjectivity and unfettered autonomy' (Munro, 2008, p. 923). Doing so may help to generate more nuanced definitions of sexual consent capable of handling the complexity of sexual practices and in the process, may prompt shifts in the law towards more realistic understandings of socio-sexual life and relational agency.

In this chapter, we have argued that insofar as the law aims to achieve justice for victims of sexual violence or indecent assault, legal actors are engaged in a performative political process (Race, 2018; Seear, 2020). To return to Race, whose comments on legal performativity we began with, we ask: does the law do what it purports to do and are its manifold effects desirable? Insofar as the court denied the appellant's appeal and upheld the counts of indecent assault and theft, the law's mobilisation and handling of intoxication can be understood in one sense as ethical and effective. However, our analysis has demonstrated that the law relies on intoxication to uphold the ideal of the rational, consenting sober sexual subject, which is a model of subjecthood that is in fact a poor fit for the complex realities of sexual practice and the vast array of non-ideal but highly significant political, social and material constraints on agency. In this way, the law produces the less-than-desirable effects of constituting intoxicated women and intoxicated sexual practices as suspect, problematic and, crucially, as straightforwardly undermining the capacity to consent. Despite these limitations, the performance of reason, and the investigation and interpretation of 'contextual factors' work to secure the authority and sovereignty of the law, even as it struggles to handle intoxicated practices. As well as buttressing the liberal subject, intoxication, like all 'non-ideal' conditions, can also be understood as immanent to the 'force' of the law (McGee, 2015). Conventional conceptions of intoxication are also thoroughly gendered: through the association of intoxication with qualities traditionally ascribed as feminine – for example, unpredictability, vulnerability and irrationality – intoxication strengthens and *highlights* the masculine nature of the law itself and its capacity to render particular subjects and practices, as beyond rational (legal) comprehension.

References

Benedet, J. (2010). The sexual assault of intoxicated women. *Canadian Journal of Women and the Law*, 22(2), 435–62.

Bowker, G. C., & Star, S. L. (1999). *Sorting things out: Classification and its consequences*. The MIT Press.

Bows, H. (2018). The 'ideal' rape victim and the elderly woman: A contradiction in terms? In M. Duggan (Ed.), *Revisiting the 'ideal victim': Developments in critical victimology* (pp. 229–42). Bristol University Press.

Buchhandler-Raphael, M. (2017). The conundrum of voluntary intoxication and sex. *Brooklyn Law Review*, 82(3), 1031–108.

Butler, J. (1990). *Gender trouble: Feminism and the subversion of identity*. Routledge.

Butler, J. (1993). *Bodies that matter: On the discursive limits of 'sex'*. Routledge.

Cahn, N. R. (1992). Looseness of legal language: The reasonable woman standard in theory and in practice. *Cornell Law Review*, 77(6), 1398–454.

Cole, K. (2017). Sex and the single malt girl: How voluntary intoxication affects consent. *Montana Law Review*, 78(1), 155–76.

Clough, A. (2019). Finding the balance: Intoxication and consent. *Liverpool Law Review*, 40(1), 49–64.

Cowan, S. (2008). The trouble with drink: Intoxication, (in)capacity, and the evaporation of consent to sex. *Akron Law Review*, 41(4), 899–922.

Craig, E. (2020). Sexual assault and intoxication: Defining (in)capacity to consent. *Canadian Bar Review*, 98(1), 70–105.

Fahs, B. (2016). Naming sexual trauma: On the political necessity of nuance in rape and sex offender discourses. In M. J. Casper & E. Wertheimer (Eds.), *Critical trauma studies: Understanding violence, conflict, and memory in everyday life* (pp. 61–77). New York University Press.

Farrugia, A. (2023). 'Something serious': Biopedagogies of young people, sex and drugs in Australian drug education. *Pedagogy, Culture & Society*, 33(3), 1–17.

Finch, E., & Munro, V. E. (2005). Juror stereotypes and blame attribution in rape cases involving intoxicants: The findings of a pilot study. *British Journal of Criminology*, 45(1), 25–38.

Finch, E., & Munro, V. E. (2007). The demon drink and the demonized woman: Socio-sexual stereotypes and responsibility attribution in rape trials involving intoxicants. *Social & Legal Studies*, 16(4), 591–614.

Fraser, S., Moore, D., Farrugia, A. & Fomiatti, R. (2022). Passion, reason and the politics of intoxication: Ontopolitically-oriented approaches to alcohol and other drug intoxication. In G. Hunt, T. Antin & V. Asmussen Frank (Eds.), *Routledge handbook of intoxicants and intoxication* (pp. 342–57). Routledge.

Gotell, L. (2008). Rethinking affirmative consent in Canadian sexual assault law: Neoliberal sexual subjects and risky women. *Akron Law Review*, 41(4), 865–98.

Goodman, C. C. (2009). Protecting the party girl: A new approach for evaluating intoxicated consent. *Brigham Young University Law Review*, 2009(1), 57–116.

Hindes, S. (2022). Beyond consent. In *The Palgrave encyclopedia of sexuality education* (pp. 1–9). Springer International Publishing.

Hunt, G., Sanders, E., Petersen, M. A. & Bogren, A. (2022). 'Blurring the line': Intoxication, gender, consent, and sexual encounters among young adults. *Contemporary Drug Problems*, 49(1), 84–105.

Keane, H. (2020). Smoking and intoxication: From control to the buzz. In *Cultures of intoxication: Key issues and debates* (pp. 45–66). Springer International Publishing.

Kukla, Q. R. (2021). A nonideal theory of sexual consent. *Ethics*, 131(2), 270–92.

McGee, K. (2015). *Latour and the passage of law*. Edinburgh University Press.

Larcombe, W. (2002). The 'ideal' victim v successful rape complainants: Not what you might expect. *Feminist Legal Studies*, 10, 131–48.

Latour, B. (2009). *The making of law: An ethnography of the Conseil d'État*. Polity Press.

McNamara, L., Quilter, J., Seear, K. & Room, R. (2017). Evidence of intoxication in Australian criminal courts: A complex variable with multiple effects. *Monash University Law Review*, 43(1), 148–94.

Munro, V. E. (2008). Constructing consent: Legislating freedom and legitimating constraint in the expression of sexual autonomy. *Akron Law Review*, 41(4), 923–56.

Pienaar, K., Murphy, D., Race, K. & Lea, T. (2020). Sexualities and intoxication: 'To be intoxicated is to still be me, just a little blurry' – Drugs, enhancement and transformation in lesbian, gay, bisexual, transgender and queer cultures. In F. F. Kjellgren (Ed.), *Cultures of intoxication: Key issues and debates* (pp. 139–63). Springer International Publishing.

Race, K. (2018). *The gay science: Intimate experiments with the problem of HIV*. Routledge.

Race, K., Pienaar, K., Murphy, D. & Lea, T. (2022). 'Uninhibited play': The political and pragmatic dimensions of intoxication within queer cultures. In G. Hunt, T. Antin & V. Asmussen Frank (Eds.), *Routledge handbook of intoxicants and intoxication* (pp. 272–89). Routledge.

Reinarman, C. (2023). Intoxications and their meanings. In G. Hunt, T. Antin & V. Asmussen Frank (Eds.), *Routledge handbook of intoxicants and intoxication* (pp. 19–32). Routledge.

Reith, G. (2022). Intoxicating consumption: Capitalism and the commodification of pleasure. In G. Hunt, T. Antin & V. Asmussen Frank (Eds.), *Routledge handbook of intoxicants and intoxication* (pp. 89–100). Routledge.

Richards, C. (2020). Intoxication, a drunk science: Expertise in cases of sexual assault regarding capacity to consent. *Canadian Journal of Law and Justice*, 2(1), 137–73.

Ryan, V. M. (2004). Intoxicating encounters: Allocating responsibility in the law of rape. *California Western Law Review*, 40(2), 407–30.

Seear, K. (2020). *Law, drugs and the making of addiction: Just habits.* Routledge.

Seear, K., & Fraser, S. (2013). Mia Freedman et al. are wrong: Being drunk doesn't cause rape. *The Conversation.* https://theconversation.com/mia-freedman-et-al-are-wrong-being-drunk-doesnt-cause-rape-19745.

Seear, K., & Mulcahy, S. (2022). Making rights and realities: How Australian human rights make gender, alcohol and other drugs. *Australian Feminist Studies*, 37(113), 347–64.

Timmermans, S., & Epstein, S. (2010). A world of standards but not a standard world: Toward a sociology of standards and standardization. *Annual Review of Sociology*, 36(1), 69–89.

Wallerstein, S. (2009). 'A drunken consent is still consent': Or is it? A critical analysis of the law on a drunken consent to sex following Bree. *The Journal of Criminal Law*, 73(4), 318–44.

Wertheimer, A. (2001). Intoxicated consent to sexual relations. *Law and Philosophy*, 20(4), 373–401.

10

Revisiting the Entrepreneurial 'Dealer'

The Case of Shiny Flakes

AYSEL SULTAN

Introduction

The field of drug studies is increasingly challenged by the rapid digitalisation of drug markets, raising the importance of reconsidering how drug laws and policies respond to the role of technologies in the drug trade, and their social impact. This chapter considers the famous case of Maximilian Schmidt, who was accused of setting up Germany's largest digital drug shop under the alias Shiny Flakes and became the subject of media stories and Netflix TV productions. The case offers an opportunity to explore how the move to digitally mediated drug supply has altered the ways in which phenomena such as the 'dealer' and 'dealing' are constituted in socio-technical and legal contexts.[1] Research shows that digital drug markets pose serious challenges to jurisdictional and regulatory frameworks and governments require costly and laborious police operations to adapt to the rapid development of these markets (EU Drugs Strategy 2021–2025, 2021; UNODC, 2022). Following the transition of drug markets and traditional dealer activities to digitally mediated formats, it has become important to consider how drug dealers and dealing are constituted and handled in law, and whether the technological means of dealing are reshaping how questions of responsibility, 'harm' and entrepreneurship are being understood. These questions are important for a range of reasons. People who deal drugs are often conceptualised, in public policy and legal discourses, as profoundly immoral, as well as malicious and powerful compared to drug users (Coomber, 2006; Flacks, 2021). The media has played an important role in amplifying these discourses, creating popular anti-hero storylines drawing on real-life figures like Pablo Escobar or George Jung who symbolise political,

[1] The terms 'dealer' and 'dealing' are preserved intentionally for consistency and when referring to existing literature.

economic and social power (Gutierrez, 2020). But the digitalisation of drug supply (Linder, 2019; Søgaard et al., 2019; Demant et al., 2020) presents a unique opportunity to challenge these conventional stories of drug dealing (e.g., Korshøj & Søgaard, 2024). The case of Shiny Flakes thus provides an opportunity to examine the ways in which discourses on drug laws, technology and media shape and co-constitute each other in relation to drug dealing.

Case Summary: *Regional Court of Leipzig v Schmidt*

At the age of eighteen, Schmidt set up a digital shop for illicit drugs in the apartment he shared with his parents in Leipzig, Germany. He used his childhood bedroom to store the drugs, scale, proportion and package them for individual shipments, for which the German media labelled him *Kinderzimmerdealer* (childhood bedroom dealer). In 2015, at the age of twenty, Schmidt was sentenced to seven years imprisonment and was required to pay three million euros to the state from the proceeds of his business. The regional court found him guilty of commercial dealings of narcotics in large quantities under Sections 29 and 29a of the German Narcotics Act (BtMG).[2] Although the prosecutor initially demanded a sentence of eight years and eight months, the judges agreed on a shorter period given that Schmidt was under the age of twenty-one when committing the crime. Psychological assessments indicated Schmidt's emotional immaturity, leading to imprisonment in a juvenile facility and vocational training. He was released after serving four years and seven months. However, in 2023, Schmidt was charged again based on new evidence that he, together with four collaborators, opened and co-operated a new digital drug shop. Schmidt allegedly set up this second shop – Candylove – during his first detention in youth custody, where he met a collaborator. This time, he was charged under Section 30a of the BtMG for organised drug trafficking, entailing a harsher punishment for repeat offending.[3] He was expected to be sentenced to an additional four and a half years; however, this verdict was overturned due to disputed new evidence, and the court's decision to review the involvement of co-conspirators in respect of Candylove. All five defendants including the four collaborators, and Schmidt himself, pleaded guilty for trafficking

[2] Under the Betäubungsmittelgesetz (BtMG), these sections on criminal offences are invoked for selling or trafficking large amounts of illicit narcotics.

[3] Section 30a is for aggravated offences, such as organised crime and trafficking of considerable amounts that could cause harm to public health.

20 kilograms of drugs in 400 shipments between 2019 and 2021. Schmidt pled guilty to the charges of running the website and operating the IT side of the business, but not to being involved in actual sales. It has been reported that Schmidt could now be punished only for aiding and abetting (LTO, 2023). At the time of writing this chapter, he and all four collaborators remain free pending the next hearing.

Schmidt's entrepreneurial career was highly publicised and inspired two Netflix productions – a three-season series entitled *How to sell drugs online (fast)*, which is loosely based on the first trial, and an investigative documentary starring Schmidt himself called *Shiny_Flakes: The Teenage Drug Lord*. The documentary (Müller and Schmitt, 2021) was screened in court and used as evidence during the second trial in 2023. Schmidt, who had also been working as a waiter, lived with his family until his first detention in 2016. The Netflix documentary starring Schmidt suggests that he was living an isolated life and, at the time of his first prosecution, had no friends or other social contacts. He shipped the drugs using the German Postal Service and DHL, which were the starting point for the authorities' investigation as several undelivered packages without a return address began to surface around Leipzig. Consequently, the police asked twenty-three post offices around Germany for similar instances, followed by a three-month surveillance of Schmidt's apartment, and finally, his arrest. At that moment, Schmidt managed to unplug cables connected to his external hard drives, however, police officers confiscated one that contained the addresses of every customer he had shipped to. Further investigations eventually concluded that he trafficked 914 kilograms of illicit drugs and made approximately three million euros revenue in cryptocurrencies between 2013 and 2015. Given its size and impact, it is possible that the case of Shiny Flakes, along with growing rates of other cybercrimes, aided in shaping Germany's legislative measures for digital surveillance and informed local intelligence responses to digital drug markets. Germany is among the European countries with highest drug supply over the darknet (Europol, 2017), and, over the past few years, the country's Federal Criminal Police have shut down some of the world's largest darknet marketplaces, such as DarkMarket and Hydra, often in cooperation with US intelligence (Daly & Shortis, 2024).

Theoretical Approach

Social studies on the drug-crime link have explored drug dealing in small-scale, social supply contexts, both online and offline, but there is a need for a more nuanced understanding of major scale digital drug dealing. In the early 2010s, with the emergence of the first big darknet marketplace, Silk Road, researchers noted the importance of digital drug markets (e.g., Barratt, 2012; Aldridge & Décary-Hétu, 2014), and predicted that these markets would grow rapidly, followed by increased decentralisation and a likely move to clearnet platforms. Darknet markets grew exponentially during the COVID-19 pandemic, with small-scale social supply becoming more popular over social media and messenger apps (Demant & Aagesen, 2022; Korshøj & Søgaard, 2024). Studies also suggested that prohibitive drug policies would remain largely ineffective in curbing the spread of these markets, and would likely create a whack-a-mole effect, with new platforms quickly replacing those shut down (Shortis et al., 2020). However, corresponding legal frameworks, and especially the role of technology in this field, remain under-theorised (Rhodes & Lancaster, 2021; Bakken et al., 2022).

Earlier studies of traditional drug dealing highlighted the importance of cultural capital or 'street capital', and how this aided in building networks to sustain such high-risk activities (Bourgois, 1995; Sandberg, 2008). These studies identified the neoliberal economy as a crucial force in understanding how street-level drug dealing careers were embedded in complex and dynamic conditions. However, the sheer scale of technological transformation has changed the face of drug dealing (Childs & Bernot, 2024). It is generally acknowledged that digitally mediated supply reduces violence and other direct harms associated with traditional drug markets (Linder, 2019; Gomes and Sultan, 2024). In addition, the internet reduces the visibility of communication between the dealers and buyers, while also introducing new ways of establishing trust, such as through review systems, encrypted payments and other anonymity features that offer more protection for both dealers and buyers (Martin et al., 2019). Potential dangers remain, however, such as the risks of being deceived or receiving poor quality products (Barratt et al., 2016), as users relearn how to establish trust in this medium and invent other ways of ensuring safety and security. Digitalisation also means that transactions on the internet become difficult to identify and trace. As the analyses will show, this 'invisibilisation' presents a dilemma for legal processes in both determining and justifying an appropriate punishment.

The popularisation of Silk Road and Shiny Flakes, in particular, through media and film discourses, has raised awareness of digital drug markets, both locally and internationally. Previous works have examined the media portrayal of drug dealing, highlighting the moralising strategies involved in dehumanising drug dealers, who are often depicted as malicious actors entrapping innocent young people (Coomber, 2006). Some scholars have challenged such simplified portrayals, highlighting the complexity of drug markets and the reductive portrayals of dealers despite the rapidly changing drug trade context (Flacks, 2021). With digitalisation and the growth in hybrid forms of drug dealing, there is a need to rethink these ideas, and particularly the notion of the 'entrepreneurial drug dealer' (Potter, 2009; Friis Søgaard et al., 2019; Gutierrez, 2021). Normative ideas about drug dealing and 'harm' are thus being refigured as the relationship between technology and the drug trade, and relations themselves, are re-constituted in digital contexts. Against this backdrop, the case of Shiny Flakes presents an opportunity to explore how the law is responding to these changes.

The discussion therefore integrates interdisciplinary insights from digital drug market studies, critical drug studies and Science and Technology Studies (STS). Science and technology studies offers an array of theoretical and methodological approaches that can be applied to examine these markets and dynamics, not least of which is the critique of technology as a value-neutral and universal force shaped in social interaction (Bijker et al., 1993; Feenberg, 2017). Until today, most studies on digital drug markets have addressed how technologies changed the market and user behaviour, identifying these as different forms of paradigm shifting innovations (Aldridge & Décary-Hétu, 2014). More recent studies focusing on socio-materiality look at how technologies such as drug checking could help re-evaluate epistemic authority in legal responses to drug markets, and reposition users as both having control over their drug use practices while resisting punitive laws (Carroll, 2021). Yet, the potential for understanding how these technologies are ascribed new meanings through user-technology interactions, and novel understandings of drugs and drugs laws, remains underexplored (Paul & Egbert, 2021). In this framework, where digital drug dealing figures as a socio-technical innovation, partly revealing deficits in legal responses the analytical focus shifts to the role of technology in constituting or permitting different realities (Winner, 1980; Akrich, 1992). In particular, the focus is on what technology *affords* (Latour, 2002), rather than defines or determines. Latour argues that human encounters with technology can produce multiple capacities and possibilities at the same time. In the case of Shiny Flakes, this involves considering internet devices in relation to drug supply not as stable processes or systems, but as relationally produced technologies that co-produce and afford multiple realities. This approach involves a departure from technological determinism (Feenberg, 2017), namely that technology, even as shaped through society and social negotiations, always 'takes a certain form', affecting human life in very specific ways (Berg, 1998, p. 464). Instead, Latour's approach invites us to consider the possibilities and capacities for action (or 'affordances') that can emerge through relations between humans and technologies in specific contexts, moments and encounters (Davis, 2020).

The analytic focus in this chapter, therefore, is on what the technology affords; Schmidt and 'drug dealing' both emerge differently/become anew as a result of the digitally mediated form of supply, resulting in challenges that the law is unable to overcome. In particular, these challenges include: the difficulty to establish the source of supply and the income generated; the inability to establish the 'harm' caused; and the apparent inability of the law to process the entrepreneurial elements of the offending, which included the customer service that Schmidt provided to his clients. Instead, the law sought to 'read' the source of the offending in terms of normative relational dynamics and conventional drug dealing scripts, whereby the dealer is powerful and predatory, and the victims are innocent and corrupted. This is illustrated in the empirical analysis that follows through popular and legal media coverage of the case, and consideration of the ways in which the law is co-produced by technology and media (Schiølin, 2023). The aim here is not simply to reassert that law is lagging behind technological advancements, but to understand the affordances that emerge out of relations between humans and technologies, and how these relate to each other within legal frameworks and court processes (Callon, 1998). In this way, the selected case prompts a range of questions, ones that require analysis of how technologies afford new meanings relating to entrepreneurial dealership, what and who the law identifies as punishable, and who defines 'harm' and in what terms.

Methods and Materials

The chapter draws on online news media articles and a documentary film. The data analysis was informed by two goals: first, to critically explore the role of media in shaping and recounting aspects of the legal process for public audiences, and second, to consider how the figure of the drug dealer is conceptualised in law and media as co-created, or 'afforded', by socio-technical innovations. Initially, a broad search of

German newspapers was conducted via Factiva using the main keyword 'Shiny Flakes' and various combinations including 'Shiny Flakes' AND 'Schmidt' OR 'Kinderzimmerdealer' OR 'Candylove'. The timeframe was set for the period between January 2015 and October 2024 and gave 2,008 results. These were further filtered by removing duplicates, and then for relevance. The resulting seventeen news media articles were supplemented by further forty articles drawn from two local websites – *Legal Tribune Online* (LTO) and the *Leipziger Zeitung* (L-iZ) – which were not accessible through Factiva. The two websites were selected because they published consistent and chronological coverage of both of the Schmidt cases, with fourteen LTO articles reporting on the specifics of the Candylove process from 2023 onwards, and twenty-six L-iZ articles covering the outcomes and implications of both cases in more succinct summaries. While both of Schmidt's legal cases received attention across local and international media outlets, the choice of these two local news websites was because of their more consistent and detailed reporting. In terms of format, LTO is published specifically for legal practitioners and is hence different to standard news media outlets in its tone and style of reporting. The second source for the empirical material was the Netflix documentary, released in 2021, six years after the first trial, where Schmidt took centre stage in re-enacting and retelling his case from setting up the shop to being detained. It includes interviews with the prosecutor, the presiding judge, a psychiatrist, Schmidt's previous employers, lawyers and members of the local police administration.

The selected materials were analysed by exporting the fifty-seven articles and the full transcript of the documentary into the MAXQDA software for coding.[4] This was followed by reflexive thematic coding (Braun & Clarke, 2022). The thematic analysis was guided by the following research question: in what ways can the case of Shiny Flakes help revisit the idea of an entrepreneurial dealer as a result of socio-technical innovation? Two themes were developed out of this material in accordance with the reflexive coding, focusing on judging 'harm' in relation to drug dealing, and a 'new' entrepreneurial narrative that challenges

[4] The selection of these particular media materials over the archives of court hearings and legal documents is due to heavy restrictions on the release of case file transcripts. German civil court case files are not public records, and the German code of criminal procedure (StPO) maintains only a limited record of a court case, as laid down in Article 272. However, access even to this record is limited to parties directly involved in a case. Any externally requested access to record or detailed archives of a case is subject to review, approval and subsequent perusal fees.

normative and criminalising discourses on drug dealing. The implications of this analysis are relevant to the growing interest in digital drug markets, inviting new reflections upon how technologies co-shape the (legal) discourse around drugs, as well as practices of drug sales.

Analysis

Judging 'Harm'

The German Narcotics Act (BtMG) lays out several regulations regarding the possession, manufacturing, sale and trafficking of illicit drugs. In a case like Shiny Flakes, judges typically consider the extent of the crime, such as the amount of trafficked drugs, the impact on society, including public health threats, as well as the intent of the accused. 'Harm' is conceptualised in court in relation to the impact on the purported victim. Popular discourses frame 'harm' in familiar and conventional ways, typically assuming that illicit drugs are inherently damaging, and that dealers prey on vulnerable victims (e.g., Coomber, 2006; Flacks, 2018). However, the lack of apparent 'harm' in Schmidt's operations fascinated the media and confused the police when analysing his character, and particularly his skills as an innovator and prodigy. For example, the psychiatrist who worked with Schmidt throughout the legal process, and was interviewed in the documentary, said:

> Other people probably wouldn't manage it because they would be worried, or because they would be afraid, or think: 'I can't do that, it's unthinkable to do something like that. I could harm a lot of people.' He didn't have scruples like this. And that's why he was able to behave in such a cold-blooded manner. 'I control everything. I'm above everything. I can do this.' That's dangerous.
>
> (Documentary, 00:16:44)

This quote demonstrates the ambivalent characterisation of his personality and motives, and was mirrored in other media documents analysed. The discussion of 'harm' across various media often hinged on these judgments about Schmidt's character and decision-making. He is conceptualised as two different characters at the same time – an innovative, confident and charismatic entrepreneur, yet also a criminal mastermind. It often appears that judges and other actors involved in the legal process seemed sympathetic to Schmidt. Besides agreeing to shorter and milder forms of detention, the presiding judges provided statements such as: 'We are not the legislators; we are the executors. We have to respect the law', or 'A constitutional state is neither to win nor to lose, it is to exist' (LTO, 1 June 2023). These were usually in response to defence arguments that Schmidt caused no direct 'harm' and did not himself use drugs. Moreover, the head of the youth correctional facility pointed out that judging 'harm' in his case was more difficult than in more 'obvious' situations, with an apparent victim. As he put it, 'harm' is difficult to identify and 'measure' in legal terms: 'Yes, there is direct harm if I hit someone, I see their injured face or their bruised eye, for example, but with this case the harm is anonymous, and perhaps for that reason the thought-process is different here' (Documentary, 00:40:04). This quote indicates, in accordance with the previous psychological analysis of Schmidt's actions and personality, that it was presumed to be easier to carry out this scale of drug dealership because potential victims and the direct 'harm' were invisible. It implies once again, the seeming invisibility of the efforts required to run such a large shop. Since the police were only able to observe Schmidt in the few months leading up to his arrest, internet operations and even courier deliveries mainly stayed out of sight for the investigating officers. Media reports thus referred to Schmidt's case as a 'victimless crime' [. . .] 'because neither party has an interest in reporting it' (von Hein, 2020). The psychological assessment is equally a powerful actor in this constellation, as it aids significantly in both achieving a shorter prison sentence, and in helping to constitute Schmidt as the innovative mastermind who is either uninterested in perpetrating 'harm' or is incapable of recognising the indirect harms of his acts. This disrupts the standard dealer script, perhaps in other ways besides the entrepreneurship narrative, and can be seen in statements from the defence lawyers such as 'for him it was about fame [. . .] it was about glory and honor' (Documentary, 01:14:53). Defence lawyers went on to stress Schmidt's skills, and the importance of his commitment to customer service when attempting to overturn the detention verdicts. For example, in the first trial, the defence attorney pleaded for six and a half years arguing: 'It wasn't about the goods for him. It wasn't about the money for him, he was interested in building something that had a kick' (Schöler, 2015). In this way, attorneys emphasised the non-violent character of Schmidt's dealing. Studies have previously suggested that arguments about the limited harm caused by drug supply are neutralisation techniques, in which the dealer denies full responsibility (e.g., Potter, 2009; Martin et al., 2019). However, the earlier claims about customer service, afforded by technological innovation, serve not only to indicate reduced culpability but to reshape how drug dealing is constituted, especially in respect of non-material gains such as reputation and respect (Hardy & Norgaard, 2015; Martin et al., 2019).

In addition, customer service is one of the technological affordances of digital platforms that allow and demand the establishment of a certain level of trust. This requires a different form of labour, such as creating a detailed page for frequently asked questions, like Schmidt did, and offering an open platform for customer ratings for the service, which could help alleviate some forms of 'harm' by enhancing transparency (see also Linder 2019). Because the law considers selling and using illicit drugs as intrinsically harmful, for example, with regard to the potential public health threat as outlined in BtMG (s. 29), it suggests the need for legal reform in this area.

The question of customer pleasure also has the potential to destabilise standard or normative accounts of harm. The documentary begins with Schmidt laughing out loud with satisfaction when reading a customer's review that says: 'Guys, two of my teeth fell out straight away. This stuff really fucks you up. Definitely recommended'. Schmidt then adds: 'Seems he was satisfied'. In contrast to the interviews with prosecutors who might have viewed this as evidence that selling illicit drugs are 'inherently harmful', the customer reviews point to ambivalence about the nature of 'harm', and particularly its relationship with pleasure. For the customer here, drugs 'fuck you up' but are 'highly recommended', pointing to the complexity of ways in which users could experience, and derive enjoyment, from drug use (see, for example, O'Malley & Valverde, 2004). Once again, customer satisfaction for Schmidt is about offering a service and a choice of products. This was important for publicising the documentary too. The film poster features Schmidt sitting behind a table that has a large pile of colourful gummy bears on it. As he later explained, he enjoyed sending a packet of gummy bears together with the ordered drugs as a gesture of appreciation: 'basically, it was just an idea, to add another feature to the customer service' (Documentary, 00:37:34). Such an entrepreneurial style sensitises us to other kind of affordances mediated by technology, and the nuances of providing service on a large scale where the anonymity of customers may require establishing trust and reputation through innovative means, such as personal touches (see also Hardy & Norgaard, 2015; Linder, 2019).

The 'New' Entrepreneurial Narrative

Some literature on drug dealing has explored the practice as a form of entrepreneurship, focusing for example on questions of autonomy and self-employment (Fairlie, 2002), socio-economic-status and cultural capital (Bakken et al., 2022). A certain set of skills and practices such as communication and knowing the 'street code' (or 'street talk') has been found to be important to maintaining networks, in addition to generating feelings of trust and safety, particularly in respect of forms of dealing that do not involve 'social supply' (Coomber & Moyle, 2014). Recent studies suggest that adapting these skills to digitally mediated platforms could be understood as a form of socio-technical capital (Bakken et al., 2022), although this implies that one is already in possession of such capital and relevant knowledge. Still, it was notable that Schmidt mostly lived a socially isolated life and did not possess prior street knowledge. According to the data, he was diagnosed with ADHD as a child, and spent his teenage years in isolation, mostly on the internet. This is how he eventually discovered the darknet and became fascinated with the conduct of business in that space, which eventually enabled him to establish his own dealing enterprise. Schmidt himself describes how spending years in the darknet, starting at around the age of fourteen, and using various tools afforded by darknet platforms eventually helped him ease his way into sourcing and selling illicit drugs. For example, he explains below the manifold steps he considered in order to organise shipping and remain as unnoticeable as possible:

> Being relatively well-versed and connected within the world of cybercrime proved to be an advantage. You need the package pick-up stations to be able to receive anything. You need a postage account to buy stamps. You need bank accounts to convert the Bitcoin into cash. How can I conceal my identity? How can I avoid getting caught? On the street, someone could see you, but on the Internet it's more about, don't leave any traces, and if you do, in what form?
>
> (Documentary, 00:34:53)

The role of technology and the lack of investigative means to identify digital operations on the darknet in time became very important to the case, as the local intelligence discovered his business after almost two years of operation only due to local postage delivery failures. The offline aspects of managing his shop were largely dependent on him personally picking up the delivered drugs, sometimes hundreds of kilograms at once, and after sorting individual orders in his room, carrying packages to postal stations for shipment. He did not use postal offices but pack stations, and usually five minutes before they would close for collection. As his business grew, he began working with the help of a courier who would deliver to his house the large quantities Schmidt would order over the darknet. Still, the operations ran quietly, and no other person was involved in the in-person transactions with Schmidt. The former president of the State Criminal Police Office of Saxony, interviewed in the documentary, marvelled at the skills demonstrated by Schmidt in the course of these operations: 'Is it even possible for such a young person, 19 at the time, and then later 20, to run something like this on their own? We had serious doubts [...], simply because of all the effort that was required, and because of all the logistics, which were enormous' (Documentary, 00:41:33). In line with psychological assessments discussed previously, the archetypal, 'lone genius' storyline of a young entrepreneur fed the news media's interest in the case. For example, his family do not appear in any of the court sittings, nor are they mentioned in any media reports following each hearing. In the documentary, however, when asked about his family, Schmidt simply says: 'no family' (Documentary, 00:19:32). Although his contact with family members seemed limited, he still carried his share of household duties including cooking, helping with laundry and recycling, as the attorney general shares: 'The investigation showed that the son, independently from his millions in revenue, would actually return the family's recyclables as part of the national recycling scheme, and they had agreed that he could then keep the money he got from that scheme as a kind of supplement to his pocket money' (Documentary, 00:43:45). This and other aspects mentioned about his family are important in the documentary because the viewer sees that Schmidt maintained family responsibilities while dealing drugs. The law also appeared ill-equipped to address these new forms of entrepreneurial drug dealing. Schmidt was found guilty of selling large quantities of narcotic drugs, but the ways in which he created and operated the digital shops were not subject to legal sanction. This is derived from the attorney general's following remarks: 'It's one of the peculiarities of this case that someone who wasn't technically a criminal ... Not only 'technically' but not at all a criminal ... this person, with the help of the Internet is capable, in a very short time, of committing crimes on this scale' (Documentary, 00:44:38). This quote underpins the aspect of socio-technical innovation that explains the media's repeated focus on something that legal judgments were not able to consider. It was also instructive that the court and investigative experts used the Netflix documentary as evidence in the second trial. According to a media report: 'Investigators hope that clues and unguarded remarks in the documentary will help them link Schmidt to [his second shop]. They also hope the new trial will help them track down Schmidt's drug-dealing fortune, much of which has vanished without trace' (Scally, 2023). In this way, the film also affords new ways of conceptualising Schmidt's activities, filling in gaps in the prosecution's case. In trying to revisit the notion of a (young) entrepreneurial drug dealer, two links become important here. First, the court's investigative and deliberative processes were outrun by Schmidt's technological skills. The investigative forces admitted not having the necessary technological means and timely interventions that led to late and still partial discovery of all Schmidt's activities. His encrypted drives were never opened, and the revenue remains untraceable. In other words, the authorities' success was mainly due to traditional investigative methods, such as monitoring suspicious mail packages, rather than advanced digital surveillance. Here the presentation of investigative forces challenged by the use of technology stands out. As the chief public prosecutor says:

> Well, you feel really powerless, and you have to realise there's no equality of arms between the perpetrators and law enforcement. The reason is simply because we don't have many legal options available to use and the perpetrators have better options available, and yet we still had leads that we could continue working with.
>
> (Documentary, 00:55:31)

In other words, the prosecutor understands the technologies to have afforded certain benefits to Schmidt, including the ability to obscure evidence and evade prosecution for some aspects of his alleged offending.

Conclusion

This chapter has considered digital drug dealing and the ways in which it has altered how phenomena such as the 'dealer' and 'dealing' are constituted in socio-technical and legal contexts.[5] Through a critical analysis of Germany's largest digital drug market case, the chapter has explored not only the law's struggle to adapt to new and emerging technologies but also what digitalisation *affords*. This was illustrated by how emerging drug market dynamics complicate what the law can imagine, or do, including its ability to confidently and definitively identify and isolate 'harm'. It showed that media reports of the case fail to acknowledge the importance of technologies in reshaping ideas around drug laws, and the

[5] The terms 'dealer' and 'dealing' are preserved intentionally for consistency and when referring to existing literature.

dynamics of certain kinds of drug-related offending as well as our assumptions about drug dealers. As an example of a 'new' entrepreneurial drug dealer, Schmidt's case indicates a potential move away from a criminalised, immoral and powerful image of a drug dealer to one that pays attention to a more complex entanglement of drug laws, technologies and meanings. This is not to deny the ambivalence in assessments of his character in court – which the media amplified – as he was simultaneously deviant and cunning, and an admired entrepreneur, both fully culpable for his actions and deserving of sympathy. It also afforded ambivalence in relation to the conceptualisation of 'harm', which was assumed rather than demonstrated by the court and by media reports. As a result, a more hesitant legal process emerged, as the court carefully sought to assign responsibility to Schmidt within the limits of what the investigation was able to uncover.

The analysis also considered internet technologies in relation to drug supply not as stable processes or systems but as relationally produced technologies that co-produce multiple affordances. Both technology and humans are remade in such encounters, creating difficulties for the law in making decisions about responsibility since these interactions trouble conventional accounts of 'harm', culpability and drug dealing. Like Silk Road, the Shiny Flakes case challenged how local and international drug and cybercrime laws can operate in the future. Critical literature often highlights prohibition as the main flaw in current drug laws, and many studies have shown how the media has participated in prohibitionist ideologies (e.g., Ash & Poyker, 2023). This chapter suggested a more uncertain and ambivalent role for the media, since it both furthered the criminalisation narrative yet also celebrated the ingenuity of Schmidt operating at the forefront of technological advancement.

The chapter contributes to drug scholarship that identifies the need for novel theoretical frameworks to aid in the study of digitalised drug dealing (Bakken et al., 2022; Childs & Bernot, 2024). Digitalisation has changed the ways in which drugs are sold and bought, and legal frameworks are increasingly confronted with the need to adapt to, and navigate, the complex web of technological challenges. New research is needed to understand how digital drug dealing has altered the ways in which we comprehend and constitute drugs and the drug trade, as well as the notion of perceived 'harm'. The analysis also raises further questions about the suitability of the criminal law as the prime means of addressing the use and supply of psychoactive drugs, and particularly the ways in which 'harm' is attributed when there is no apparently visible victim.

Acknowledgements

I would like to thank the editors of the volume for their invaluable feedback and improvements they made to the earlier versions of this chapter.

References

Akrich, M. (1992). The de-description of technical objects. In W. Bijker & J. Law (Eds.), *Shaping technology/building society: Studies in sociotechnical change* (pp. 205–24). MIT Press.

Aldridge, J., & Décary-Hétu, D. (2014). Not an 'Ebay for drugs': The cryptomarket 'Silk Road' as a paradigm shifting criminal innovation. In *SSRN*. https://doi.org/10.2139/ssrn.2436643.

Ash, E., & Poyker, M. (2023). Conservative news media and criminal justice: Evidence from exposure to the Fox News Channel. *Economic Journal*, 134(660), 1331–55.

Bakken, S. A., Oksanen, A. & Demant, J. (2022). Capital in illegal online drug markets: How digital capital changes the cultural environment of drug dealing. *Theoretical Criminology*, 27(3), 421–38.

Barratt, M. J. (2012). Silk Road: eBay for drugs. *Addiction*, 107(3), 683.

Barratt, M. J., Ferris, J. A. & Winstock, A. R. (2016). Safer scoring? Cryptomarkets, social supply and drug market violence. *The International Journal on Drug Policy*, 35, 24–31.

Berg, M. (1998). The politics of technology: On bringing social theory into technological design. *Science, Technology & Human Values*, 23(4), 456–90.

Bijker, W. E., Hughes, T. P. & Pinch, T. (Eds.). (1993). *The social construction of technological systems: New directions in the sociology and history of technology*. MIT Press.

Bourgois, P. I. (1995). *In search of respect: Selling crack in El Barrio*. Cambridge University Press.

Braun, V., & Clarke, V. (2022). *Thematic analysis: A practical guide*. SAGE Publications.

Callon M. (1998). An essay on framing and overflowing: economic externalities revisited by sociology. *The Sociological Review*, 46(1), 244–69.

Carroll, J. J. (2021). Auras of detection: Power and knowledge in drug prohibition. *Contemporary Drug Problems*, 48(4), 327–45.

Childs, A., & Bernot, A. (2024). The platformisation of illicit drug markets: How datafication, technological affordances, and platform-mediated labour practices shape illicit drug markets. *Crime, Media, Culture*, 21(2), 149–68.

Coomber, R. (2006). *Pusher myths: Resituating the drug dealer*. Free Association Books.

Coomber, R., & Moyle, L. (2014). Beyond drug dealing: Developing and extending the concept of 'social supply' of illicit drugs to 'minimally commercial supply'. *Drugs*, 21(2), 157–64.

Daly, M., & Shortis, P. (2024). *Breaking Klad: Russia's dead drop drug revolution.* Global Initiative Against Transnational Organized Crime (GITOC).

Davis, J. L. (2020). *How artifacts afford: The power and politics of everyday things.* MIT Press.

Demant, J., & Aagesen, K. M. B. (2022). *An analysis of drug dealing via social media: Background paper commissioned by the EMCDDA.* European Monitoring Centre for Drugs and Drug Addiction (EMCDDA).

Demant, J., Anderdal, B. S. & Hall, A. (2020). Social media markets for prescription drugs: Platforms as virtual mortars for drug types and dealers. *Drugs and Alcohol Today*, 20(1), 36–49.

EU Drugs Strategy 2021–2025, (2021). 64 Official Journal of the European Union No. 2021/C 102 I/01. https://eur-lex.europa.eu/legal-content/EN/TXT/PDF/?uri=OJ:C:2021:102I:FULL.

Europol, E. A. (2017). *Drugs and the darknet: Perspectives for enforcement, research and policy.* European Monitoring Centre for Drugs and Drug Addiction (EMCDDA) and Europol.

Fairlie, R. (2002). Drug dealing and legitimate self-employment. *Journal of Labor Economics*, 20(3), 538–67.

Feenberg, A. (2017). A critical theory of technology. In U. Felt, R. Fouché, C. A. Miller & L. Smith-Doerr (Eds.), *Handbook of science and technology studies* (pp. 635–663). MIT Press.

Flacks, S. (2018). Making drug harms: Punishments for drugs offenders who pose risks to children. *European. Journal of Criminology*, 16(6), 652–70.

Flacks, S. (2021). *Law, drugs and the politics of childhood: From protection to punishment.* Routledge.

Friis Søgaard, T., Kolind, T., Birk Haller, M. & Hunt, G. (2019). Ring and bring drug services: Delivery dealing and the social life of a drug phone. *International Journal of Drug Policy*, 69, 8–15.

Gomes, A. B., & Sultan, A. (2024). Problematizing content moderation by social media platforms and its impact on digital harm reduction. *Harm Reduction Journal*, 21(194). https://doi.org/10.1186/s12954-024-01104-9.

Gutierrez, E. D. (2020). The paradox of illicit economies: Survival, resilience, and the limits of development and drug policy orthodoxy. *Globalizations*, 17(6), 1008–1026.

Gutierrez, E. D. (2021). Criminal entrepreneurs as pioneers, intermediaries, and arbitrageurs in borderland economies. *International Journal on Drug Policy*, 89, 103091. https://doi.org/10.1016/j.drugpo.2020.103091.

Hardy, R. A., & Norgaard, J. R. (2015). Reputation in the internet black market: An empirical and theoretical analysis of the deep web. *Journal of Institutional Economics*, 12(3), 515–39.

Korshøj, N. T., & Søgaard, T. F. (2024). Hybrid drug dealing: Merging on- and offline spheres when dealing drugs via social media. *International Journal of Drug Policy*, 130, 104509. https://doi.org/10.1016/j.drugpo.2024.104509.

Latour, B. (2002). Morality and technology: The end of the means. *Theory, Culture & Society*, 19(5/6), 247–60.

Linder, C. (2019). The entrepreneurial criminal: How trust coordinates illicit drug cryptomarkets. In *Entrepreneurship and Development in the 21st Century* (pp. 171–89). Emerald Publishing Limited.

LTO (2023). Summary of the Candylove case. In: Legal Tribune Online, 1 June 2023, www.lto.de/persistent/a_id/51894.

Martin, J., Cunliffe, J. & Munksgaard, R. (2019). *Cryptomarkets: A research companion*. Emerald Group Publishing.

Martin, J., Munksgaard, R., Coomber, R., Demant, J. & Barratt, M. (2019). Selling drugs on darkweb cryptomarkets: Differentiated pathways, risks and rewards. *The British Journal of Criminology*, 60(3), 559–78.

O'Malley, P., & Valverde, M. (2004). Pleasure, freedom and drugs: The uses of 'pleasure' in liberal governance of drug and alcohol consumption. *Sociology*, 38(1), 25–42.

Paul, B., & Egbert, S. (2021). Associate editor's introduction: Sharpening the focus – taking into account the socio-materiality of drug control and prevention. *Contemporary Drug Problems*, 48(4), 299–304.

Potter, G. (2009). Exploring retail-level drug distribution: Social supply, 'real' dealers and the user/dealer interface. In Z. Demetrovics, J. Fountain & L. Kraus (Eds.), *Old and new policies, theories, research methods and drug users across Europe* (pp. 50–74). PABST Science Publishers.

Rhodes, T., & Lancaster, K. (2021). Futures-oriented drugs policy research: Events, trends, and speculating on what might become. *International Journal on Drug Policy*, 94, 103332.

Sandberg, S. (2008). Street capital: Ethnicity and violence on the streets of Oslo. *Theoretical Criminology*, 12(2), 153–71.

Scally, D. (2023, 5 February). German drug dealer who inspired Netflix show is back in court. *The Irish Times*. www.irishtimes.com/world/europe/2023/02/05/german-drug-dealer-who-inspired-netflix-show-back-in-the-habit-and-court/.

Schiølin, K. H. (2023). STS jurisprudence: Exploring the intersection between science and technology studies and law. In Brozek B., Kanevskaia O. & Palka P. (Eds.), *Research Handbook on Law and Technology* (pp. 365–78). Edward Elgar Publishing.

Schmitt, M., & Müller, E. (2021). *Shiny Flakes: The teenage drug lord* [Online]. Netflix.

Schöler, M. (2015, 2 November). Urteil im Landgericht: Shiny-Flakes-Betreiber muss für sieben Jahre hinter Gitter. *Leipziger Zeitung*. www.l-iz.de/leben/faelle-unfaelle/2015/11/urteil-im-landgericht-shiny-flakes-betreiber-muss-fuer-sieben-jahre-hinter-gitter-114142.

Shortis, P., Aldridge, J. & Barratt, M. J. (2020). Drug cryptomarket futures: Structure, function and evolution in response to law enforcement actions. In D. R. Bewley-Taylor & K. Tinasti (Eds.), *Research handbook on international drug policy* (pp. 355–79). Edward Elgar Publishing.

UNODC. (2022). *World drug report 2022*. United Nations.

von Hein, M. (2020, 4 August). Deutschlands größte Online-Dealer vor Gericht. *Deutsche Welle*. www.dw.com/de/deutschlands-gr%C3%B6%C3%9Fte-online-dealer-vor-gericht/a-54435047.

Winner, L. (1980). Do artifacts have politics? *Daedalus*, 109(1), 121–36.

INDEX

For EU product safety concerns, contact us at Calle de José Abascal, 56–1°,
28003 Madrid, Spain or eugpsr@cambridge.org.

www.ingramcontent.com/pod-product-compliance
Lightning Source LLC
Chambersburg PA
CBHW071248180926
51613CB00002B/166
9781009713351